AF531630

CREATIVE METHOD OF TEACHING ENGLISH

CREATIVE METHOD OF TEACHING ENGLISH

DR. PRAMOD KUMAR PRUSTY
Ph.D., D.Litt. (Education)
Former Senior Lecturer in Education
Harakamaya College of Education
Gangtok, Sikkim
District Welfare Officer and DPC, SSA
Jagatsinghpur, Orissa.

Foreword by

PROF. (DR.) JAGANNATH MOHANTY
Former UGC Emeritus Fellow
Ravenshaw Autonomous College, Cuttack
and Former Prof. of Education and
Retd. Principal, Radhanath IASE
Cuttack, Orissa

DEEP & DEEP PUBLICATIONS PVT. LTD.
F-159, Rajouri Garden, New Delhi - 110 027

CREATIVE METHOD OF TEACHING ENGLISH

ISBN 978-81-8450-258-9

Printed in India at MAYUR ENTERPRISES
WZ Plot No. 3, Gujjar Market, Tihar Village, New Delhi - 110 018

Published by DEEP & DEEP PUBLICATIONS PVT. LTD.,
F-159, Rajouri Garden, New Delhi - 110 027 • Phone : 25435369, 25440916
E-mail : ddpubs@gmail.com • ddpbooks@yahoo.co.in
Showroom :
2/13, Ansari Road, Daryaganj, New Delhi - 110 002 • Telefax : 23245122

Contents

Foreword

Teaching of English as a foreign language has always been a challenge for teachers and learners. In spite of its international importance, English has been accepted as second language in India. But as a language it has no less importance and contribution in developing students' imagination, creative talents and ability to generate new things. As an international language it has ample scope to accelerate the creative expressions among learners

This book is the outcome of a study conducted by the author for his doctoral research degree under Utkal University, Orissa. The title of the study was 'Effect of Creative Methods of Teaching English [CMTE] on the Development of Creative Thinking of Secondary School Students'. Here, the author had developed a new method of teaching English language, i.e., Creative Method of Teaching English [CMTE]. This new method of English teaching is meant for secondary school level. The method is specially designed to develop students' creative thinking ability as well as their achievement in English. This method was also proved equally beneficial for boys and girls. The significance of this method is it is specially designed to enhance creative talents among learners. But such development of creative talents of the learners go hand in hand with development of academic achievement.

The study followed Randomized Matched Groups Pre-test Post-test Design. The tests on intelligence, achievement, socio-economic status and creative thinking were administered at pre-test stage. Since intelligence and SES were accepted as control variables, tests on achievement and creative thinking were administered at post-test stage. There was a Listening-Speaking Achievement Test in English, which was administered before and after the intervention. It was designed because the Achievement test in English developed by OSSTA was specifically meant for measuring reading and writing skills of the learners. The intervention method was designed mainly to see the enhancement of creative thinking and expressions of students through teaching English language. Since listening and speaking are the important means of expressing creative talents and tests of OSSTA lacked it, this test was felt very much necessary for the study.

Overall CMTE is a unique method of teaching English. In comparision with all other existing methods of teaching English it is proved better. A comparative experiment of CMTE with other methods of teaching English may be conducted to prove formers effectiveness. This method, no doubt, would be very popular if will be used in our classroom by our effective teachers. Our training institutions and curriculum of secondary level teacher training should include it to enhance creative talents among students. Institutionalization of this method will prove its credentials and will be helpful in correcting the limitations and extending its implications.

PROF. JAGANNATH MOHANTY

Acknowledgements

Creativity has been accepted as a challenging area of research. A creativogenic society is always congenial for developing creative personnel. In turn, the creative people help in creating a creative society. Though some view it as hereditary power, it is widely accepted that training can enhance creative power. It has been experimentally proved in Gordon's synactic, Osborn's Brain stoming, Tylor's PAKSA, Bono's CoRT and several other methods of teaching. Under this process, Creative Method of Teaching English is a novel method developed and experimented by the author and has been proved effective in developing creative thinking and academic achievement. It was an experimental study conducted on the secondary school students. However, this research study showed a new dimension of teaching English language through which creative thinking and achievement of students can be enhanced.

The author, with profound sense of gratitude, acknowledges his indebtedness to Dr. R.C. Das, Retired Professor and Head, Department of Teacher Education, NCERT, New Delhi and Ex-Vice-Chancellor, Berhampur University, for his constant guidance, inspiration and valuable suggestions without which this research work would not have been completed.

I also expresses my indebtedness to Prof. J. Mohanty, UGC Emeritus Fellow and Retired Professor and Principal, Radhanath IASE, Cuttack, Dr. S. Samal, former Head, Department of Education, Ravenshaw College, Dr. M.M.

Mohanty, Former Director SIEMAT, Orissa, Prof. S.L. Jena, Former Director TE & SCERT, Orissa, Dr. D.S. Ray, Former Principal, CTE, Orissa for their valuable suggestions.

I am grateful to teachers and students of the schools where experiment of the study was carried on, to the Directors of NCERT, New Delhi, ICSSR, New Delhi, NUEPA, New Delhi, CHETANA, Orissa who were gracious enough to allow their library for the use of the researcher's study.

I must acknowledge special thanks to Deep and Deep Publications Pvt. Ltd., New Delhi for publishing this book·with interest and care. I am also thankful to my spouse Mrs. Sajna Sagarika Mohapatra who has been a permanent source of inspiration for this endeavour.

DR. PRAMOD KUMAR PRUSTY

CHAPTER 1

CREATIVITY
A Conceptual Analysis

1.1 Creativity and Civilization

1.2 Creativity—It's Meaning

1.3 Creativity—The Theoretical Speculations

1.4 Measurement of Creativity

1.5 Creativity and Education

1.6 Creativity and Methods of Teaching

CHAPTER 1

Creativity
A Conceptual Analysis

1.1 CREATIVITY AND CIVILIZATION

"Man is not content with the world that he has been given. From his primitive days, he has been busy creating a world of his own resources from the raw materials that lie around him".

—Rabindranath Tagore

Creativity is interlinked with civilization. The anthropological evolution asserts that it is the creative potentiality which has improved the status of the individual from primitive cave-dwellers to the man of space. Absence of creative thoughts and ideas, no doubt, sterilizes the civilizational progress and paralyses human imagination. The future of a civilization and the survival of its members in a developed status depends on the quality of their creative imagination. A creative generation begets creative civilization. In turn, a creative social condition nurtures creative potentials of the people. Creativity, by nature, relies on extreme individualism and democratism It is antagonistic to sociologism. In contrast both are bent in constructive unity. Berdyaev (1964) aptly stated, "The nineteenth and twentieth centuries are a period of unprecedented quickening of social consciousness and unprecedented sharpening of individualism. We live under the sign both of an extreme sociologism (the generally accepted consciousness today is sociological consciousness: sociology has replaced theology) and an extreme individualistic isolation of personality."

Plato, Aristotle, Socrates had unputdownable contributions for the then Greek civilization and also for the present human society in different fields of life. Voltaire, Montesque, Rousseau were the forerunners of establishing democracy on the ash heap of autocratic French monarchy. Garlibady's imagination became helpful for Italy's unification. Marx and Engles established communism. Helmout Khol's persistent endeavour united West and East-Germany by demolishing Great Berlin Wall. The gospel of Renaissance in Europe and Movement of Green Revolution in India were the products of creative outlook and attempt of talented personnel. Likewise, Einstein, Galileo, Dalton, Robert Koch, Ronald Ross, Alexandar Fleming, Cartwright, Newton, Graham Bell were some creative personnel, creative acts of whom have been leading the civilization to an unanticipated level of achievement. There are literary and musical persons, artists and sculptors those have thrilled the world with their excellent contributions. There are also a number of unknown and mistekenly forgotten creative persons whose achievements are the bases of our life and development. The mankind is obliged to them and history pays homage to their ingenuity. So Crawford (1954) states, "Civilization represents millions of pieces of creations, each put thereby someone or other. Ideas are piled on top of the other and thereby make history".

Everywhere and every time creative people are less in number, but their contributions are uncountable and worthwhile. They lead the civilization to a unique position and energize the people with progressive aspiration and action for generations to come. This is the basic cause for which a few people always govern or direct the mass or a people of a nation or a society. But extreme sociologism is hypocritical and vicious against such microcosmic of man. It denies the creative secrets of communion because it denies and does not want to recognize the cosmic nature of man that evolved New Testaments, metamorphoses and epistemologies with perennial values. That is why, Jesus Christ was crusified and Socrates was forced to drink hemloc. On the other hand, the openness and multi-dimensionality of democracy have recognized and fostered these uncommon potentialities with all of their norms and actions. It regards human resources as most precious resources of all and takes long-term interest and utmost care in cultivating those talents for excellence. The society which recognizes the talent and gives prestige and support to the bearer achieves hydra-hearted development in science, technology, literature, music, economics, politics, culture, language, etc. The creative people naturally, desire to stay under the umbrella of such societal conditions which are conducive and congenial for flowering their budding thoughts and actions. This resulted in increasing rate of brain drain in developing countries like India to the developed countries which show magnanimity and cosmopolitan attitude to their creative endoments and propensities.

The existing human civilization is confronted with diverse array of problems in the field of politics, business management, economics, culture, science and technology. Dehumanization, conspiracy, treachery and mistrust are becoming the means of survival. The world is facing challenges such as pollution, starvation, terrorism and threat of nuclear war. In this connection, Ackoff and Vergara (1988) state,

> "The accelerating rate of change is accompanied by a corresponding rate of absolescence. An increasing number of problems have few or no precedents; hence, there is a decreasing number of opportunities to solve them effectively in familiar ways. The greater the need for new ways of doing things, the greater the need for creativity" (p. 77).

Alongwith, our society strives to solve the problems of war, greed, pestilence, famine, and of peace by cultivating humanitarian values and trustworthiness. To achieve the same, it is essential to concentrate on the creative minds which lie dormant and untapped. Toynbee (1964) states, "Creativity is the outcome of an encounter". This talent may be channelized for national reconstruction, social upliftment and preservation of world peace. Creative people are not only precious national human resource but also the most important asset of the civilization and are therefore responsible for its development and decay. Toynbee (1964) says, "To give a fair chance to potential creativity is a matter of life and death for any society" (p. 4). Creativity is a central factor in our ability to continue and to adapt to the changing environment (Rogers, 1959). But conscious community support must help in generating a new world order beneficial both for mankind and for the future civilization. Toynbee (1967) has rightly pointed out that if a nation actively seeks to nurture creativity, it will play a part in making history. However, if a nation ignores the creative potentials of its people it will surely be surpassed by other nation. Since social, economic and scientific progress relies upon creativity and innovation, it is crucial for this potential to be developed wherever it is found in society (Mumford and Gustafson, 1988). Hartley (1958) states "in the present international tug of war, survival itself may depend upon making the most effective use of the nation's intellectual resources".

The creation of this universe is the culmination of the creative persuit of the Almighty—His imaginative thinking and novel ideas. Thinking is also the greatest power which enables man to be an exception in nature by generating some extraordinary thoughts or matters, producing novels, plays, musical compositions, paintings, etc. Every individual has his own creative set of mind and thinks about many things which he wants to know and thereby becomes the grandee of exceptionals. Naturally, these propensities of human endeavour are held in high esteem and also enjoy higher social status and prestige. The society shows obligation to creative people and values them and their creations with most reverence. It is regarded as the highest form of mental operation in the field of science, industry, business organisations, art, architecture, music, painting, human relation and overall, in the area of solving divergent problems of the modern world and in creating situations for amicable co-existance of the people of this world.

History records their unprerishable rather stimulating contributions for civilizational upliftment Creative people have made seminal contribution to the advancement of modern world as they have unique strand of mental abilities, interest, attitudes, temperaments and other variables characterising thoughts feelings and behaviour (Tuli 1988). According to Torrance (1965), "the capacity of the creativeness is the central part of History—a man with the capacity of creativity can transform material factors, reshape goals and bring vision to reality." It is fair to say that the progress of a nation does not depend so much upon natural resources it has as it depends upon the persons of high brilliance, on whose shoulders ultimately lies the task of exploitation of natural, physical and human resources. The fuller use of a nation's potential demands that children with abilities other than intelligence be identified earlier and their talents be developed. Similarly, in our rapidly changing world, the cultivation of a creative-personality, sensitive and open to problems in his environment is not only important but also of immense urgency. Hence, Rogers (1961) states, "In a time when knowledge, constructive and destructive, is advancing by the most incredible leaps and bounds into fantastic atomic age, genuinely creative adaptation seems to represent the only possibility that man can keep abreast of the Kaleidoscopic change in his world. Unless individuals, groups and nations can imagine, construct and creatively revise new ways of relating to these complete changes the light will go out. Unless man can make new and original adaptations to his environment as rapidly as science can change the environment, our culture will perish".

1.2 CREATIVITY—ITS MEANING

An etymological search propounds that the word creativity has been derived from the Latin word "Creare" : "to make" and from the Greek word "Krainein" : "to fulfill". An approach on these two derivations avails a bifurcated connotation. On one side, the Greek derivation stressed on the product, whereas, on the other side, the Latin derivation favours utilitarian aspect of the creation. Creativity, in real sense, is the paradoxical integration of two polarities of doing and being. It is the integration of our logical side with our intuitive side, our left brain with our right (Young, 1985). Creativity is the concrete imagination. The individual always uses his imagination to 'make up' something 'new' and 'valuable' and thereby actualizes the potentialities of his imagination which are in abstract thought. Lesner and Hillman (1983) accepted creativity as the process of transforming creative idea into "concrete reality." The creator always adds something exceptional to the existing schemata and improves the outmoded and traditional values. Creativity is the most fertile intellectual property which impregnates the creator with productive uniqueness. The creative-productive gifted persons are distinctive from the school-house gifted (Renzulli, 1986) by their creative excellence against any traditional excellence (Taylor, 1987). People, inclined to this aspect of human personality, do use a number of synonyms to express creativity. Some of those are "reflective thinking", "productive thinking", "divergent thinking", "lateral thinking", "adventurous thinking", "independent thinking", "original thinking", "intuition", "insight", "imagination", "exploration", "giftedness", "spontaneity", "ingenuity", "inquisitiveness", "productivity" and "inventiveness". Bloom *et. al.* (1956) assert that creative learning involves the ability to organize, interpret, analyze, criticize, synthesize and evaluate possibilities.

1.2.1 Definitions of Creativity

Although varied definitions visualize creativity in divergent ways, most of them reflect a great deal of essential agreement (Torrance, 1971). Some of the definitions read as follows:

Simpson (1922)

"Creativity is the initiative that one manifests by his power to break away from the usual sequence of thought".

Spearman (1931)

"Creativity is the power of the human mind to create new contents by transforming relations and thereby generating new correlates".

Kunkel and Dickerson (1947)

". . . . for the source of creativity is not the individual but God who manifests himself in the We, of which the self is a part. . . . "

Ghiselin (1952)

"Creativity is the process of change of development of evolution, in the organisation of subjective life. . . . It begins in a state characterized by confusion and suspense."

Drevdahl (1956)

"Creativity is the capacity of a person to produce compositions/products or ideas which are essentially new or novel and previously unknown to the producer".

DeHaan and Havinghurst (1957)

"Creativity is the production of anything new, whether be it a new invention or a discovery in science or a new artistic performance or musical composition".

Bartlett (1958)

"Creativity is an adventurous thinking or a getting away from the main track, breaking out of the mould, being open to experience and permitting one thing to lead another".

Murray (1959)

"Creativity is a process that results in the occurence of a composition which is both new and valuable."

Maslow (1959)

"Creativity is the capacity of certain individuals to produce compositions of any sort (work of art, mechanical devices, etc.) which are essentially novel or which were previously unknown to the producer."

Rogers (1959)

"Creativity is the emergence in action of a novel relational product growing out of the uniqueness of the individual on the one hand and the materials, events, peoples or circumstances of his life on the other."

Rollo May (1959)

"Creativity is the process of bringing something new into birth."

Getzelsand Jackson (1962)

"Creativity is the ability to produce new forms and to restructure stereotyped situations."

Hoefele (1962)

"Creativity is the ability to formulate new combinations from two or more concepts already in the mind."

Mac Kinnon (1962)

"Creativity is a process extended in time and characterized by originality, adaptiveness and realization."

Torrance (1962)

"Creativity is the process of becoming sensitive to problems, deficiencies, gaps in knowledge, missing elements, disharmonies and so forth; identifying the difficulty, searching for solutions making guesses or formulating hypotheses about the deficiencies (and possibly modifying and testing them); and finally communicating the results."

David Ausubel (1963)

"Creativity is a generalized constellation of intellectual abilities, personality variables and problem-solving traits."

Ralph Mallaman (1963)

"Creativeness is everywhere the same and that it has a divine origin."

Mednick (1964)

"Creative thinking consists of forming new combinations of associative elements which combinations either meet specified requirements or are in some way useful. The more mutually remote the elements of the new combination, the more creative is the process of solution."

Yamamoto (1964)

"Creativity is the process of framing new ideas or

hypotheses, testing those ideas or hypotheses and communicating the result."

Wallach and Kogan (1965)

"Creativity lies in producing more associations and in producing more that are unique."

Hitt (1965)

"Original thinking and logical reasoning are the complementary aspects of creative thinking."

Parnes (1967)

"Creativity is the process of recombining known elements to produce more valuable (satisfying) ideas than previously existed in the mind of the thinker."

Barren (1969)

"Creativity is the ability to bring something new into existence."

Strnger and Karwoski (1973)

"Creativity implies that production of a totally or partially novel identity."

Stein (1974)

"Creativity is a process which results in novel work that is accepted as tenable, useful or satisfying to a group of people at some point of time."

Wilson, Guilford and Christensen (1974)

"The creative process by which something new is produced—an idea or an object including a new form or arrangement of old elements. The new creation must contribute to the solution of some problems."

Arieti (1976)

"Creativity, a prerogative of man can be seen as a humble human counterpart of God's creation."

Garrett (1976)

"Creativity is a process of transformation of creative

impulse through the use of techniques and sign manipulation into a communicable product. All the parts of the brain are called upon to work together; the right brain responsible for vision, the impulse, the intuition and the left brain for the manipulation of tools of the language appropriate for expression of vision, whether the language be words, colours, sounds, movements or physics. Both hemispheres must work together using their own specialities in the formation of a new idea or a work of art."

Levin (1978)

"Creativity is the ability to discover new solutions to problems or to produce new ideas, inventions or works of art. It is a special form of thinking, a way of viewing the world and interacting with it in a manner different from that of the general population."

Page and Thomas (1979)

"Creativity is the ability for divergent thinking or open-ended thought."

Paplia and Olds (1987)

"Creativity is the ability to see things in a new and unusual light/to see problems that no one else may even realize exist and then to come up with new, unusual and effective solutions."

Ford and Harries (1992)

"Creativity is a modifiable and deliberate process which is verified through the uniqueness and utility of the product created."

Greenberg (1992)

"Creativity is a process which results in novel creation or output."

Amalgamately, the above viewpoints approach creativity as a gift, process, product and above all as the higher order mental function. Some assert creativity as supernatural mystries spirited by blessings of the Almighty (Arieti, 1976; Mallaman, 1963). The theologists accept it as the metaphysical power or spiritual spark that activated the individual to be creative or to be exception from the ordinary. It is not found among all as it is a gift of the supreme power and meant only for the deserving few.

1.2.2 Creativity as the Process

Psychologists who accept and define creativity as the process are totally concerned to the psycho-physical systems which function in the individual organism and inspire him/her to imagine and think in an extraordinary manner. Thinking is the basis of creation. Reflective thinking generates new and unique products. It sensitizes the individual regarding the nature of a problem, process of taking hunches, testing and modifying those for effective result (Torrance, 1967). Guilford (1959) emphasized on divergent thinking as the essence of creativity, identified generalized sensitivity to problems, fluency, flexibility, originality, redefinition and elaboration as important components of such divergent thinking. Creativity is a functional process which is described in terms of "sensitivity", "synergy" and "serendipity" (Parnes,1967). The mental metabolism helps the person, prepares him to incubate problem—its nature and possible ideas for solution, illuminates him with ideas and thoughts for application and verifies the ideas for final product (Wallas, 1926). By applying the originality, the person constructs new combinations and associations and through reflective logistics justifies his views on product and stand. Such process is influenced by experience, evolution, adaptation and bio-social interaction. Abstractness in thought, here, is concretized. The researches on hemispheric functioning (Garrett, 1976) state that creativity is the product of right hemispheric process, whereas, logical thinking and rationality are the products of left hemispheric process. But creative potentiality, to some extent, is influenced by logic and rationality, intuition and insight. So both the hemispheres must have collaborative contribution with their specific specialities towards the germination and formation of new ideas, thoughts and products. Creativity is also the most exhuberant intellectual field on and by which the creator multiplies his qualitative and productive potentialities. But creativity can never be synonymous to intelligence.

Arieti's (1976) view on "Creativogenic Society" accepts creativity as a bio-social process, which brings new things into existance. In this connection MacKinnon (1962) states, "True creativeness fulfils at least three conditions :

(i) It involves a response or an idea that is novel or at the very least statistically infrequent novelity and originality though an aspect of creativity is not sufficient.
(ii) If a response is to lay claim to bring a part of the creative process it must to some extent be adaptive to or of reality. It must serve to solve a problem, fit a situation or accomplish some recognizable goal.
(iii) True creativeness involves a sustaining of the original insight an evaluation and elaboration of it and developing it into the full."

It shows that creativity is a process extended in time—short-term or long term and characterized by originality, adaptiveness and realization. It is an improved process of solving problems : personal and social, for effective adjustment. Such problem-solving thinking has novelity and value, unconventionality and persistence. Hunches are inspiring sparks which break through and the creative germ (Young,1985) which help in outbursting new and tenable ideas and make the person self-disciplined to solve different problems.

Guilford's (1956) "divergent thinking" is not all that makes the person creative or enables the individual to create new things. The thinking process, no doubt, is many-faceted. But the end or the product synthesizes the diverged attempts and means of thinking in a single point. It is the process of synchronization of multiple supra-rational or supra-logical paradoxes (Barren, 1969; Farm, 1970) which result in abduction (Fann, 1970) that is, the tendency of integrating, unifying and synthesizing the exhibited phenomena into a transparent metamorphosis by knowing and recognizing (Kaha,1983). Kaha again states, "creative process is an activity of mind characterized by an optimum level of unity." It is not the predominant area of primary process or unconsciousness state of an individual as viewed by Freud (1958). As Maslow (1957) states, creative thinking results from suitable cooperation between primary and secondary processes. It is not the product of right hemispheric function, but the combined effort of both right and left hemispheres. A synchronized brain facilitates the release of creative potential. In seventies, cognitive metaphor for creativity was regarded as left-right integration, i.e., integration of cognitive and affective metaphors for creativity. According to Elliott (1986) will was omitted in this right-left brain synchronization. The volitional metaphor, based on will, calls for not only right-left and top-bottom brain sychronization, but also front-back synchronization—in short, total brain synchronization. In the field of creative problem-solving also the rationales or insights of the individual converge in a new solution. Here, the difference lies between creative thinking and the creation. Can we praise and reward a person who has abundant creative thoughts and had never expressed, communicated, materialized or produced any of those thoughts? The answer would be an emphatic no. It is because creative thinking has a must relationship with creative product. At the very time a product comes to exist it carries the synthesized and converged ideas, endeavours and thoughts drawn from a series of divergent thoughts. Hence, the creativity or the creative outcome is the product of divergent-*cum*-convergent thought process and also of total brain synchronization.

Pre-consciousness is represented by incubation (Wallas, 1926) which results in illumination or insights. Some persons speak of incubation in terms of hemispheric functions. They refer to incubation as any technique of relaxation of conscious cognition (left cerebral hemispheric function). . . which allows subliminal processes (right hemispheric function) to operate (Gowan, 1979). Sometimes creative process gives rise to surprise permuations—the unexpected insight, the unsolicited twist that confers new dimensions. That kind of thought is creative. As stated by Dial (1991) such creative thinking "leaves one feeling singled out, affected by something external, grateful for privilege; paradoxically the peaceful aftermath to surrender of the will is a feeling of consumed and transcendent integration." Jung (1960, 1966), hence, says that creative process itself is dependent upon principle of synchronicity, the simultaneous occurrence of two meaningful but not casually connected events. Both Freud and Jung envisioned creativity as "a process that is of particular service to the individual by helping to make the unconscious conscious" (Lesner and Hillman, 1983).

Although imagination and fantasy seem to be the breeding grounds for creativity (Pickard, 1990), such higher-order cognitive activity (Gruber, 1980) or metacognitive activity (Scobee, 1983) which may be attributed as meta-creativity (Bruch, 1988) is "goal-directed" and thereby becomes a subject to an "intentional act" (Pickard, 1990). This idea questions the Freudian 'unconscious' basis of carrying on creative thinking and determines that creativity is a conscious and goal-directed process. Still this explanation needs more empirical analysis for generalization.

1.2.3 Creativity as the Product

The product-oriented approach measures the creative potentiality of the person in terms of his creation or product. The product should be unique and new or novel to be called creative creation. Man's capacity to produce new ideas, insights, inventions, discoveries artistic performance or musical compositions are accepted as being of social, spiritual, aesthetic, scientific or technological value. This emphasizes novelity and originality in production of new combination of familiar patterns, reorganisation of concepts and theories. To be creative, the product may be recognized by capable people and should posses social usefulness. If the product is proved to be creative, the concerned creator could be considered as creative. Rogers (1959) and Maslow (1959) also stressed on such new and novel production of the creative personnel. Unreplicated product idea or matter attests the creative talent of the person. Guilford's (1956) "originality" and Maslow's (1962) "product approach" also stress on the unconventional product. It is antithetical to the existing values and trends, old Testaments and traditional orthodoxy. As stated by Bartlett (1959) "creativity is getting away from main track, breaking out of the old..." Barren identified it as "the ability of bringing something new into existence." Newness and value characterise the worth of the product. The assessment of creativeness thus depends upon the quality of the product itself. The man may have a lot of good ideas and conjectures, but unless and until he communicates those to others, those bear no fruit. "The greatness of a work is not intrinsic to it, it is independent of the creator except in a case where an individual tailors a work to satisfy some audience. To become great, a work must be judged positively by those within the field says Weisberg (1992). Mihalyi Csikszentmihalyi also asserted that social acceptance of product makes the thing creative by saying ". . . if one produces something novel that is not accepted by the field and therefore does not become part of the domain, neither the work nor the person can be called creative. Conversely if a previously ignored work now becomes valued in the field, the work and the person who produced it, become creative."

1.2.4 Creativity as the Power

As stated by Simpson (1922), Bartlett (1959) and Mednick (1962) creativity is accepted as the "power". What does this power mean? Can this power be eliminated from the process of thinking? Can we suppose that one's mental mechanism operates with no potentiality and energy? Probably 'no'. When we do talk about creative thinking, we must concern to some "extraordinary power" or "rare talent" but not mere "power". The creative people are just ordinary people with extraordinary gifts and abilities. It is because, the thought, idea and attitude of the creative in almost all cases, deviate from those of ordinary individuals. Layman never finds courage to break the prevailing order, tradition, usages and beliefs, whereas, the creative never cares to those constraints and philosophies and does what he thinks right, what he rationalizes good and what he views as perfect with futuristic socio-individual view. The sequence of thought becomes asymmetric for creatives. They think unequivocally and they have a number of fruitful unconditioned responses to any conditioned stimulus. In the light of foregoing discussion, it can be concluded that creativity is the extraordinary power or the unique thinking process that inspires the person to produce unusual and unique ideas and matters which have socio-individual values and necessity.

1.3 CREATIVITY—THE THEORETICAL SPECULATIONS

Many psychologists and philosophers have developed different theories of creativity with varied meaning, scope and methods. Several purport to describe the nature of the creative process by using unique terms and mechanisms.

1.3.1 Psychoanalytical Theory of Creativity

The Freudian psychoanalytic or psychodynamic fascination approached creativity with the breeding field of catharsis of libidinal energy. Unconscious incubation or primary process originates creative thinking keeping pace with the psycho-sexual stages of individual's development. Individual's creativity originates as the individual encounters conflict that is caused due to tension of the conscious reality-bound processes with unsatisfied and unconscious biological drives. Creativity is the emotional purging and the sublimation of individual's repressed sexual desires into a socially acceptable and personally gratifying channel. Primary-process thought produces an association of irrational and illogical ideas that strike the thinker and creates the field for the unconventionality and uniqueness. Psychoanalysts also emphasize neurotic or schizophrenic root of primary-process thought which generates creativity. Many psychologists accept creativity as "madness" or as "affective disorder" or as "abnormality"-maniac depression and cyclothymia (which involve cycling between highly elated mood states-mania or less severely hypomania) and depression (less severely dysthymia). To them mania brings about changes in thought processes resulting in creativity of thinking. In maniac stage, the individual feels extraordinarily elated and energetic and during it the thought processes "loosened" as stated by Emil Kraepelin, to be resulted in production of new ideas that would not be possible in non-maniac stage. Still enormous empirical scrutiny are required to dig out the truth underlying this concept.

The Neo-Freudians shifted the psychoanalytic locus of creativity from the unconscious level to the pre-conscious level. The close kinship of creative thinking with that of neuroticism or psychopathological condition subsequently changed into phenomenological attributes. Jung, Sullivan and Erikson viewed creativity as the product of "bio-social" elements. Environmental feeding generates creative potential. Jung (1928) accounted for creativity of artists and poets when he said, "The unsatisfied yearnings of the artist reaches back to the prime-dial image in the unconsciousness. . . . The unborn work in the psyche of the artist is a force of nature that achieves its end either with tyrannical might with the subtle cunning of nature herself, quite regardless of the personal fate of the man, who is its vehicle. The creative urge lives and grows in him like a tree in the earth from which it draws its nourishment. We would do well, therefore, to think of the creative process, as a living thing implanted in human psyche." May (1975) asserted that, "creativeness is the unconsciousness (i.e., mindless awareness) breaking through into consciousness (i.e., mindful understanding)". To him creativity is the encounter of intensively conscious human being with his or her world. Kris (1952) viewed creativeness as "a fantasy and relaxation (regression) of age functions. . . . In fantasy and dreams, in states of intoxication and fatigue, such functional regression is especially prominent, in particular it characterizes the process of inspiration." The creative thinking may be connoted as "the cognitive unconscious" or "affective" state to produce novelties.

1.3.2 Cognitive Theory of Creativity

Cognitive theories of thinking developed by Piaget and Lewin stress on thinking, reasoning, intellectual exercise and reflex actions as the primary assests for inspiring creative thoughts. The cognitive domain predominates the person's creative thinking. The Gestalt theories (Wertheimer, 1945), creative problem-solving approaches (Osborn, 1963; Parnes, Noller and Biondi, 1977), Associative theories (Maltzman, 1960; Midnick, 1962; Koestler, 1964) and Cognitive abilities (Guilford, 1967; Torrance, 1974) also characterize creative thinking as the product of intellectual property. Keeping tune with different stages of Piaget's cognitive development, that is from sensori-moter through formal operation, the imagination, accomodation, assimilation, organisation and adaptation get modified and creative thoughts emerge. Stage of "equilibration" is the conflicting state of ideas, which in latter state brings equilibrium and adaptation to the creator. Novelity is addressed in the "process" aspects of Piagetian theory stemming from equilibration model, from the relative conception of reflective abstraction and from Piaget's notion of the cognitive unconscious. Hence, creativity is regarded as the higher sensori-motor, or metacognitive activity which gives rise to abstract reality in the imagination. It is the process of logical sequence from which, at many instances, leaps of insights are evident. Gestalt psychologists also believed in the creative problem solving which was experimented by Wolfgang Koheler's work on problem-solving in apes. This theory stresses on the utilization of cognitive or intellectual insights in spontaneous restructuring of the creative problem-solving process. Guilfords "divergent thinking" and Edward de Bono's "lateral thinking" also accept creativity as a definite pattern of horizontal expansion of "Judicial Mind" for generation of new ideas and thoughts and thereby enabling the individual for creative problem-solving means. Simonton's Remote Association Theory speaks of the function of remotely associated mental elements to generate novel ideas. He calls it the "chance permutation", where the higher mental elements and reasonings combined together for creative production.

1.3.3 Divine Inspiration Theory of Creativity

Theologists assert creativity as the gift of God. The person is not capable of being creative due either to his heredity or to his environment. Rather he is endowed with divine power to create something new and to think in some new pattern. As all are not divinely inclined, a rare number of persons are found to be creative. The best singer, the popular dramatist and the renowned scientist are inspired by unseen power of the Almighty, as these theorists view. So Arieti (1976) maintained that "Creativity, a prerogative of man, can be seen as the humble human counterpart of God's creation." Descartes, the great philosopher asserted creativity as some sort of divine inspiration. Mallaman (1963) also says, "Creativeness is everywhere the same and it has a divine origin." For the metaphysists, this human potentiality is accepted as unanalyzable supernatural mystery.

1.4 MEASUREMENT OF CREATIVITY

Creativity is a behavioural disposition. It can be quantified. Standardized tests or batteries and non-standardized tools are used to operationalize the term specifically. The operational definition of creativity defines the term by the name and activity of the measuring instrument. So as the meaning and definition, varied measures emerged to assess creative potentiality of the individual. Besides the standardized tools, check lists, rating scales, observation, analysis of cumulative records and personality data blanks throw light on the procedure of measuring creativity. Still the standardized tests give more reliable and valid information on creativity than the non-standardized tools. As creativity is very closely related with intelligence, motivation, achievement, cultural and social factors, its measurement seems cumbersome even by standardized tests. The process of assessment becomes more complicated when we talk about the creative potentiality in relation to sex, grades, race, socio-economic status, culture, education and environmental situations. Despite all shortcomings, researchers venture to find out validity, reliability and usefulness of different creativity tests. The tests (verbal or figural) may be administered to an individual or a group of individuals, the validity of the test does not establish any appreciable standard. The concept of normality and exceptionality still worsening the truthfulness and appropriateness of the test. Besides these the irregularities concerned with testing period, the testee, the administrator and scoring account much for unconformity of the results of creativity measures.

Assessment of creative talent began with Guilford's (1959) "Structure of Intellect Model." Though Guilford identified 120 different factors or abilities of intelligence, fifty factors are known (Andal, Krishnan and Thomas, 1995) and out of those some like fluency, flexibility, originality and elaboration are generally found to be measured by different tests. A number of creativity tests were developed following the suggestions of Guilford, Wilson and Christensen (1952). Their rationales mainly based on Guilford's three dimensional morphological model of human intellect. During the last two or three decades a number of creativity tests have been developed and published in USA for commercial purpose. In addition, a good number of creativity tests have been developed and used, not for commercial purpose but for research activities. Kaltsounis (1971) has listed thirty-six commercially available creativity tests which are useful in studying creative talents. Davis (1971) and Kaltsounis (1972) have also furnished information about the non-commercially available creativity tests and those would be about sixty in number.

Torrance Test of Creative Thinking (1962) consisted of seven verbal and three non-verbal sub-tests with 45 minutes and 30 minutes time duration for administration respectively. Verbal sub-tests include Ask and Guess Questions, Product-improvement Tasks, Unusual Uses, Just Suppose Questions, Unusual Questions and other types. The non-verbal sub-tests were Picture Construction Test, Complete the Figure Test and Parallel Line Test. The test-retest reliability of TTCT ranged from +0.70 to +0.92. Fluency, flexibility originality and elaboration are measured by this test. The popularity demanded its translation into different foreign languages for world-wide use. Getzels and Jackson's Test of Creativity was developed in 1962. It has five sub-tests and the test was entirely based on Guilford's model of divergent thinking and on its measurement. Minnesota Test of Creative Thinking was made available in 1958 by the Bureau of Educational Research, University of Minnesota. It has three verbal tests and four non-verbal tests. The verbal tests are—Ask and Guess Test, Product Improvement Tasks, Just Suppose Test, whereas the non-verbal tests are—Drawing Completion Test, Incomplete Figure Test, Circle and Square Tasks and Shape Test. Mednick's Remote Association Test (RAT) was prepared and standardized by Mednick and his wife in 1964. The test is prepared separately for two levels of students-school level and college level. Wallach-Kogan Test of Creativity is of great use all over the world at present time. It was based on Getzels and Jackson's study and prepared by M.N. Wallach and N. Kogan in 1965. It has verbal and non-verbal sub-tests. The test, as per instruction is to be administered in a game-like or free condition. Mainly the test is used to measure the originality and fluency. Calvi (1965) developed a test namely "Espressioni" at the University of Milan to identify gifted children in the early teens. Recently it was translated into English and adapted for use in Irland and administered to groups of boys and girls attending different types of post-primary schools.

In India also many researchers have developed a number of tests on creativity. Some of them are verbal, whereas others non-verbal. Mehdi's Test on Creative Thinking is the only commercially available test. Others are used for research purposes but are not commercially available. Mehdi's test is available both in Hindi and English languages. A detailed discussion of it is made in chapter III of this study. Besides Medhi's test, Passi's Test of Creativity (1972) Acharyulu's (1981) "Think Creatively" creativity battery, Basanti's Remote Associates Test (1984), Shan's (1992) Verbal and Non-verbal Tests on Creative Thinking for high school students have been used by researchers to operationalize the creative talent. Although researchers express creative potentiality through any of the creativity test scores the validity of such tests always remain in ambiguity. Still attempts should be made to neutralize the influence of the factors relating to external and internal validity of a test.

Some research has also been conducted on the nature and uses of creativity tests. Nicholls (1971) contrasted test-like and game-like conditions for investigating divergent thinking by using Wallach-Kogan's procedure. One group received a game-like followed by test-like and other group a test-like only. The results showed high correlation between tests administered in game-like condition and test-like condition. Hattie (1974) also studied the conditions for administering creativity tests. Three different conditions of creativity test administration—game-like, untimed and formal testing conditions were tested on two equivalent groups. One group was administered Wallach-Kogan Creativity Battery and TTCT in a game-like and untimed conditions and other group was exposed to formal testing conditions on two consecutive days. The results of creativity tests administered under three conditions were not found equivalent. Indian investigators have also attempted to study in the field of measurement of creativity. Raina's (1969, 1971) reviews showed that TTCTs are indeed popular with Indian researchers and are also translated into various Indian languages. Gakhar and Luthra (1973) reported high test-retest reliability of coefficient of correlation for all the seven sub-tests and for the complete battery. Indian research on creativity still is in search of the technically satisfying creativity measures which are condusive to specific national conditions.

1.5 CREATIVITY AND EDUCATION

Education aims at natural, harmonious and progressive development of an individual. This can never be achieved unless and until we pay positive attention to the creative aspect of the person alongwith other attributes. Modern world speaks of the democratization of educational system for individualized development. The approaches and methods have been eclecticised. The plans and policies view to develop human potentialities to optimum. Still we have failed to give proper recognition to creative potentials of individuals those are a few in their number. Starting from the four walls of a general classroom to the national policy framework the creatives realize a negligible importance. Till the present time, the creatives of the world are not recognized, accepted and appreciated by others. Our present educational structure is hampering development of creativity. As pointed out by Getzels and Jackson (1962) ". . . . There are indications that our whole educational structure is unable to assess creativity and actually is biased against it. Most teachers do not care much for the usual 'off-beat' child who gives answers that do not conform to some predetermined idea of what is correct." Our education is so tradition or convention-bound that even generous teachers underestimate and supress the budding creative exceptionality of students. Educational achievements are also measured by seeing the students' reproduction of crammed, "what is taught" or "book-bound" information. So Vernon (1967) says, "The present system is criticized for favouring the conformists mentality—the pupil or student who is good at accepting the learning what his teachers and lecturers tell him and thinking and writing along conventional lines, whereas it discourages spontaneous and independent thinking. . ."

Education for creative thinking seems to be the central issue around which revolve many problems of education. But our education system has neglected and too often supressed the natural creativity of the young and emphasized convergent thinking abilities. The eagerness with which a happy and secure child starts school, his curiosity, his capacity for different tasks, his fascination with his living world—everything becomes foreign to him as he learns what his teachers teach and expect from him. "How to do it instructions"—the dead knowledge snatches away all his opportunities of being creative. The child is made a stranger to his own potentialities.

The goal of education is to develop productive capabilities, personal expression, inventiveness and gifted leadership. It is to acknowledge the intuitive brain skills which are left underutilized and to improve their status for productive management. It is of great concern that our educational centres should be managed to enhance such human capital for unconventional problem-solving approaches for future survival (Agor, 1991). Dewey (1933) identified an appropriate emphasis for education to be the process of reflective thinking. He charged teachers with the responsibility to know this process and facilitate its development in students by providing appropriate condition to stimulate and guide thinking. Foshay (1981) pointed out, "there is a long history to the type of goal statement, which is supportive of creative learning." Citing some notables, ". . . including Plato, Montaigne, Milton, Franklin, Rousseau, Jefferson, Newman, Spencer, Dewey and Whitehead. . ." he opined that such development of creative potentials can be achieved by full acquisition of adequate and accurate knowledge of creativity. The creative thinking abilities contribute significantly to the acquisition of information and various educational skills (Getzels and Jackson, 1958; Torrance, 1960). Torrance (1962) realized the importance of guiding the growth of creative thinking abilities in children for ensuring their mental health, fully functioning personalities, educational achievement, vocational success, social importance and for providing different guidance roles. Sengupta (1976 and 1977) states that creative people of scientific and engineering persuits are inclined towards higher autonomy in actions and decisions and are more persistent in efforts, curiosity in them remains strong and they do possess high intelligence. Many studies (Pathak, 1961; Joshi, 1973 and Bhargava, 1979) asserted positive and significant relationship between creativity and educational attainment. Covington (1967) researched the effectiveness of creative learning and provided support for it being a central concern for education and concluded, "The nurturing of the cognitive skills of productive thinking should assume a central place in the curriculum not a secondary or incidental one. Training of these skills should not be subordinated to the overriding demands of subject matter acquisition as at present, but should be dealt with directly. What we need, in short, is a curriculum. . . which nurtures the process of productive thinking in its own right and yet in such a manner as to be fully coordinated with the other more traditional content-centred curricula." The creative learning transcends mere recall, providing the learner with the opportunity to synthesize and apply previously learned materials to novel situations. Thus, creative learning stresses on the importance of using knowledge by focussing on analysis and synthesis. The learner, here, is regarded as the "raw-material to be processed and transformed into a product" (Molnar and Zahorik, 1977). So Treffinger (1980) summarized the rationale for creative learning by stating that this type of learning is important because it helps learners to be more effective when teachers or trainers are not around, it creates possibilities of solving future problems that cannot be anticipated, it may lead to powerful consequences in our lives and because it can produce great satisfaction and joy.

During the last four decades a considerable amount of research has accumulated on the development, measurement, nature and nurture of creativity. The world of today including India, has attested the great influence of creativity on the educational theory and practice. Most of the developed and developing countries of the world are programming viable plans and instructional media to expose their students and teachers to the world of creativity to convey them about the uses of those research outcomes for optimum development of students' creative potentials. In this connection, Brandt (1984), studying the creativity researches of USA, states, "Educators across the country are reviewing their curricula and looking for assistance in planning thinking skills programs. . . they stress on intellectual development voiced in the recent national reports, makes it prudent for schools to provide for teaching thinking throughout the curriculum."

The first significant step towards creative education was the establishment of the "Creative Education Foundation" in the University of Buffalo, USA in 1957 by Alex Osborn. A decade later, the foundation started "The Journal of Creative Behavior" " which, till today, is also continuing in disseminating information concerning the investigations in the area of creativity on a wider scale. The Institute of Creative Problem-solving is also another brain child of Osborn which remained as an ever-influencing institute of creativity. Edwarad DeBono's Cognitive Research Trust (CoRT) has also developed some creativity lessons and "CoRT Thinking Teacher's Notes" for enhancement of creativity. Australia, Phillipines, Great Britain are setting their pace and developing in slow rateon creativity researches. Comparatively, researches and organisational consolidation on creativity are not up to standard in India. At present, in Utkal University, M.S. University, Baroda, Devi Ahilya University, Indore, NCERT are some centres which conducted a large number of research studies and have established a positive influence of creativity on education. Parnes (1967) states, "We receive so much spoon-feeding in our present society in terms of how-to-do it instructions in school, at home and at work that most of us lack almost any opportunity for being creative. . . . Education can help provide for this need by building the environmental turnpikes on which the individual may drive once he has removed the mental governors that restrict his creative ability". Rogers speaks that education provides "psychological safety" or "psychological freedom" necessary to the creative individual.

1.6 CREATIVITY AND METHODS OF TEACHING

"Creativity does not just happen. It needs appropriate seed, soil and climate. How to identify creative individual and foster creative abilities is most crucial endeavour for national reconstruction", says Murphy (1966). In any field of endeavour, creativity is regarded as a highly valued ability in our society. It is the ability of producing valuable and novel products. Hence, researchers of the world are in search of innovative means of its enhancement. Still, our achievement is negligible. "Educators have laboured for years over the problem of helping children to become more creative, usually with considerable frustration without notable success" (Eisner, 1977). Golman (1963) surprisingly laments on the role of teachers as they can not know with certainty whether their job is one of creating opportunities or of designing and delivering instruction.

However, it is the foremost responsibility of education and educational scientists to develop creative thinking among students. The place may be within the four walls of the classroom or in the business and marketing areas where the individual faces challenges of solving innumerable problems. The well-prepared creative method fertilizes the creative ideas of an individual in geometrical proportion and in divergent or lateral sphere by trespassing into the sterilized bonds. As educators, we have no control over genetic factors. Our control is confined exclusively to environmental variables in children's development. So our environment in all respects should be exploited and poised to stimulation of the creative potential of students to excellence. Rose and Lin (1984) acknowledged that creative thinking is both a skill and an innate ability. The skill can be developed and the innate abilities can be stimulated and nourished through education and training. There are a good deal of studies which have experimentally established the significant and positive effect of different methods of teaching on escalation of creativity. Some methods capitalized on Osborn's "brainstorming" or Gordon's "synectic", whereas, others followed Guilford's divergent method or any other methods to see the development of creativity. Some researchers have also developed their own methods which develop originality, elaboration, fluency and flexibility among students. Audio-visual teaching aids and use of computer packages are some innovative means through which students' creative abilities can be materialized and enhanced. Creative potentials are not something confined to a gifted few and determined at birth. Increasingly we are recognizing creativity as a normally distributed human potentiality. Evidence seems to support the view that no one is without creative potential; when we talk about creative behaviour we refer to every man rather than to the unique man. Hence, an appropriate method can enhance creativity among all the individuals of the society. Torrance (1967) gave six principles to encourage creativity. The principles are—be respectful of unusual questions, be respectful of the unusual ideas of children, show children that their ideas have value, provide opportunities for self-initiated learning and give credit for it and provide for periods of non-evaluated practice or learning. However, such unique talent should be optimized through improved teaching-learning programmes.

CHAPTER 2: REVIEW OF RESEARCH STUDIES ON CREATIVITY

2.1 Relation of Creativity with Intelligence

2.2 Relation of Creativity with Achievement

2.3 Creativity and Socio-economic Status

2.4 Sex-Difference in Creativity

2.5 Effect of Training on Creativity

CHAPTER 2

Review of Research Studies on Creativity

Although creativity to a certain extent is synonymous with unique or exceptional production or process, it can never be accounted as an independent factor, as it is basically a behavioural disposition of an individual organism. No behaviour of any organism can be treated separately, even though we call it in different symbolic words. Likewise, creativity is correlated with so many factors for its development and nurture. But here, the researcher has confined the analysis to its relationship with intelligence, achievement, socio-economic status and sex.

2.1 RELATION OF CREATIVITY WITH INTELLIGENCE

The scientific study of creativity started since Guilford introduced the morphological model of intelligence, i.e., "The Structure of Intellect". He identified creativity with divergent thinking category of mental operations. Guilford's presidential address to American Psychological Association (APA) in 1950 on creativity and its low relationship with intelligence, in later time, provoked a large amount of research both in America and other countries of the world (Acharyulu, 1977). Guilford's address in the Sixteenth Annual Convention of Creative Problem-solving Institute at State University College of New York at Buffalo (1970) cited examples of major envigorating developments in creativity after 1950s with some of his own observations on research activities conducted at the University of Southern California, University of Los Angeles, University of Minnesota, University of Georgia and State University of New York (Raina, 1980).

Research on the inter-dependence of creativity and intelligence resulted in what Cropley (1966) calls "two quite incompatible views : first that "divergent" tests do not cluster separately from convergent measures and secondly, that do" (p. 260). To be sure, the independence of creativity and intelligence as two separate domains is still a conflicting issue. Freeman, Butcher and Christie (1971) have suggested, "one way to demonstrate the independence of creativity and intelligence would be to construct a battery of tests designed to assess creativity and the other to assess intelligence. If the correlations between tests within each battery were high, but the correlations between tests in different batteries were low, there would be a good case for accepting the existence of distinct traits. Actual research results have more commonly revealed high correlations between tests of intelligence, low correlations between tests of creativity and correlations between the two kinds of tests that have varied from zero to very high. A brief review of some of the more important studies will show that this generalization requires all sorts of qualifications about the kind of tests used, the sample of people chosen and the circumstances and atmosphere in which the test scores and other measures were obtained" (p. 9). Some studies related to intelligence and creativity are presented here to clarify the idea on the relationship between the two variables.

2.1.1 Studies conducted in India and Abroad on the Low Creativity-Intelligence Relationship

Getzels and Jackson had taken a study on 533 pupils (292 boys and 241 girls) drawn from grade six to senior year of high schools of Mid-Western Private Secondary School, situated in

Chicago. The IQ of each student was obtained from the office record which were calculated by using Stanford-Binet or Henmon-Nelson or WISC. All scores were converted into Binet's IQs for easy comparison. For creativity scores, five creativity tests were administered, those were adapted from Guilford's test, Cattle's test and some devised by the authors specifically for the study. The measures included tests like; Word Association, Use of Things, Hidden Shapes, Fables and Make-up Problems. The experimental groups were formed taking the high creative group (top 20% in the creativity measures) and high intelligence group (top 20% in intelligence test scores). The former group had 26 subjects among whom 15 were boys and 11 were girls and the latter group had 28 subjects which included 17 boys and 11 girls. After analysis, the investigators reported low correlations between their tests of creativity and IQ measures. Those low correlations may be due to the fact that, those were based on a selected group and did not cover the whole group of pupils who were heterogenous in ability.

Torrance and his associates (1962) at the University of Minnesota reported results from eight partial replications of Getzels and Jackson design. There were five replications at the elementary level, single at high school level and double at graduate school level. Same procedures were followed by Torrance and his associates to identify high intelligence group and high creative group in all eight studies as was done in Getzels and Jackson study. But, in all these replications they had used a battery of Tests of Creative Thinking (1959) developed by them, instead of Getzels-Jackson Tests. Their test which was known as Form DZ consisted of Product Improvement, Toy Dog, Unusual Uses of Toy Dog, Unusual Uses of Tin Cans, Circles and Ask and Guess. Varied measures of intelligence were used in the study as different schools used different intelligence tests to record the IQs of their students. The major findings of the study had shown a tendency for highly creatives to be highly intelligent as well. Torrance (1962) felt that this may be due to the nature of the measures of the intellectual talent used" (p. 59). Two, out of eight replications did not support the Getzels-Jackson phenomenon. Torrance cited two explanations to it. Firstly, greater emphasis on traditional kind of learning provide no opportunity for highly creative group to develop their abilities to maximum. Secondly, the IQ means for the highly creative groups were low. In the words of Torrance, "it will be noted that the average IQ of the highly creative groups was lowest...." Citing the studies of Anderson (1960) and Roe (1960), Torrance concluded that upto a certain level of IQ, perhaps at a cut-off point of around an IQ of 120 intelligence will be the predictor of achievement, but beyond this point, the influence of intelligence decreases and the creativity factor becomes discriminating.

Mille and Merrifield (1962) questioned the classification procedure and the creativity tests used by Getzels and Jackson.

But Torrance acalimed it as the century's most notable study that called for a change in the educational theory and practice.

Mc Nemar (1964) criticized the authors' rationale as "half-blind logic".

Burt from U.K (1962) favourably reacted to Getzels-Jackson findings by saying that teachers and more academic type of parents preferred the intelligent pupils to the creative pupils and questioned the intelligence-creativity dichotomy.

Guilford and Christensen's (1956) factor analytic study reveals that the correlations between general intelligence and divergent thinking were approximately of the same size (r=0.25) as the inter-correlations among creativity tests themselves.

Yamamoto (1964) studied 272 high school students drawn from grade nine through grade twelve and found mostly low degree of correlation between intelligence and creativity, which ranged from +0.16 to +0.18.

Clark, Veblman and Thrope (1965) in a study on 192 (87 boys, 105 girls) students of University Junior High School in Austin, Texas reported a low correlation between creativity and intelligence. Such low degree of relationship between creativity and intelligence had been corroborated in the research studies of Wallach and Kogan (1965), Hudson (1966), Madaus (1967) and Cameron (1968) having their correlation values +0.10, +0.30, +0.33 and +0.08 respectively. But these studies show a wide diversity in their method, sample, tools and the procedures of analysis of data. Boersma and O'Bryan (1968) investigated the relationship of creativity with intelligence on a sample of Canadian School Children and found a negative and non-significant correlation. Comeron (1968) in a study on English school boys and reported a very low median correlation of +0.08 between the two divergent thinking and two convergent thinking tests. Soloman (1968) exploring the creative and intelligent behavior of 722 first, third and fifth graders of Columbia elementary schools by using Peabody Picture Vocabulary Test and Torrance Test of Creative Thinking reported that the measures of creativity were uncorrelated with intelligence. Massad's (1969) study used Wallach-Kogan Test of Creativity on 132 sixth graders of Ohio Public School, who belonged to different SES groups. The investigator tried to find out the relationship of creativity with intelligence. The study reported independence of creativity from intelligence. Clark and Mirels (1970) conducted a study on 93 students of the age group 09-15 years by adopting Torrance Tests of Creative Thinking (TTCT) and Helmon-Nelson Test of Mental Ability. The study reported a low degree of correlation (r=0.09) between creativity and intelligence.

Bruiniks and Feldman (1970) studied the relationship among creativity, intelligence and achievement on 72 (36 boys and 36 girls) disadvantaged children of Tennesse State. Collecting data by Peabody Picture Vocabulary Test, Stanford-Binet Scale of Intelligence and by TTCT, analysed those data through correlational procedure. The study reported low correlation (+0.18) between creativity and intelligence.

Reid (1970), in a study on 87 boys and 79 girls (Total sample 166) of intermediate schools of New Zealand found moderate to low interrelationship, i.e., around +0.30 between creativity and intelligence.

Davis and Belcher (1971) conducted a study on 51 students (22 boys and 29 girls) of Wisconsin High School by using three kinds of creativity tests such as Mednick's Remote Association Test (RAT), TTCT (Verbal, Form A) and Alpha Biographical Inventory (ABI). In analysis, the study reported the correlation of each of these tests with intelligence as non-significant which ranged from +0.04 to - +3.26.

Guilford and Chirstenson (1974) reported a low degree of correlation (r=0.25) between creativity and intelligence by analysing the data gathered through Lorge-Thorndike Scale of Intelligence and Verbal-Figural DP Tests. The sample consisted of 435 students reading in four to six grades of two schools.

Dudek (1974, 1976) examined the creativity of young children in relation to their intelligence and other personality attributes. Torrance Test of Creative Thinking and Wechsler Intelligence Scale for Children (WISC) were used for the measures of creativity and intelligence respectively. Analysis showed that by grade four and age 10 most variables except IQ were positively related. Intelligence, was inferred to have a low or negative correlation with that of creativity.

Jershild (1978) in a study on creativity and intelligence found very low and positive correlational value. Milgram (1984) in her review papers claimed that intelligence and creativity are separate and distinct dimensions. Here, supporting Getzels and Jackson findings, she cited some studies which dealt with gifted (high IQ) adolescents. Perhaps, at this end of IQ range the association between creativity and intelligence was not found as strong as it was at other points of the IQ range.

Freeman (1995) in a study on the gifted and non-gifted students' school performance and creativity examined the data by applying three way ANOVA. The analysis reported a negligible correlation between creativity and intelligence. The investigator felt that as the highly intelligent pupils are pressurized to excel in scholastic achievement, their creative potentialities naturally are getting sterilized and it resulted in producing low degree of correlation with that of intelligence.

2.1.2 Indian Research Studies Reporting Non-significant Creativity-intelligence Relationship

Khire (1971) conducted a study on 1054 eighth and ninth grade boys by using Guilford's Tests of Creativity and Raven's Advanced Progressive Matrices. The study found that different dimensions of creativity such as : fluency, flexibility, originality and elaboration had low degree of relationship with intelligence. The composite score of creativity had zero correlation with that of total intelligence score.

Weinstein and Bobko (1980) in their study suggested that creativity is not related to intelligence. Further their analysis reported that; this lack of association is only applied above an intelligence threshold.

Gupta (1972) in the study on a sample of Indian class IX students reported a low and positive correlation of +0.26 between creativity and intelligence.

Rajyalakshmi (1972) conducted a study on the relationship of intelligence and creativity taking 82 Indian industrial workers as sample. Wallach-Kogan Creativity Test was used to obtain creativity scores and Raven's Progressive Matrices were used to collect intelligence scores. The analysis reported no relationship between these two variables. Mehdi (1973) reported a study of Fatima who used Mehdi's Non-verbal test of creative thinking and reported very low range of correlation (r = -0.179 to +0.125) between intelligence and creativity.

Mehdi (1977) had undertaken a study on 459 urban and rural boys with age range of 12 to 13 years. The investigator used his own Verbal and Non-verbal tests of creativity for creativity measures and Mohsin's Group Test of General Intelligence and Raven's Progressive Matrices for intelligence measures. The analysis of data reported negative correlation between creativity and intelligence. The same study also reported a non-significant correlation between intelligence and creativity scores of rural and urban samples.

Sharma (1979) reported a non-significant correlation between creativity and intelligence through conducting a study on 200 high school students (Class IX and X) of Indore City and collecting data by administering Jalota's Group General Ability Test for intelligence scores and Passi's Test of Creativity for creativity measures.

Mehdi (1979) in a study on socio-psychological factors in creativity found low correlation between intelligence and creativity after administering his own creativity test on 857 boys and 337 girls of Class VII and VIII drawn from Uttar Pradesh and Madhya Pradesh. Menon (1980) conducted a study on 301 English Medium school students of Delhi and through correlational analysis found that intelligence is very negligibly related with creativity having the correlation value +0.29 only.

Chadha and Sen (1981) reported a low and positive correlation between TTCT scores and Ravens Progressive Matrices (RPM) scores of 116 students of Class XII of Delhi school. Pandey (1982) conducted a study on eighth and tenth graders of Kumaun Division and found no positive relationship between creativity and intelligence.

Pandey (1990) administered Mehdi's Test of Creative Thinking and Raven's Progressive Matrices on Class VIII students. Data collected and analysed by application of 't' test. The study reported negative and non-significant relationship between creativity and intelligence.

Chaudhary (1983) conducted a study on the pupils of age group 11+ to 13+ by administering own Creative Thinking Ability Test and other required tests to obtain data on creativity and intelligence measures. A statistical analysis of data reported that the students with high IQ did not have more creative potentiality than the students having low IQ.

Pal (1991) in a canonical analysis (Hotelling,1936) of inter-domain relationship between creativity and intelligence, powerfully established a low degree of relationship. The measures of creativity variance can explain 08% variance of the measures of intelligence domain and *vice-versa.*

Hota (1993) conducted a study on 580 Class IX students drawn from 24 schools of Western Orissa by using Wallach-Kogan Test of Creativity (1965) adopted in Oriya by Tripathy (1979) and Cattle's Culture Fair Test of Intelligence Form 'A', Factor 'G', Scale II (1965). The analysed result reported low and significant relationship between creativity and intelligence.

2.1.3 Studies Reporting Positive and Significant Relation Between Creativity and Intelligence

Historic finding of the Getzels and Jackson study (1962) on the separate dimension of creativity and intelligence found a nullified impact of 'g' factor of intelligence on creativity. This, in latter stage, raised antagonistic findings by several research studies which established a positive and significant correlation and hence the presence of 'g' factor in creativity. Burt (1962) and Marsh (1964) strongly supported significant and positive correlation between intelligence and creativity and hence concluded that these two dimensions can never be separated. Marsh, after a statistical analysis of Getzels and Jackson's data observed, "the detailed analysis of the author's correlations would seem to indicate that creativity is determined by different phenomena than those Getzels and Jackson assume. Rather than being almost independent of the general factor of intelligence, this factor is the most constant and conspicuous ingredient. Also, the ordinary type of intelligence test, particularly those used by Getzels and Jackson, were not fully representative of all aspects of intelligence" (p. 93). Hence this analysis showed that difficulties of measures of intelligence might be a factor of Getzels and Jackson's study which failed to measure the influence of intelligence on creativity. However, the reanalysis of Marsh (1964) did not provide much evidence for a different dimensionality for both these variables. Vernon (1964) also expressed his doubt on the long-term realiability or predictive value of divergent thinking tests of Getzels and Jackson study and suggested divergent thinking as an aspect of 'g' factor.

Yamamoto (1964), in his study on 461 fifth graders found +0.14 (P<0.01) correlation between creativity and intelligence and did not see Getzels-Jackson effect. Cline, Richards and Needham (1964) reported positive and significant median correlation (+0.40) between five of the Guilford's Creativity Test and the California Test of Mental Maturity (CTMM). Wodtke (1964), being conscious of the adverse effect of selective sample, used an unrestricted sample of four elementary schools of Salt Lake city which included students reading in classes II, III, IV and V. Torrance's Test of Creative Thinking (Verbal) and Lorge-Thorndike Intelligence Test were administered to obtain data on creativity and intelligence respectively. The analysed data reported statistically significant correlation (P>0.05) between intelligence and creativity for classes II, III, IV and V.

Yamamoto (1964) conducting a study on 272 High School students (Class IX to XII) reported a positive and statistically significant correlation (r = +0.30, P<0.01) between creativity and intelligence. For it, he used Test of Imagination and the Ask and Guess Test for obtaining creativity data and the Lorge-Thorndike Intelligence Test for obtaining intelligence scores. Kelly (1965) studied the relationship between creativity and intelligence on 492 fourth, sixth and eighth graders, sampled from the Public Schools in New Mexico. The Unusual Uses (Tin Cans) and the Circles Tests of TTCT battery were used as creativity measures and the California Test of Mental Maturity Short Form (57-S) was used as the measure of intelligence. The study reported grade wise correlations which were positive and statistically significant. Correlations between verbal creativity and intelligence for both sexes ranged from +0.33 to +0.54 (P<0.01) and the correlations between non-verbal creativity and intelligence for either sex ranged from +0.27 to +0.48 (P<0.02).

Pogue (1965), conducted a study on 263 Negro and White children, drawn from grades four through six of a school located in low SES area of Muncie of Indiana. Using Minnesota Tests of Creative Thinking for getting the creative measure, he found a positive and significant correlation between intelligence and creativity. Castiglione (1996) used Otis Quick Scoring Test of Mental Ability (Gamma Form C) and Remote Association Test (RAT) to find out intelligence and creativity scores respectively from a sample of New York University under-graduates. The study reported positive correlation between the RAT and the Otis IQ, Robenstein (1966) in a study on 350 fourth grade students reported a positive correlation between intelligence and creativity test scores.

Carey (1966) conducted a study on 196 sixth graders of a small metropolitan school in south central district of Indiana. Minnesota Tests of Creative Thinking and Kulhman-Anderson Intelligence Tests were used for creativity and intelligence measures respectively. The correlation between intelligence and creativity scores was reported to be ranged from +0.10 to +0.20. The correlation between IQ and flexibility ($r = +0.20$, $P < 0.01$ and $r = +0.17$, $P < 0.05$) were found to be statistically significant. Guilford and Hoepfner (1966) found an average correlation (+0.32) between I.Q. and 45 divergent thinking tests. The correlations were based on samples having wide range of I.Q.

Hassan and Butcher (1966), for the first time replecated Getzels and Jackson's study in U.K. with 12-years-old Scottish School children. The sample consisted of 175 (100 boys and 75 girls) children drawn from a Scottish Local Authority comprehensive school. The Moray House Verbal Reasoning Test provided the measures of intelligence. Creativity scores were based on Getzel-Jackson's Test of Creativity, Word Fluency of Thurstone's Primary Mental Abililities Battery, Guilford's Expressional Fluency Test, Mednick's Remote Associates Tests and Torrance's Circle Test. The creativity scores on each of these tests of creativity correlated positively and significantly with intelligence. These correlations were also high. The correlations of intelligence with scores on Word Association, Uses of Things and Fables Tests were +0.77, +0.55 and +0.73 respectively for boys.

Yamamoto, Lembright and Corrigan (1966) studied the intelligence and creativity of 730 (346 boys and 384 girls) fifth graders by administering Lorge-Thorndike Intelligence Test (Verbal) and Minnesota Test of Creative Thinking as measures for respective variables. The correlation between creativity and IQ for total sample was +0.26 (P<0.01) and the correlation between creativity and IQ for either sex was +0.25 (P<0.01).

Mednick and Andrews (1967) correlated the RAT scores and the IQ scores obtained through the Lorge-Thorndike Intelligence Test and WISC from 106 high school students. They reported that the correlation between L-T verbal score and RAT, L-T quantitative and RAT and L-T total score and RAT were +0.41, +0.34 and+0.43 respectively. The same authors also reported positive and significant correlation (r=+0.55) between RAT and WISC scores of 269 students belonging to grade VII to XII. Boersma and O'Bryan (1968) investigated the relationship between creativity and intelligence under two conditions-standard and playful way of testing. The sample consisted of 46 fourth grade boys drawn from an elementary school in Canada. Lorge-Thorndike Intelligence Test and Figure Completion & Unusual Uses Tests of TTCT were used as the means of acquiring intelligence and creativity measures respectively. For both the groups the correlation of verbal and non-verbal creativity measures with each of the verbal and non-verbal measures of intelligence were found to be positive and statistically significant. Under standardized conditions all correlations between creativity and intelligence/excepting that between verbal creativity and nonverbal intelligence, were found to be positive and statistically significant ranging from +0.21 to +0.56.

Ginsberg and Whitemore (1968) compared the intelligence and achievement scores obtained through Verbal Intelligence Measures and RAT respectively from 292 freshmen of University of Nevada. The result reported that the RAT and the verbal intelligence measures were positively and linearly related across the full range of obtained scores. In a separate study on an Australian sample they have reported a correlation as high as +0.60 between creativity and IQ.

Torrance (1968) reported a small but positively significant relationship between IQ and creativity. The study reported a higher correlation for boys than girls in the verbal tests. Tabulating 178 product-moment coefficients of correlations between creativity (Verbal, Figural and Total) and intelligence, the author found a median correlation of +0.20 between IQ and total creativity. The median correlation based on 88 coefficients of correlation between intelligence and verbal creativity was +0.21, while the coefficient of correlation between intelligence and figural creativity based on 114 coefficients of correlation was +0.06.

Wade (1968) studied the relationship between creativity and intelligence on a sample of 105 tenth grade pupils. He used Guilford's Test of Creativity and Lorge-Thorndike Intelligence Tests and reported a correlation of +0.37 between creativity and intelligence. Wallach and Kogan (1965 and 1969) using fifth grade pupils and college freshmen as sample reported correlations of + 0.41 and + 0.51 respectively between creativity and intelligence.

Cave (1970) conducted a study on a sample of 447 (370 White and 77 Negro) children of classes nine through eleven drawn from two high schools of Alcoa in Tennessee. Lorge-Thorndike Intelligence Test (Level 5, Form A) was used for intelligence measures. The creativity test used for the study included three of Getzels-Jackson's Tests (Uses Tests, Word Association Test and Make-up problems Test) and two of Torrance's Tests of Creative Thinking (Circle Test and Incomplete Figure Task). He reported a statistically significant correlation (+0. 38) between intelligence and creativity.

Damm (1970) explored the relationship between creativity and intelligence using a sample of 208 (95 boys, 113 girls) high-school students of Willamettee high school of Eugene, Oregaon. California Test of Mental Maturity (CTMM) was used as measure of intelligence. RAT and Biographical Information Inventory (developed by Tylor and Ellison) were used as the measures of creativity scores of the sample. The CTMM and RAT correlated significantly having correlation value +0.33 ($P<0.01$).

Dewing (1970) studied the relationship between creativity and intelligence on 394 seventh graders drawn from 10 Metropolitan Schools in Perth of Western Australia. IQs were based on ACER Intermediate Test-'D'—a verbal group intelligence test. Four of the Minnesota Tests of Creative Thinking-Alternate Uses (Tin Cans), Alternate Uses (bricks), Circle Test and Square Test, provided the creativity scores of the sample. The study reported a positive and significant correlation between IQ and creativity for the total group of sample (r=0.14, P<0.05). The correlation of verbal creativity with intelligence was +0.20 (P<0.01) while non-verbal creativity correlated +0.13 (P<0.05) with intelligence.

Davis and Belcher (1971) studied 51 students (22 boys and 29 girls) drawn from Wisconsin High Schools by using Mednick's Remote Association Test, Alpha Biographical Inventory and Torrance's Test of Creative Thinking and the Henmon-Nelson Test of Intelligence. They reported a positive and statistically significant correlation of+0.76 (P<0.05) for boys and +0.60 (P<0.05) for girls between IQ and RAT scores. In case of girls, the originality scores of TTCT correlated positively and significantly (r=0.45, P<0.01) with IQ scores.

Anastasi and Schaefer (1971) have explored creativity-intelligence relationship by conducting a study on 989 boys and girls reading in class X, XI and XII in New York Metropolitan area. Guilford's Test of Alternative Uses and Consequences provided the measure of creativity and Pintner General Ability Test provided the measure of intelligence. The study reported that IQ correlated +0.274 (P<0.01) and +0.103 (P<0.01) with Alternate uses and consequences respectively. Jershild (1978) in an extensive study on creativity and intelligence reported a low but positively significant correlation.

Torrance (1984) reaffirmed his position by saying that creativity points to academic achievement and intelligence and only 30 percent of students are both intellectually and creatively gifted. Hall (1985) demonstrated complex interrelationship between creativity and achievement by measuring both creativity and IQ of eighth grade and twelfth grade. She reported a little relationship between high creativity and high IQ.

Mc Cabe (1991) conducted a study on 126 seventh grader, (ages 12-13) and 84 ninth grader, (ages 14-16) girls enrolled in segregated high schools. Creativity was measured by Torrance Test of Creative Thinking (Form B) and intelligence was measured by using the ACERML and MQ tests of Intelligence

(Developed by Australian Council of Educational Research 1981). The finding reported that high creativity was positively and significantly associated with high verbal and quantitative IQ scores. However, the study accounted creativity for about 15 percent variance in IQ scores.

Carroll and Howieson (1992) conducted a study on 48 Australian ninth graders by using Torrance Test of Creative Thinking and comparing its score with IQ measures. The study reported that high creativity was significantly associated with high intelligence in different fields of activity.

Mumford, Connelly, Baughman and Marks (1995) studied the cognitive capacities of the gifted and talented students. From their study on the means of solving problems, generating new ideas, values, beliefs, developing skills the researchers found no significant difference between the gifted and creatives. Hence, from this., they concluded that both intelligence and creativity were significantly related.

Runco and Nemiro (1995) of California State University found a strong relationship between creative components with giftedness. They also reported the strong inclination of both creative and gifted students towards problem finding, problem identification and their solution.

2.1.4 Indian Studies Reporting Significant Creativity-Intelligence Relationship

Pathak (1962) conducted a study on 32 sixth grade pupils (17 boys and 15 girls) of a high school in Baroda. Circle Test and Incomplete Figures Test of MTCT and 'Draw-a-Man' Test were used for measuring creativity and intelligence respectively. The finding supported a positive and significant correlation ($r=0.343$, $P<0.05$) between creativity and intelligence.

Sharma (1972) reported a positive and statistically significant correlation of +0.44 between creativity and intelligence by conducting a study on 204 tenth graders of Agra city and collecting data on intelligence and creativity using Jalota's Mental Ability Test and Two Creative Tests (developed by Chauhan and Tiwari) respectively.

Passi (1972) studied 600 higher secondary students of Punjab, Haryana and Chandigarh by collecting creativity data through his self-developed test and intelligence scores through

Jalota's Group Test of General Mental Ability and Raven's Progressive Matrices. He reported a correlation of 0.266 (P<0.01) between creativity and intelligence.

Sharma (1974) studied the relationship between creativity and intelligence on 423 tenth graders by using 'Sri janatmaka Pariksha', "Varna Parichaya Pariksha" and Jalota's Mental Ability' test for obtaining measures of creativity and intelligence respectively. He reported that the students of high intelligence had significantly higher scores in creativity than the students of low intelligence.

Acharyulu (1977) conducted a study on a sample of 481 students of class VIII drawn from the schools located in West Godavari and Guntur districts of Andhra Pradesh. Torrance's Test of Creative Thinking and Cattell's Culture Fair Intelligence Test (Scale-2) were used as the measures for creativity and intelligence respectively. He reported positive and statistically significant correlations between TTCT and intelligence measures (r ranged from –0.163 to +0.287).

Rawat (1977) reported a positive and statistically significant relationship between creativity and intelligence by conducting a study on 300 high school students (class VIII and X) of Agra city. He used his own creativity tests for .obtaining measures of creativity and Jalota's Test on Mental Ability for intelligence scores.

Badrinath and Satyanarayan (1979) conducted a study on 114 ninth graders of Bangalore Central School by using Mehdi's verbal and Non-verbal Test of Creative Thinking and Nair's Non-verbal Test of Intelligence to obtain creativity and intelligence scores respectively. The study reported that the highly intelligent students had significantly higher scores on verbal and non-verbal and total creativity scores than low intelligent students.

Gupta (1979) by administering Mohsin's Intelligence Test and Mehdi's Creative Thinking Test on 100 high school students (class VII & VIII) reported a positive and statistically significant correlation of +0.39 between creativity and intelligence. Jarial and Sharma (1980a, 1986) administered Passi's Test of Creative Thinking and Jalota's Mental Ability Test on 200 Indore City High School students and reported statistically significant difference in fluency, flexibility and total creativity scores of high and low intelligent students.

Jarial (1981) conducted a study on 200 male and female students of class IX of Indore and administered Torrance's Test of Creative Thinking and Jalota's Mental Ability Test. The study reported that verbal and nonverbal creativity correlated positively and significantly with intelligence.

Safaya (1981) explored the relationship between creativity and intelligence of 68 B.Ed., degree girl students drawn from Urban Teacher-Training College of Punjab State by administering TTCT (verbal and non-verbal) and Jalota's Group Test of General Mental Ability for obtaining measures of creativity (fluency, flexibility and originality) and intelligence respectively. He reported a positive and significant correlation between verbal measures of creativity and intelligence.

Maddu (1982) studied the "relationship between creativity and intelligence as a sample of 475 male students drawn from different high schools of Hyderabad. Passi's Test of Creativity and Jadota's Group Test of General Mental Ability were administered as the measures of creatity and intelligence respectively. The study reported correlations of +0.124, +0.114 and +0.125 between fluency and intelligence, flexibility and intelligence & originality and intelligence respectively.

Mishra (1982) conducted a study on 200 urban boys drawn from five middle schools of Bhubaneswar, Orissa. Raven's Progressive Matrices (coloured) and Acharyulu Chandrasekhar Remote Association Test were used to measure intelligence and creativity respectively. Analysis reported a positive and statistically significant correlation between creativity and intelligence ($r=0.13$, $P<0.05$).

Chakraborty (1984) in her study on National Rural Talent Search (NRTS) awardees of Orissa used self-developed test for creativity measure (Basantic Remote Association Test) and Raven's Standard Progressive Matrices for intelligence measures. The study reported a positive and statistically significant relationship between creativity and intelligence.

Mishra (1986) conducted a study on 350 tenth graders (209 boys, 141 girls) by using Wallach-Kogan Test of Creativity and a standard intelligence test for creativity and intelligence measures. He reported that high intelligent persons have high creative ability and low intelligent persons have low creative potentiality.

Ramkrishna (1986) in a study on 600 secondary school students tried to find out the correlates of creativity through administration of the standardized tools on intelligence, creativity and achievement. The result revealed positive and significant correlation between creativity and intelligence.

Brar (1987) studied the effect of intelligence on the development of creativity of 637 students reading in class VII through XII with age ranges from 13 to 18 years/drawn from rural areas of Faridkot and Punjab. After the collection of data through the standardized tests of intelligence and creativity, the analysis found a considerable increase in the growth of all components of creativity (fluency, flexibility, originality and elaboration) keeping positive and developmental pace with the level of intelligence and progress of the grades, i.e. from Class VII through Class XII.

Sharma and Bhartiya (1988) in a study on 84 ninth graders (40 boys and 44 girls) collected the intelligence and creative measures through standard tools and analysed the data by unweighted means analysis and ANCOVA. The study found that intelligence and creativity are positively related to each other.

Chadha and Chandna (1990) found a positive and significant relationship (P<0.01) between intelligence and creativity. The study was conducted on 79 eleventh graders (42 boys and 37 girls) and TTCT and Raven's Advanced Progressive matrices are used as the measures of creativity and intelligence.

Padhi (1990) using Mehdi's Creative Thinking Ability Test and Raven's Progressive Matrices on a sample of eighth graders reported a positive significant correlation of intelligence with creativity. Pal (1991) in a study established a positive and significant relationship between creativity and intelligence through cannonical analysis of the factorial structure of creativity and intelligence.

Mishra and Mishra (1993) conducted the study on 90 class V (age: 9-10 years) students of five different schools of Bhubaneswar. The sample consisted of 45 educable mentally retarded and 45 normal students on the basis of IQ. Ravens Coloured Progressive Matrices (RPM) and Acharyulu's Think

Creativity Test (ATC) were used to measure intelligence and creative abilities of students. The study reported a significant relationship between creativity and intelligence by showing that normal students (non-retarded students) are more creative than the EMRs whose intellectual capacity is comparatively lower than normal pupils.

2.2 RELATION OF CREATIVITY WITH ACHIEVEMENT

There have been quite a few studies dealing with the relationship between creativity and achievement in different school subjects. Some of these studies reported positive and significant relationship between creativity and achievement while, others contradicted this.

2.2.1 Studies Reporting Significant Relationships Between Creativity and Achievement

Torrance (1959) conducted a study on 75 children (25 each in grades fourth to sixth) in Laboratory School by using his own creativity tests. He reported statistically significant correlation between creativity and achievement measures which ranged from +0.13 to +0.56, after the effects of IQ were partialled out.

Bentley (1966) conducted a study with a purpose to test the hypothesis that certain creative abilities might contribute to certain kind of achievement so that the creativeless intelligent student can achieve equal to or better than less creative-more intelligent student. For it, 75 graduate level students of University of Minnesota were administered Product Improvement and Ask-and-Guess Tests of TTCT for creativity measure which was compared with students' Total Achievement. The analysis reported a statistically significant correlation +0.34 ($P<0.01$) between creativity and achievement.

Carey (1966) studied 196 sixth graders drawn from four schools in a Metropolitan School District of South Indiana. Torrance Test of Creative Thinking (Abbreviated Form VII) and IOWA Tests of Basic Skills gave the measures of creativity and achievement respectively. The study reported positive and significant correlations between +0.14 to +0.21 between TTCT originality and IOWA measures of achievement and TTCT flexibility and IOWA achievement measures.

Mayhem (1966) conducted a study on 265 ninth grade students drawn from eight small high schools by using Torrance's Test of Creative Thinking (Abbreviated Form VII) and nine sub-tests of IOWA Tests of Educational Development for obtaining measures of creativity and achievement respectively. The study reported statistically significant correlation between achievement and creativity measures.

Yamamoto and Chimbidis (1966) took a correlational study on 790 fifth grade (366 boys and 426 girls) children drawn from 10 elementary schools in North-Eastern Ohio. The Minnesota Test of Creative Thinking and Stanford Achievement Test (Intermediate Battery) were used for creativity and achievement measures. They reported statistically significant correlations ranged from +0.15 to -+0.31 between creativity and achievement.

Torrance (1968) summarised the relationships between creativity and various measures of school achievement based on standard tests and Teacher Grades that have been reported in the Minnesota Studies of Creative Behaviour. Analysing 65 coefficients of correlation between creativity and standard achievement tests he reported a median correlation +0.28 between these two measures. He used TTCT and Stanford Achievement tests for creativity and achievement measures.

Gilchrist (1970), studying architecture students' creative and achievement potentialities through standardized tests, reported that high levels of creativity were more common among high academic achievers than among students who achieved less well.

Brin, Barenbaum and Schwarz (1971) conducted a study on 70 educationally deprived and 64 educationally non-deprived sixth grade students of Israel through administering a battery of creative thinking ability test. The result showed significant difference in the level of creative thinking and the language ability of the two groups.

Rechardson (1989) conducted a study on 308 adolescents (146 boys and 162 girls) reading in Grade X of high schools in five territories of the eastern Caribbean, namely, Antigua, Dominica, Montserrat, St. Lucia and St.Vincent. The mean age of the sample was 15.4 years. The Approaches to Studying Inventory (Entwistle, 1981) which comprised three main orientations including achievement and two creativity measures, one figural (Circles Test; Torrance, 1962) and one verbal (Unusual Uses Test; Guilford & Hoepfner, 1966) were administered to measure achievement approach and creativity respectively. The study reported a significant coefficient of correlation of +0.24 between achievement and creativity measures.

Mc Cabe (1991) studied the influence of creativity on achievement of 126 grade 7 (ages 12-13) and 84 grade 9 (ages 14-16) female students enrolled in seggregated high schools. Creativity was measured by Torrance Test of Creative Thinking, Form B (Torrance, 1974) and the academic performance was assessed in three subject areas : English, Mathematics and Art by two measures (1. Report Card Mark, and 2. Teachers' Rating) used for each subject. The result reported that high creativity scores are positively and significantly associated with high test scores and high assessment scores in English and with high test scores in Mathematics and Art.

Carroll and Howieson (1992), by using Torrance Test of Creative Thinking on 48 Australian ninth graders tried to find out the relationship of creativity with total achievement scores. They reported that, high creative subjects scored higher in their academic performance and resourcefulness. Bawa and Kaur (1995) conducted a study on the creativity and achievement in language through administration of standardized tests. The result reported that creativity is strongly correlated with the achievement of students in language.

In India, there also exist a good deal of studies on the positive and significant relationship of creativity with that of academic achievement.

Khire (1971) administered a battery of creativity test and some non-cognitive measures on 1054 eighth and ninth grade boys and reported that creativity has higher correlation with scholastic performance.

Joshi (1974) in a study on 3503 high school students of Gujurat administered Torrance Test of Creative Thinking and Achievement Test in English. The analysis of data revealed a positive and significant relationship between the two variables.

Dhaliwal and Saini (1976) used the Torrance Test of Creative Thinking (TTCT) on a sample of 118 urban high school boys and reported that their achievement in English, Geography and History was positively and significantly related to the two attributes of TTCT (viz. fluency and flexibility).

Acharyulu (1977) studied the relationship between achievement and creativity measures of 400 eighth graders of Andhra Pradesh. He used the TTCT (Telugu version) as the measure for creativity and school achievement marks as the achievement scores. The correlations between verbal creativity and achievement scores in Telugu, English, Mathematics, General Science and Social Studies were found positive and statistically significant.

Mehdi (1977) studied the relationship of creativity with academic achievement of 459 boys (259 urban and 200 rural) of class VII and VIII by using his own Battery of Verbal and Non-Verbal Creativity Tests. Statistically significant relationships were reported between creativity and school marks in different subjects.

Singh and Mathur (1977) revealed a significant and positive correlation (0.56) between creativity and school marks of 100 secondary school students. Chauhan-Tiwari Verbal Test of Creativity was used for creativity measures and school marks were used as the achievement scores of pupils.

Awasthy (1979) conducted a study on 300 higher secondary school students, drawn from Indore city. Mehdi's Test of Creative Thinking (Verbal) was used for creativity measures and the school achievement marks were used as the achievement performance scores. The study reported that creativity scores are positively and significantly related with school marks secured by students in different subjects.

Gupta (1979) used Mehdi's Tests of Creative Thinking in studying the creativity and achievement of 100 seventh and eighth grade students. He found a positive and statistically significant correlation (+0.70) between creativity scores and achievement scores (school marks) in different subjects.

Sandhu (1979) undertook a study on 217 class X boys, administered Passi's Tests of Creativity for creativity measure and collected school marks as achievement scores. The analysis established statistically significant relationship between creativity and achievement.

Asha (1980) sampled 800 (400 boys and 400 girls) tenth graders and administered Wallach-Kogan Creativity Tests for creativity score and took school marks as achievement measure. The analysis showed a positive and significant relationship between these two variables.

Menon (1980) conducted a study on 301 higher secondary school students drawn from some English Medium Schools of Delhi. Administering standard tools on creativity and achievement of students, the author analysed the data through correlational methods. The study reported a positive and significant relationship between creativity and achievement variables which was found to be +0.45.

Vijayalaxmi (1980) conducted a study on 425 secondary school students of Trivandrum by administering Kerala Test of Creative Thinking for creativity measure and finding out school marks for achievement scores. She reported statistically significant differences in achievement between the high and low creative students.

Jarial (1981) studied 200 high school boys and girls of Indore city. Torrance Tests of Creative Thinking (Verbal and non-verbal) were administered for creative measures and school marks were collected as academic achievement measure. The analysis supported a positive and significant relationship of both verbal and non-verbal creativity with that of academic achievement.

Pandey (1981) conducted a study on some high school students (both boys and girls) of Kumaun Division by administering creativity test and achievement test. From analysis he reported that creativity has a positive and significant relationship with various levels of education, which is indirectly related to academic achievement.

Safaya (1981) gave the TTCT to a sample of 68 female B.Ed., students. The B.Ed. students skills in teaching were assessed internally and externally. The internal assessment in Arts and Crafts correlated positively and significantly with verbal originality, while external assessment in these subjects correlated positively and significantly with non-verbal fluency and the arts and crafts correlated positively and significantly with nonverbal elaboration.

Joshi (1982) revealed a significant coefficient of correlation between achievement in Marathi and verbal creativity scores of 830 students of Maharastra. Dey (1984) in a study on NRTS students used own creativity test (BRAT) for creativity measures and accepted NRTS examination scores as achievement measures. The study reported positive relationship between creativity and marks in different school subjects and a significant relationship between creativity and achievement in Mathematics.

Kamila (1986) conducted a study to know the relationship between creativity and scholastic achievement of blind and normal students comparatively. In total 170 students (120 Normal and 50 Blind) were recruited from classes VIII, IX and X. Acharyulu's Think Creatively Test and School Achievement scores represented the creativity and scholastic achievement measures respectively. The analysis of the study reported low but positive relationship between creativity measures and scholastic achievement of the blind students. Normal students were found to excel the blind students in their creativity thinking ability.

Mishra (1986) studied relationship of achievement with creativity using Mehdi's Test on Creative Thinking and school marks for the creativity measures and achievement measures respectively. ANOVA and 't' tests were used for analysis of data. The study reported a high and positive correlation between creativity and achievement.

Ramkrishna (1986) studied the achievement and creativity scores of 600 secondary school children through standard tools. The analysis of the data found a significant relationship between achievement and creativity scores.

Brar (1986) studied the relationship between creativity and achievement measures of B.Ed., students of northern India and reported that high creative subjects scored higher in their academic performance.

Sharma and Bhartiya (1988) studied the influence of creativity (divergent thinking) on mathematical learning of 84 ninth graders (40 boys and 44 girls) through a factorial analysis. Unweighted means analysis reported that the achievement of high creatives appeared to be highest and that of low creatives found to be lowest.

Singh and Gautam (1988) conducted a study on 240 students reading in class VI, VIII and X both from urban and rural settings of Himachal Pradesh. Singh's Verbal Test and

Creative thinking was used for creativity scores. The relationship of creativity with achievement of different grades of students was found to be significant.

Mukhopadhyay, Chakrabarti and Kundu (1980) conducted a study on 80 most creatives and 80 least creatives of the age group 10-11 years reading in class V and studied the relationshipship of creativity scores with parental education. TTCT was used for creativity score and an Information Sheet was developed to find out the levels of parental education. Analysis of variance reported that parents' higher level education is a favourable factor for development of creativity of their children. Here parental level of education has become a factor which has contributed significantly ($P<.05$) for the development of creative thinking of their children.

Pandey (1992) studied 349 tenth graders (both boys and girls) drawn from Boys', Girls' and co-educational schools of rural and urban areas of the districts of North 24-Praganas, South 24-Praganas and Nadia (West Bengal, India). Torrance Test of Creative Thinking-Verbal and Figural (Form A and B) and a Scholastic Achievement Test, standardized by the author, were used as creativity and achievement measures. A product moment correlational analysis reported a significant relationship between creativity and scholastic achievement and established the fact that divergent thinking production is due to high scholastic achievement.

Hota (1993) conducted a study on 580 randomly drawn students of Class IX from urban, rural and tribal areas (204 urban, 213 rural and 163 tribal) and administered Wallach Kogan Test of Creativity (1965) adopted in Oriya by Tripathy (1979) for creativity measures and Achievement Motivation test (Non-verbal) by Mohan (1971) for achievement measures. The study reported significant relationship of creativity with achievement motivation which is the base of achievement.

Padhi (1995) took 636 ninth graders (379 boys and 257 girls) drawn from 15 schools (8 urban and 7 rural) in Orissa to study the relationship of creativity scores with total achievement scores and with achievement scores in each of five different subject areas. Acharyulu's Think Creatively Test (Verbal) was administered for creativity measures and school marks provided the achievement scores in different subject areas. The study revealed that all correlations of creative abilities with achievement in subjects are positive and significant at 0.001 level. All creativity scores correlated significantly and positively with achievement in English ranging from +0.26 to +0.34. Achievement in Mathematics correlated positively and significantly with verbal flexibility, fluency and originality. Further, achievement in science correlated positively and significantly with all creativity scores (r=0.29 to 0.37). The total achievement score has a high and positive correlation with total creativity scores (r=0.34 to 0.42). High creative group was found superior in their achievement (significant at 0.01 level) in comparison to low creative group.

2.2.2 Studies Revealing Low and Negative Relationship between Creativity and Achievement.

Holland (1961) conducted a study on a random sample of 649 National Merit Finalists (Approximately 9,868 high scoring students). High school grades were taken as criteria of school achievement. The criteria of school performance included awards, prizes or publications for notable scientific or artistic performance. Basing on this criteria, two scales (Creativity Science Scale and Creativity Arts Scale) were developed and used. The study reported that for students having high scholastic aptitude, creative performance is generally unrelated to scholastic aptitude. The investigator, seeing such result recommended the use of non-intellectual criteria for awarding scholarships and fellowships to students.

Pathak (1962) investigated the relationship of creativity with achievement on a sample of 32 sixth grade pupils of Baroda. Two Non-Verbal tests from Minnesota Tests of Creative Thinking and 'Draw-a-Man' test were used. The school marks collected from school records represented the achievement measure. The correlation between creativity and achievement was reported to be low and statistically non-significant.

Flescher (1963) through his study did not find any evidence on the close relationship of creativity with achievement. Torrance (1964) differentiated highly creative students, identified by the Minnesota Test of Creative Thinking, from students' achievement standard, measured by Gates Reading

Test and by the IOWA Test of Basic skills. He reported no significant relation between the measures of these two variables.

Edwards and Tyler (1965) in their study on 181 ninth graders used Incomplete Figures Test and the Unusual Uses Test of the TTCT, the SCAT and STEP tests for obtaining scores on creativity, intelligence and achievement respectively. Achievement results based on STEP and GPA were in favour of high SCAT group and not in favour of high creativity group. Success with creativity tests was found to be unrelated to achievement.

Jacobson (1966) conducted the study on 206 Boys living in Middle Class Community (with IQ 105 and above) drawn from 25 heterogenously grouped classrooms of seven schools. The Creative Thinking Ability (CTA) measure was based on 10 paper-pencil tests of creativity. Six of CTA were devised by Guilford and other four were Torrance Tests. The California Achievement test provided the measure of achievement. The study reported low correlation between creative thinking test score and measures of school achievement.

Bruininks and Feldman (1970) studied 72 disadvantaged children of the third and fourth grades by using four of the verbal activities of Torrance's Test of Creative Thinking (TTCT) and the written language portion of the Metropolitan Achievement Test (Elementary Battery) were used to obtain achievement scores. The correlation between the two measures was reported to be ranged from +0.04 to +0.18 which is low in nature. This low correlation revealed the unrelatedness of creativity measures to the measures of school achievement.

Dewing (1970) reported almost zero correlation between creativity and achievement. The study was conducted on ten schools and the result indicated zero correlation in nine schools. In one school correlation between creativity and intelligence was found significant ($r=0.28$, $P<0.05$). The average correlation between creativity and intelligence was as low as +0.07.

Bagga (1973) studied the relationship of Verbal and Non-Verbal creativity with the achievement of students in science subject. The result reported a negative and non-significant coefficient of correlation between creativity (Verbal and Non-verbal) and achievement measures in science.

Paramesh (1973) reported a non-significant correlation between creativity and achievement of 155 male students who had passed the secondary school examination. The Wallach-Kogan Test of creativity was used to measure creativity and school marks were used as achievement measure of the students. The study reported non-significant relationship between creativity and achievement.

Zetenyi (1976) conducted a study on relationship between scientific productivity (number of publications and lectures held, academic degrees in science, etc.) and performance on creativity tests in a group of professionals in chemistry. Results indicated that there was no significant relationship between scientific productivity and creativity.

Dhaliwal and Saini (1976) studied 183 urban male students. Torrance Test of Creative Thinking and Achievement in Mathematics were used as the measures of creativity and achievement respectively. The analysis reported very low correlation between the two indices.

Sharma (1981) conducted a study on 62 ninth class students by measuring the verbal creativity of students by Passi's Test of Creativity and using school marks as the measure for achievement. The study reported that high and low achievers did not differ significantly from their verbal 'creativity measures'.

Dey (1984) undertook a study on NETS awardees and compared their creativity with academic achievement. The investigator had used own creativity test (Basantic Remote Association Test) and Total School Achievement Scores of NRTS awardees as the measures of creativity and achievement respectively. The study reported that the relationship of creativity (BRAT) to State Level Award Selection Test Scores and the subsequent corresponding achievement in different subjects, though found positive, was low and too weak to be statistically significant.

Richardson (1989), in a study took 380 adolescents (146 boys and 162 girls), randomly selected from grade 10 population of high schools, situated in five territories of Eastern Caribbean-Antigue, Dominica, Montserrat, St. Lucia and St. Vincent. The mean age of the sample was 15.4 years. Entwistle Approaches to Study Inventory and two creativity tests (figural-circle test of TTCT; and verbal-Guilford and Hoepfner' Unusual Uses Test) were used for measures of achievement and creativity respectively. The result analysed by Pearson product-moment correlation showed no significant relationship between the two components-approaches of studying and creativity. This result showed that creative production would hardly be facilitated by perspective approaches to learning.

Chadha and Chandna (1990) conducted a study on 79 students (42 boys and 37 girls) of eleventh grade under 10+2+3 pattern of education from a reputed Delhi Administration School. Torrance Test of Creative Thinking (Product improvement activity, unusual uses activity unusual question activity and just suppose activity) and Annual Marks of llth class result taken from the school record were considered for measures of creativity and achievement respectively. The analysis reported negative and significant correlation ($P<0.01$) between creativity and achievement, which was found while the effect of intelligence was partialled out.

Toth and Baker (1990) studied 116 public school students studying in Grade six, eight and ten. Torrance Test of Creative Thinking (Form A) and Renzulli Learning Styles Inventory with Metropolitan Achievement Test (MAT) were used to determine the creativity and achievement scores. MAT scores were obtained from the current academic files. T-tests were used to analyse the data which reported a non-significant difference between these two variables.

Freeman (1995) conducted a study on 210 gifted and non-gifted students of age group 5-14 years in their family and school context. A 3-way comparison was made among 70 children identified and graded as gifted, a first control group of 70 non-graded but equally able children and a second control group of 70 children taken at random. The study though indicated that intense academic study could inhibit creative development, admit the possible loss of creative potential of intellectually gifted students as they found vulnerable to pressure imposed from parents and teachers to excel at school work.

Kapoor (1996) studied creativity and achievement of 300 secondary school students of Papum Pare district of Arunachal

Pradesh which included 110 tribal and 190 non-tribal pupils. Passi's Creativity Test (1972) and school marks were used as measures of creativity and achievement respectively. The study reported no significant relation between creativity and achievement at 0.01 level of confidence.

2.3 CREATIVITY AND SOCIO-ECONOMIC STATUS

2.3.1 Studies Reporting the Relationship Between Creativity and SES

Socio-Economic Status (SES) has been accepted as one of the major elements of the environment to be the causal factor for creativity. Still, researchers are not in agreement on the relationship of these two variables.

Ogletree (1971) in a study tried to establish the relationship between creativity and SES. He administered the Torrance Test of Creative Thinking on 1165 elementary public and private school children in Scotland, England and Germany. The investigator found that social class had a definite effect on creativity, favouring the upper and middle class groups. Ogletree and Ujiaki (1973) studied the effect of social class status on tests of creative behaviour by using TTCT on the same sample taken in last study. They confirmed that creativity scores were a function of socio-economic background. In all countries, subjects from upper class families obtained significantly higher creativity scores (both verbal and non-verbal) than subjects from middle and lower class families. The same significant difference was evident in comparison of middle class to lower class subjects. This was found true when analysed within countries by age, grade and sex. There was no evidence to support the contention that children from lower class background perform better on non-verbal tests than high class children, although they did make a better showing on the non-verbal tests than on the verbal.

Dudek and Strobel (1974) found marked difference in development of divergent thinking as a function of socio-economic status. They conducted the study on 1,450 fifth and sixth graders drawn from high, medium and low socio-economic strata. The study reported that, although analysis of socio-economic variables revealed divergent thinking ability to be markedly lower in lower socio-economic groups, exception in both high and low groups were frequent enough to indicate that school and classroom in the question (i.e., proximal influence) played an important part in developing and eliciting divergent thinking.

Pandit (1976) used a sample of 240 tenth class students of Indore. Kuppuswamy's SES scale provided the measures of SES. The study reported a positive and statistically significant correlation between creativity and SES.

Seetharam and Vednayagam (1979) found statistically non-significant differences in the creativity scores of High, Middle and Low SES students.

Jarial (1979) conducted a study on 200 class IX and X students of different high schools located in Indore city. Passi's Test of Creativity and Kuppuswamy's Socio-Economic Status Scale were used to obtain the creativity measures and SES scores respectively. Students of high socio-economic status scored significantly higher than those of Upper-Middle, Lower-Middle and low SES levels. The students of Upper Middle SES scored significantly higher than those of the low socio-economic status group on creativity. There was no significant differences in the creativity of the students of the upper and lower middle socio-economic status levels.

Sharma (1979) studied the relationship between creativity and SES on 200 students reading in Class IX and X in Indore City. Passi's Test of Creativity was used as the means to obtain creativity measures. The study reported a corresponding increase in the creativity scores keeping pace with the level of SES.

Sharma and Jarial (1980) administered Kuppuswamy's Socio-Economic Status Scale and Passi's Test of Creativity to a sample of 200 male and female students of class IX and X. The study reported that students of high SES background were superior to those of low SES background on the fluency component of creativity.

Sekhar (1980), in his study, tried to find out relationship between creativity and home environment factor. He studied the influence of home environment factor in terms of differential groups-high creative high IQ *v.* High creative low IQ and High creative high IQ *v.* Low creative-high IQ. The findings reported that the factor of home environment has direct positive relationship with creativity. The relation of creativity and SES was found positive and curvilinear in nature.

Chadha and Sen (1981) conducted an investigation on 116 class XII students reading in Delhi Schools. Torrance Test of Creative Thinking and Socio-Economic Status Scale developed by Kuleshrestha were adopted as measures of creativity and SES. The analysis reported no significant relation between creativity and SES.

Pandey (1981) studied the eighth and tenth graders of Kumaun hilly area schools by administration of standard creativity and SES measures. The study reported a positive trend in case of upper SES group and a negative trend of lower SES group with creativity.

Srivastava (1982) found that culture and SES exerted a significant effect upon creative abilities. Subjects of middle SES scored higher than those of lower SES. This finding was based on 80 high school students randomly recruited for the study.

Chaudhary (1983), in an investigation into the trends of creative thinking ability of pupils of age group 11 to 13 years with that of SES,used his own Creative Thinking Ability Test and adopted a SES scale. The findings showed that higher socio-economic status positively influences the higher creative thinking among pupils. Hussain and Hussain (1983) also reported that high socio-economic group was at a higher level than the low socio-economic group in verbal creativity scores.

Ramkrishna (1986) conducted a study on 600 secondary school children and tried to find out the relationship of their creative potentialities with their socio-economic status. The findings reported a positive and significant relationship between these two variables.

Rao (1988) developed and standardized test on literary creativity and tried to find out its relationship with sex and community background. The study was based on 900 ninth graders (both boys and girls). A correlation analysis of the creativity and SES scores of students reported a positive relationship between creativity and SES measures.

Singh (1988) studied the difference in mathematical creative potentials of Hindus and Muslims, who differed in their respective socio-cultural style and processes of living, freedom of action, religious rigidity etc. A mathematical creativity test, developed by the investigator and Mehdi's Biographical Inventory with a SES scale were used to measure different variables of the study. The analysis reported a non-significant difference between the Hindus and Muslims in their mathematical creativity ($P>.05$). But rural Hindus and Muslims differed significantly in their mathematical creative abilities favouring the rural Hindus.

Singh (1988) studied 240 school students comprising class VI, VIII and X selected both from urban and rural areas of Himachal Pradesh. The investigator used his own Test of Creative Thinking and Koul's SES Scale to obtain data on creativity and SES respectively. Analysis of data revealed that the rural-urban and high-low SES groups differed in their creative thinking significantly.

Pandey (1990) established positive and significant relationship of creative thinking of VIII graders of Kumaun division with their socio-economic status. The data were collected by administration of Mehdi's Test on Creative Thinking and by a standard SES scale.

Kumar (1992) studied the relationship between creativity and some socio-educational variables of 200 secondary school students, selected at random from two government high schools and one central school of Subansiri and West Siang Districts of Arunachal Pradesh. Creativity Test developed in the Department of Education, North Eastern Hill University, Aizawl (1987) adopted to Arunachal Pradesh was used to obtain creativity measures and Latrinkimi's Socio-Economic Status Index was used to findout the SES scores. The result reported a significant and positive relationship of creativity and SES.

Kaur (1993) studied the impact of school and home environment on creativity of 144 respondents (with equal number of boys and girls) drawn from four schools of Hissar district. The age level of students was 10 to 12 years. Mehdi's Test on Non-Verbal Creativity and Kuleshrestha's SES scale were used as the measures of creativity and SES respectively. The result reported a significant and positive correlation between creativity and SES.

Roy (1993) studied the impact of various dimensions of home and school environment on the development of scientific creativity of +2 science students reading in Government, Government-aided and Private schools situated in Delhi. Majumdar's Scientific Creativity Test and Two Environmental Questionnaires (School and Home) were administered to obtain the creativity and SES scores. The findings reported on various dimensions of home and school environment and on their relation with scientific creativity. The high scientific creative adolescents felt that they got more creative support from their parents than the low Scientific Creative (LSC) group. With regard to the school environment, the HSC groups confessed that they felt the importance of full support, possible help and full freedom provided by teachers for the increase of their creative potentials.

Hussain (1995) studied the creative potentials of students of industrial and non-industrial belts of Bihar. He reported that students belonging to industrial belt were superior to their non-industrial counterparts in their creative abilities. Patwardhan (1995) conducted a study on creative thinking of 216 illiterate women (105 from rural and 111 from urban) drawn from Pune District of Maharashtra. The result showed no difference between urban and rural illiterate women on inferential and creative thinking skills.

Verma (1995) studied the creativity styles of women students in relation to their rural-urban backgrounds. The sample consisted of 274 University Women students (153 rural and 121 urban) studying in facaulties of sciences, social sciences and languages. Creativity styles were measured by Creative Style Questionnaire of Kumar and Holman (1992). The result shown no statistically significant difference between rural and urban women on their creative style.

Behera (1996) tried to find out rural-urban differences in verbal creativity of Navodaya Vidyalaya Sixth graders. In total 80 students (40 from rural and 40 from urban) were selected from two Navodaya Vidyalayas of Orissa. Torrance Test of Creative Thinking was administered to findout the creativity measure. The findings revealed that the urban students of Navodaya Vidyalayas do not differ significantly in creative scores from their rural counterparts, except in the scores of verbal originality,

2.4 SEX DIFFERENCE IN CREATIVITY

Sex is regarded as one of the important variables whose influence on creativity has been extensively studied. But researches carried out both in the west and in India seem to be contradictory in determining the relationship of sex with that of creativity. Some research findings support the excellence of girls in creativity, whereas, others support the excellence of boys. A few studies indicated 'no sex difference1 in creativity.

2.4.1 Studies Favouring the Excellence of Girls in Creativity Measures

Torrance (1961) reported sex difference in his tests of creative thinking. He found that the boys of elementary school age-level scored lower than the girls, in most of the tests of the TTCT.

Torrance (1963)/while investigating on sex difference in creativity of the students from first grade to fourth grade, found that, by fourth grade, boys begin losing their battle showing a sharp measured decline in the abilities of originality and flexibility.

Klausmeier and Wiersma (1964) conducted a study on 160 fifth and 160 seventh grade children drawn from a larger population of high IQ children enrolled in two school systems-one located in a larger city and another in a smaller city. IQs were based on four tests viz. Current Events, Work Study Skills, Problem Solving Judgement and Analogies. Creativity scores were based on seven divergent thinking tests viz. Object Uses, Word Uses, Plot Titles, Expressional Fluency, Plot Questions, Object Improvement and Sentence Improvement. They reported a significant difference between the sexes on five out of the seven creativity measures and in all significant results girls excelled the boys in their creativity scores. On the convergent thinking measures, sex was also found as an important variable to influence that. On the three, out of four tests, boys were found to excel girls.

Gregor and Smith (1965) studied the originality component of creativity among high school boys and girls. The analysis of the result showed that girls were higher than boys in their creativity test scores. Naufield (1965) also found that girls significantly scored higher on word fluency, ideational fluency, expressional fluency and average fluency than boys.

Yamamoto, Lembright and Corrigan (1966) used a sample of 730 fifth grade children (346 boys and 384 girls) drawn from 10 elementary schools. Torrance Test of Creative Thinking and Lorge-Thorndike Intelligence Test (Verbal battery, Level 3, Form A) were used to obtain creativity scores and IQs respectively. He found significant sex differences in both creativity and intelligence measures with higher scores of girls.

Motlagh (1968) used a sample of 168 college students and reported significant sex differences. The scores of females were reported to be higher than those of males.

Ogletree (1968) made a cross-cultural study involving 1165 pupils (557 boys and 608 girls) of grades three through six drawn from the State Schools and Steiner Schools in England, Scotland and Germany. The third graders were administered TTCT Verbal Section of Form A and the Figural Section of Form B. The fourth, fifth and sixth graders were given the TTCT (Form B, Verbal and Figural). The TTCT was orally administered to all the grades. In the English and German samples (N=479 and N=493) girls significantly outscored boys on all creativity measures-both verbal and figural. In Scottish sample (N=193), girls excelled boys significantly on verbal creativity measures. The Scottish boys obtained higher scores on Figural creativity tests compared to girls, although the difference in scores was not statistically significant.

Soliman (1968) administered the TTCT to a sample of 484 senior high school boys and girls. The result reported signiciant sex difference in creativity. Girls scored significantly higher than boys on elaboration (Figural, Verbal and Total), While boys scored higher than the girls on verbal and total originality measures of creativity.

Soloman (1968) also used the Torrance Test of Creative Thinking and reported sex differences in creativity. The results favoured the girls. More instances of significant sex differences on both verbal and figural forms were reported at the third grade level than at other grade levels of the elementary school.

Torrance (1968) reported on the basis of his cross-cultural studies that, Indian children did well on verbal tests than on figural tests. He found sex differences in creativity, both in

American and Indian samples. Indian boys were found to excel girls in verbal creativity measures but not on the measures of figural creativity. In contrast, the American girls were found to score significantly higher than boys on verbal tests and not on figural tests. These differences in the performance on creativity tests of American and Indian children were attributed by him to the differences between the two cultures.

Bower (1969) in a study administered different batteries of TTCT viz. Product Improvement, Unusual Uses, Incomplete figures, Ask and Guess-Guess Causes-Guess Consequences, Arithmetic Problems and Climate Problems and Circles and some few other creativity tests on a sample of 278 ninth grade pupils (135 boys and 143 girls) drawn from a Junior High School in St. Paul, Minnesota. The criteria of achievement were the GPA and a composit score based on IOWA Tests of Educational Development (Form YS). The inter-correlations among the creative measures ranged from +0.16 to +0.51 for boys and from +0.10 to +0.55 for girls. Significant sex difference was observed on product improvement, Ask and Guess, Climate Problems, Word Fluency, It is IQ and both achievement measures, and girls outscored boys on these measures.

Abney (1970) conducted a study on 168 Junior and Senior (Honours and non-honours) students of University of Arkansas. Mednick's Remote Association Test (Form I) provided the measure of creativity. Significant correlations between sex and RAT scores were found in the ease of Honours group and the females outscored males on the creativity test.

Anastasi and Schaefer (1971) administered Guilford's Tests of Alternate Uses and consequences to a sample of 989 boys and girls of grade X through Grade XII, drawn from the high schools of the New York metropolitan area. Intelligence test scores were collected from school records. The correlations for boys and girls were significant. The girls were reported to be higher scorers than the boys.

Richmond (1971) conducted a study on 70 students among which 34 were Negros and 36 were Cancasions, reading in grade VI. The study reported that the females scored higher than males in their creativity measures. Hussain and Hussain (1975) in their study on male and female samples, found significant difference in favour of girls on unusual uses test (originality measures), whereas on other three tests (novel uses, consequences and elaboration), the differences were not significant, though the girls had higher mean scores on all these tests. Maccoby and Jacklin (1975) in their exhustive review on the creativity researches came to the conclusion that verbal measure of creativity reflects the verbal superiority of girls at least from the age 07 years onwards.

Singh (1978) wanted to verify the relationship of various divergent thinking abilities with intelligence of boys and girls. 320 students (158 Boys and 162 Girls) were administered the Jalota Group Test of Intelligence and Creativity tests. The result showed that girls were at higher level than boys in different components of creative thinking-fluency, flexibility, originality etc.

Sajid and Hussain (1984) studied 400 Indian people (200 male and 200 female) and compared the mean scores of the respondents on verbal and non-verbal tests of creativity. The findings suggested that the female respondents had higher scores on verbal creativity (which includes scores on fluency, flexibility and originality as well as on the composite creativity mean scores) as compared to their male counterparts. The difference was also found significant at 0.01 level.

Ramkrishna (1986) conducted a study on the literary creativity in Hindi and its correlates like Intelligence, achievement, sex and SES on 600 secondary school students. Standard tests were administered on intelligence, creativity, SES and achievement. The study reported a significant difference in the creativity scores of boys and girls with higher creativity mean scores of girls than those of boys.

Richardson (1986) conducted a study on 320 adolescents (101 males and 219 females) selected randomly from eleven graders of eight high schools. Five creativity tests : Word Associations (Getzels and Jackson, 1962); Unusual Uses (Guilford and Hoepfner, 1966); Fables (Getzels and Jackson, 1962); Circles (Torrance, 1962); and Remote Association (Mednick, 1962) were administered to the subjects in a relaxed classroom atmosphere, without the presence of time limits. Responses were scored for both fluency and originality on circles, Unusual Uses and Word Association Tests, while only the originality dimension was considered for the Febles test and the fluency dimension for the Remote Association Test. The data were analysed by application of 't' test, which proved significant sex differences in creativity with higher mean scores of girls' on creativity measures.

Patel (1987), in an experimental study, tried to find out the impact of gender differences on the development of creative thinking as a result of "Produce Creative Thinking Programme". The study was conducted on elementary school children. The investigator also tried to find out the relationship between creativity and intelligence. In total, eight classes were included in the study, having four experimental classes, those were taught 32 programmes and four traditionally taught control classes, those were taught in traditional methods by the concerned teachers. The researcher collected data through own intelligence and creativity tests and applied ANOVA to analyse the data. The result though reported a significant impact of training programme on development of creative thinking abilities, no sex differences was found to be accounted for such increment of creative thinking among students.

Lutzer (1991) tried to differentiate the ability of pre-school boys and girls in interpreting the common metaphor. The analysis found a significant gender effect on metaphorical interpretation at 0.7106 (P<.03), indicating an overall gender effect. Girls gave significantly more correct responses in consequential metaphors than boys (P<.003), whereas, the boys gave more metaphoric correct response than girls (P<.04).

Behera (1993) conducted a study on 80 sixth graders (40 boys and 40 girls) drawn from two Navodaya Vidyalayas of Orissa and administered Torrance Test of Creative Thinking (Verbal, Form A) to get the creativity measures. The findings of the study reported that in verbal originality the girls have surpassed the boys, by giving a significant difference at 0.05 level of significance. But in other variables of verbal creativity sex played no significant difference.

Hota (1993) studied the creative potentiality of urban and rural students (both boys and girls). On the whole, 580 randomly selected sample of Class IX were administered Wallach-Kogan Test of Creativity adopted in Oriya by Tripathy (1979). The analysis of data reported that among urban adolescents, the girls were found more creative than boys in their verbal, figural and composite scores of creativity. In rural area, boys excelled girls in verbal and composite scores of creativity and in tribal areas boys surpassed girls in figural and composite creativity scores. The study also reported no sex difference with figural creativity and verbal creativity of rural and tribal students respectively.

Pandey and Rai (1995) conducted a study on 480 eighth grades drawn from high school and intermediate colleges of Kumaun Division. Mehdi's Test of Creative Thinking (non-verbal) was administered to obtain creativity measures. The study reported that female students manifested statistically significant ($P<.01$) and better creativity as compared to male students on originality factor of creativity. This factor remain same both in non-tribal and tribal settings.

2.4.2 Studies Favouring Excellence of Boys in Creativity Measures

Kelly (1965) administered the Tin Cans Test and the Circle Test of Torrance Test of Creative Thinking (Abbreviated Form-VII) to a sample of 492 boys and girls drawn from grade IV, VI and VIII. The study reported significant sex differences in non-verbal creativity of fourth grade children which went in favour of boys.

In a study of Indian and American children, Straus and Straus (1968) reported lower creativity of girls than those of boys both in America and India. The study further revealed that sex difference in creativity were greatest in India.

Harold (1968) administered a battery of perception and creativity tests on 136 sixth graders and his results indicated that there are sex differences on several creativity variables, with males being stronger than females.

Raina (1969) conducted a study on 180 (90 boys and 90 girls) drawn from six higher secondary schools in Ajmer. Torrance Tests of Creative Thinking (both Verbal and Figural Forms) were used for measuring creative thinking of students. The analysis reported significant differences in creativity and sex, favouring the higher mean score of boys over girls.

Barl (1971) studied a sample of eighth grade Arab rural subjects and observed that male subjects obtained higher scores on Torrance Test of Creative Thinking as compared to female respondents.

Mari (1973) investigated cultural and sex differences in creative performance between Modern American and traditional Israel-Arab rural eighth grade pupils. Sixty American and 60 Israel-Arab rural eighth graders (30 males and 30 females in each group) were administered the Torrance Test of Creative Thinking (Forms Verbal B and Figural B). Thirteen scores were derived from the tests for each subjects. The result yielded that, overall American subjects performed significantly better than their Israel-Arab counterparts. Israel-Arab males performed better than females in nine out of 13 dependent measures of creativity. Among Americans, however, there were no significant sex differences except two measures favouring females. These differences, as reported by the investigator, were due to different socio-cultural backgrounds of two groups, particularly, because of the factors of cultural values and traditions.

Dharmangadan (1981) in a study tried to find out the relationship of sex with creativity and reported that boys scored significantly higher than girls in the creativity measures.

Nayana (1981) conducted a study on a representative sample of 1,500 children of 13 to 15 years of age. Both verbal and figural tests of Creative Thinking, developed by Mehdi (1973) were used to obtain the creativity measures. The study reported that males excelled females on measures of verbal flexibility, figural originality and figural elaboration.

Akinbye (1982) examined the influence of age and sex variables on creativity. Over age span studies (10-17 years), the study reported that males scored higher than females on flexibility dimension.

Vora (1984) developed a divergent thinking programme in Mathematics of Standard VII and VIII students and tried to know its effectiveness in development of creative thinking keeping pace with grade and sex. The experiment was conducted on 271 students of both classes. Passi's Test on Creativity was used to collect the creativity measures. The study, reported that boys and girls do not differ significantly from each other in the development of creative scores as an impact of Divergent Thinking Programme in Mathematics.

Sajid (1984) conducted a study on creativity measures of school going boys and girls. Administering a non-verbal test on creativity, the investigator reported-that, boys were found superior to girls in their non verbal creativity scores.

Hussain (1985) studied the creative potentiality of tribal and non-tribal male and female students. The result found boys to be superior to their female counterparts on different aspects of creativity.

Lutzer (1991) studied the common metaphor retaining abilities of pre school boys and girls which was based on metaphoric or metalinguistic comprehension. Sixtysix pre-schoolers were interviewed individually in sessions lasting about 15 minutes. There were 35 three and four years olds (14 boys and 21 girls) and 31 five and six years olds (21 boys and 10 girls). Eight metaphors were presented orally to each child with the same order of presentation for all children. The children were presented with two sample tasks and their responses were recorded. The result reported that boys gave more metaphoric correct responses than girls ($P<.04$).

Pandey (1992) conducted a study on 349 tenth graders (both boys and girls) drawn from Boys', Girls' and co-educational institutions of rural and urban areas of West Bengal. TTCT was used for creativity measures. The analysis found that male students were more creative than female students.

Hota (1993) studied 580 ninth graders of tribal, rural and urban area schools of Orissa. Wallach-Kogan Test of Creativity, adopted in Oriya by Tripathy (1979) was administered for creative measures of the sample. The study found that the rural and tribal males differed significantly from their female counterparts in verbal-composite and figural-composite creativity scores. But, no significant sex difference in verbal creativity and in figural creativity of tribal and rural areas students was found.

Gelade (1995) in a study on the creative style and divergent production of some male and female adolescents reported gender difference in creative thinking with higher remote consequences for men.

Kapoor (1996) conducted a study on 300 pupils reading in secondary schools of Papurn Pare district of Arunachal Pradesh. The sample consisted of 143 boys and 157 girls. Passi's

Creativity Test (1972) was administered for creativity measures. Calculation of data through ANOVA reported a significant difference in creativity scores of boys and girls. Male pupils were found better than the females in creativity. In Unusual Uses Test, male and female pupils do not differ significantly and it is interpreted that the male and female pupils perform equally well on unusual uses test of creativity.

2.4.3 Studies Reporting No Sex Difference

Pathak (1962) found no significant sex difference in creativity. The sample in this study consisted of 32 sixth grade children of an Experimental School at Baroda. She used the Circles Test and the Incomplete Figures Test of the TTCT to obtain measures in creative thinking.

Pogue (1965) conducted a study on 263 Negro and White children and measured their creative abilities through Minnesota Tests of Creative Thinking. The finding reported no significant sex difference in creativity.

Mayhon (1966) in his study on 265 ninth graders, used Minnesota Tests of Creative Thinking (Abbreviated Form VII) and found no significant difference in creativity mean scores of boys and girls.

Raina (1970) attempted to find-out sex differences among 50 teachers in Creative Thinking ability. Results showed no significant difference between males and females in all the factors of creativity except that of originality.

Pandey (1981) conducted a study on some eighth and tenth grader boys and girls of Kumaun Division by administration of creativity test and SES scale. The finding reported no significant difference between the mean creativity scores of boys and girls.

Katiyar and Jarial (1985) in their study attempted to study the effect of training sex and SES on development of creative thinking. In this experimental study TTCT was used as the measure of creativity. Verbal Creativity Development Programme (VCDP) and Non-Verbal Creativity Development Programme (NCDP) were prepared and experimented in 50 school periods. The result though established the effectiveness of VCDP and NCDP on creativity found no significant effect of male and female students on development of creative thinking.

Singh (1986) studied 100 male and female secondary school science teachers by administering Mehdi's Verbal Test of Creative Thinking and applied 't' test for analysis of data. The analysed data reported no significant sex differences in creative thinking.

Rao (1988) developed and standardized a test on literary creativity and tried to findout the relationship between sex and creativity. In total 930 ninth graders (both boys and girls) were administered the creativity test developed by the investigator. A correlational analysis found no significant difference between boys and girls in their creativity measures.

Sharma and Bhartiya (1988) conducted a study on the convergent and divergent thinkers (both males and females) in relation to their mathematical learning. A factorial design was adopted for the study. Unweighted means analysis and ANCOVA were applied for data analysis and found that boys and girls did not differ significantly in their convergent and divergent thinking abilities.

Mukhopadhyay, Chakrabarti and Kundu (1990) tried to establish the effect of parental sex on the development of creative thinking ability. A total sample of 160 fifth graders were selected from the age group 10-11 years and the sample included both high and low creative boys and girls.

Their parental education and sex was taken into account in collection of data. It showed that father and mother, both showed equal contribution on the development of creative potentiality among their children.

Behera (1993) conducting a study on 80 sixth graders (40 boys and 40 girls) of two Novodaya Vidyalaya of Orissa, administered TTCT for finding out the creativity measures. The result revealed that, the girls do not differ significantly in all the measures of verbal creativity from boys, except in verbal originality.

Pandey and Rai (1995) studied 480 eighth graders (240 male and 240 females) selected from tribal and non-tribal sections of the intermediate colleges of Kumaun Division. Mehdi's Test of Creative Thinking (Non-Verbal) was applied to measure the creativity of the subjects. The study reported that non-tribal male students and non-tribal female students do not differ significantly in composite scores of creativity.

2.5 EFFECT OF TRAINING ON CREATIVITY

Creative endowment, at present, has become the most fertile field of research on the development of which, the psychologists, educationists and managers of creative potential place a high premium. Although the creative personnel and their creative products sometimes seem mysterious, its process now is found not at all in obscurity. As analysed by Gordon (1961), this potentiality can be described and it is possible to train persons to develop their creative potentials by conscious analysis and effective training procedures. During 1960s, researchers of the Globe capitalized on the training strategies for enhancing this uniqueness of the individual to its optimum excellence. This trend of thought and research has logically supported the environmental and training correlation with fostering creativity by discarding the importance of heredity on this ability.

Wallas (1945) described creativity as synonymous with creative thinking and proposed four sequential steps—preparation, incubation, illumination and verification for its development. Osborn (1957) introduced the technique of "Brain Storming" as a means of encouraging multifaceted thoughts or quantity of ideas. In this procedure, the teacher simply inspires the students to ask as many questions as possible, however, absurd or unreal these may be. Writing of questions or ideas which come up may not be stressed as children might forget something while answering. Sidney Parnes (1959 and 1961) found effective result of this procedure through some experimental analyses. The research work of Meadaw (1962) also supported the significance of brainstorming programme on development of creative thinking. They found the usefulness of training through brainstorming for creative problem solving and producing ideas. Students in creative problem solving courses (which included Brain-storming) obtained higher scores in Guilford's Test of Creative Abilities than the students who have not had such courses. But Taylor and his associates (1958) found that, brainstorming technique produced ideas which are inferior in quantity and quality. Torrance (1961) viewed in his study that, in group situation brainstorming may not be very effective. But when teacher asks pupils to ask questions orally, it has been found to be quite effective. He also found directions to produce as many ideas as possible without regard to quality resulted in fewer responses than did directions to produce interesting, clearer and unusual ideas. However, though not the best way, brainstroming may be regarded as a way of invoking recall of concepts and principles necessary for solution of problem.

Torrance and Harmon (1961) advocated creative reading procedure for stimulating creative thoughts and Torrance and Myers (1963) also stressed on the importance of such reading skills in developing manysided thoughts and generating a greater number of ideas from a particular stimulus.

Osborn (1960) advocated four basic rules for developing creative responses in a group procedure. The rules include ruling out the criticism, welcoming free wheeling of ideas, wanting qualitative product and seeking combination and improvement.

Taylor (1961) developed Pack Corp Scientific Approach (PAKSA) in honour of the Packaging Corporation of America for the development of creative thinking. This technique consits of nine steps-pick a problem, get knowledge, organise knowledge, refine knowledge, Digest, produce ideas, rework ideas, put ideas to work and repeat the process.

Gordon (1961) cited "Synectics" as an important problem solving method and experimented it as a means of enhancing creative potential. "Synectics" always aims at generating new alternative thoughts by using metaphors and analogies. This method is also helpful to increase problem-solving capacity, creative experiences, empathy and insight into social relations (Bruce, Joyce and Weil, 1992).

Torrance (1965) stressed on generating greater number of ideas to a particular stimulus and developed six stimulating principles for stimulating creative thinking. The principles suggested to-treat questions with respect, treat imaginative and unusual ideas with respect, show pupils that their ideas have value, give opportunities for practice without evaluation, encourage and evaluate self-initiated learning and tie in evaluation with causes and consequences.

Davis (1969) identified four techniques for creativity development. The techniques are as follows:

(a) *Part Changing Method* : In this technique the child is given a thing with specific size, colour, shape and told to change each part and think of creating something original.

(b) *Checker Board* : It is similar to cross word puzzle. On one side, for example, characteristic of one individual are written and on the other side the educational situation. The student is asked to fill up the type of technique that is to be followed to teach him. This can be made a routine work and used through conducting different games.

(c) *Check List* : In this technique seven characteristics such as colour, area, size, old or new, add or subtract, rearrangement and new model are written on a paper. Here, the students are to use these dimensions when they describe books, vehicles, etc.

(d) *Finding Something Similar* : Here a problematic situation is shown to the child with some remarks on solution of similar problems. The child may apply the knowledge to solve the problem he has encountered. For example, the child is told that your school has no large place for cars to park. But parents come with their cars. Where can they park? Along with this, they are told to keep in mind how books are arranged in a book store, shoes are kept in a shoe shop, how ants/bees live, etc. Then the child can possibly try to think of a multistoried garage.

Prasad (1979) used the "Discovery Method" to promote creativity and achievement against the traditional method. Mehdi's Creative Thinking Test and students' achievement scores were taken as the measures of creativity and achievement respectively. A statistical analysis of data proved the significant effectiveness of discovery method in developing these creative potentialities among students.

Golub and Hahn (1983) designed the study to compare the effect of a creative training programme on students in both open and traditional classrooms, as many educators expression favours open classroom due to its emphasis on self-directed education, integrated studies and responsible decision making in comparison to traditional classroom. A sample of 48 third graders served as sample of the study having 24 each from open and traditional classroom. Each class was then divided into experimental and control groups. The experiment went on for eight weeks having four thirty-minutes sessions per week. The teaching mainly stabilized on the process of brainstorming, creative problem solving and principles of stimulating new ideas. From the analysis of gain scores no significant difference was found between open classroom and traditional control groups. However, there were significant difference between control group and experimental group on all measures following exposure to training. The gain score of experimental group was significantly higher than that of control group and open classroom was found to facilitate creative growth and expression.

Hooda and Jarial (1983) experimented the effect of "Role-playing Technique" developed by Moreno and his associates in 1945. Through applying all the principles of role playing, the subjects were taught by the investigator following eight successful steps of play, such as, defining the problem situation, selecting actors and protagonists, warm up, briefing the actors and the audience, enactment, discussion on played situation, evaluation of whole session and re-playing situation. The study reported its effectiveness.

Vora (1984) developed a divergent thinking programme in mathematics of standard VII and VIII students. The researcher experimented the method in relation to gade and sex. After trying out the programme on 115 students, the investigator conducted the experiment on 271 students of both seventh and eighth class. Data on creativity were collected by Passi's Test on Creativity. A 3x2x2 factorial design was used in the study and in data analysis. The findings reported development of creativity as a result of Divergent Thinking Programme in Mathematics (DTPM). It was found equally effective for both boys-girls and high-low creative groups.

Gupta (1985) developed a Creative Training Programme (CTP) for sixth graders and experimented that on them with relation to their sex and intelligence. Analysis of data reported a great possibility of development of creativity through CTP without hampering the routine work of the school.

Katiyar and Jarial (1985), observing the possibility of training in verbal and non-verbal creativity, designed a training programme which included Verbal Creativity Developing Programme (VCDP) and Non-Verbal Creativity Development Programme (NCDP). The training programme was experimented on 160 ninth graders in a Two Group Pre-test and Post-test design. The Torrance Test of Creative Thinking was used as measuring tool of creativity and 50 school periods were utilized for the experiment. The result established a significant effectiveness of VCDP and NCDP in development of different dimensions of verbal and non-verbal creativity. SES and sex proved no significant effect on development of creative potentials-verbal and non-verbal. But low- creative female group of pre test stage gained significantly more (at post test stage) than the high creative male group's in their creativity gain scores.

Singh (1985) experimented the creative method of teaching Mathematics on 277 secondary school students. Mehdi' s Test of Creative Thinking was used as the means of obtaining creativity measures. The study reported the significant effect of the method on the development of creativity among secondary school students.

Hooda and Jarial (1986) studied the effect of teaching mathematics to sixth graders by using mastery learning on different dimensions of verbal and non-verbal creativity. Following a random control group pretest post test design, 55 sixth graders were divided into two comparable (on creative measures) groups-experimental and control. Students in the experimental group were taught eight units of Mathematics from their prescribed test book, by following the strategy of mastery learning. The criteria of mastery learning was fixed to be 80 percent mastery of the content. The same content was taught to the students of control group by traditional methods. The experiment continued for six months. Verbal form of Passi's Test of Creativity and the Non-verbal form of Torrance Test of Creative Thinking were used at pre- and post-test stages for measuring different dimensions of verbal and non-verbal creativity respectively. Analysis of data revealed that except for flexibility, experimental group students scored significantly higher than control group members on all the dimensions of verbal creativity, i.e., on fluency ($t=2.20$; $P<0.05$); on flexibility ($t=1.92$; $P<0.05$); on originality ($t=2.47$, $P>0.05$) and on composite creativity ($t=2.26$, $P<0.05$). Difference was also found significant in the post test mean creativity scores of students of experimental and control groups on all the dimensions of non-verbal creativity, i.e., on fluency ($t=6.88$, $P<0.001$), on flexibility ($t=6.24$, $P<0.001$), on originality ($t=4.61$, $P<0.001$), on elaboration ($t=4.68$, $P<0.001$) and on composite nonverbal creativity ($t= 6.33$, $P<0.001$). This shows that teaching through mastery learning helps in improving different dimensions of verbal and non-verbal creativity.

Mitchell and Wilkens (1986) investigated the changes in hemispheric functioning of college students who participated in a teacher education course in creativity. Your style of learning and thinking (SOLAT) Form A (Torrance, 78) was used as the measure of creativity. The sample consisted of 256 advanced education students, some of whom had very little teaching experience. The thirty contact hour creative course explored strategies for structuring the classroom environment to enhance development of creative thinking and conceptually based plans and activities which were designed to further creative development. The pre-post SOLAT scores were analysed by Sign Test. The result showed a statistically significant decrease in the scores of test items representing left hemisphere style of learning and thinking. There was comparatively small, non-significant positive change in the scores representing right hemisphere responses while the author expected an improvement in right hemisphere score. Hence, it was inferred that the course was not effective, may be due to either previously developed thinking pattern or due to short duration of the course.

Nandanpower (1986) hypothesizing the improvement of language achievement and linguistic creativity as the effect of creative teaching, used the equivalent groups pre-test post-test design. The experimental group now taught by self-developed creative method and the control group was taught by traditional method. The data compared by 't' test revealed that, due to the impact of creative method of teaching the experimental group was found to score significantly higher than the control group in linguistic creativity and composite creativity.

Sharma (1986) prepared an instructional package (print-pictures and its workbook; tape slides and its work book) and experimented that to know its effect on verbal and non-verbal creative abilities of secondary school students. A 4x3x3 factorial design was used which included intelligence and achievement as correlates. TTCT was used to test creative measure. Findings supported the significant impact of the instruction on the development of creative thinking. Both print-picture and tape-slide methods proved their positive impact on performance and concept learning keeping pace with different levels of creativity.

Shaw and Cliat (1986) developed a model for training of teachers for development of creative thinking. The method was also experimented by teacher trainers, who worked with pre-school children, three hours a week. They used to meet their supervisors 90 minutes a week for training in teaching techniques. In this meeting they receive feedback from their supervisors, who had observed their work with children. The experimental group was formed with 19 Pre-service teachers and the control group was formed with 18 pre-service teachers. For an eight week period, supervisors trained the experimental group on divergent thinking and questioning techniques using the model for teacher training. The control group was trained by their supervisors in classroom managements, fostering positive self-concept in children and promoting various readiness skills, but not on divergent thinking techniques. The experiment continued for eight weeks. The supervisors tested both experimental and control groups of pre-service teachers with pre- and post-tests to measure their knowledge of divergent thinking questions. Analysis of covariance proved significant difference in post test creativity scores of experimental and control groups in favour of experimental group.

Stasinos (1986) studied the effects of 16-week creativity training programme upon the creative performance and self-esteem of mentally handicapped Greek children by applying Mark 1 NDC programme (Renzulli, 1973) three times a week. Seventeen primary special state schools for MH Greek children drawn randomly from six urban areas of Greece participated in the study. Experimental and control groups were randomly identified with 45 subjects each. Pre-post tests on creativity and self-esteem were administered. Verbal and figural subtests of

TTCT and Coopersmith's (1967) self-esteem scale were administered to obtain respective measures in creativity and self-esteem. The analysis reported that the experiments made significant improvement on five out of seven creativity factors as well as on subjective self-esteem. Figural flexibility, figural elaboration and behavioural self-esteem were not significantly improved. Sex played no role to influence either creative performance or subjective self-esteem.

Torrance and Safter (1986) used TTCT (verbal and figural) and compared the change of creative performance of students acquired in 1972 to that of new norms of TTCT, computed in 1982. The result reported that at almost every grade or educational level the scores had increased beyond the scores obtained in 1975. On fluency, flexibility and originality components of creativity, from grade one through junior high school on Form A and B, the results reported a significant increase in gain scores.

Patel (1987) experimented the effect of produce Creative Thinking Programme on the creative abilities of elementary school children in relation to sex and intelligence. The researcher took four experimental classes, which were taught 32 programmes and four traditionally taught control classes for the study. After collecting data through own intelligence and creativity tests and analyzing the data by ANOVA, the researcher reported the significant effect of Produce Creative Thinking Programme (PCTP) on the development of creative thinking ability. Intelligence was also found as an important factor to influence creative development, whereas, sex had shown no significant effect on the enhancement of creativity.

Burns (1988) developed a course pattern and step-by-step guidline for teacher to teach Haiku poems and songs and for enabling elementary students to explore a process of composition of using Haiku poetry, penatonic scales, rhythmic durations and melodic contour-in other words create a song. Haiku is an unrhythmed Japanese poem of three lines containing 5, 7 and 5 syllables respectively. He also realised its effectiveness in creating new and original melodies through totally accepting, non-competitive and non-threatening environment.

Buyer (1988) studied the impact of criteriacued, Brainstorming and standard instructions on the development of creative problem solving capacities. The areas of problems included producing a title for a story, constructing a sentence using all of the words in a word set, completing the verbal portion of the last panel of a cartoon, writing a title for a table of data and writing a summary for a paragraph. The sample consisted of 75 students registered in introductory psychology classes who participated in the experiment for class credit. The subjects were randomly assigned the equal numbers to the three instructional conditions. The problems chosen represented verbal, numerical and pictorial areas of endeavour. All responses were written and none required computation or drawn responses. Two raters rated the creative progress of students in degrees. The study reported that the group working under the brainstorming instructions produced more responses (44% of total number) than either of the other two groups. Subjects in the criteria-cued and standard instruction conditions produced approximately equivalent number of responses (28% and 29% of the total number of responses respectively). Subjects in brainstorming and criteria-cued conditions produced approximately the same number of superior responses (120 and 123 respectively) and both the groups produced substantially more superior responses than subjects in the standard instruction condition (71). But in percentage of superior responses (upper 10% of rating distribution) the superiority of criteria-cued procedure (14.7%) over brainstorming (9.2%) and standard instruction (8.2%) was found.

Gurman (1988) conducted a study on the impact of travelling to foreign land in development of creative thinking. Travelling was regarded as an improved method of teaching in the study. The effect of foreign travel specifically was experimented on the improvement of creative responses diversely by exposing the individual to new problems, providing new ideas, offering fresh perspective on familiar problems and by providing time for new and original thoughts. A pre-test and post-test design was used on two groups (experimental and control groups) having 24 students in each group. Torrance Test of Creative Thinking was used as the creaivity measure and ANOVA was used for data analysis The result established the significance of effect of foreign travel on development of creative thinking among the participants.

Hennessey and Amabile (1988) had developed and experimented a story telling instructional package for fostering creativity. The sample consisted of 115 boys and girls ranging from five to 10 years old. All children participated in individual story-telling sessions in a parochial school in eastern Massachusetts. Three elementary school teachers with at least three years of teaching experience with children's writing were the story judges. Subjects began the experimental session by examining a set of detailed black and white drawings in a book with no words. Different pictures were given in the test where the subjects were to frame stories basing on those pictures. Three judges rated the stories thought up by the students on eight dimensions-creativity liking, novelity, imagination, logic, emotion, grammar, detail vocabulary and straightforwardness. A Spearman-Brown inter-judge reliability was calculated for each dimension of the judgement (Nunnallym 1967). All reached an acceptable realiability level. Six of the nine reliabilities were above 0.85, with a median reliability of 0.88. Of particular interest is the reliability of the creativity measure; this value was highly satisfactory at 0.91. In a varimax rotation factor analysis, three orthogonal factors gave significant mean values, such as; creativity (4.48), factual detail (1.68) and technical goodness (1.37); where the creativity mean value showed its most significance. Further, four dimensions of rating found loaded high and positively on the creativity factor and low on factual detail and technical goodness. Instead of certain difficulties in rating as an assessment measure for creativity and in operationalizing the novelity and appropriateness of the product, the story telling method presents a number of practical advantages within a theoretically sound methodology to assess and instigate creative potentials among story-liking elementary graders.

Joseph (1988) examined the effect of creative divergent thinking training on the creative divergent thinking. The study was conducted on 46 sixth graders in a Quasi-experimental Non-equivalent Control Group Design by administering pre-tests and post-tests on creativity. The intervention lasted for 10 weeks with three thirty minutes lessons per week. Torrance Test of Creative Thinking was used to obtain the creativity measure. The obtained gain scores were logically analysed by MANOVA.

The result reported a significant increase in verbal creative thinking and a significant decrease in figural creative thinking as an effect of creative divergent thinking programme.

Michael (1988) prepared a programme for development of creative thinking ability (CTA) and proved the effectiveness of the programme. The study was conducted on 330 students and the investigator used his own creativity test to measure creative potentiality of students. Analysis of covariance stated that, experimental groups gained more by CTA programme than the control group. The adjusted means of two experimental groups did not differ significantly, whereas, the means of control group was found significantly lower than the means of experimental group.

Nosanchuk, Ogrodink and Henigan (1988) investigated the effect of short story writing on the incubating capacity. Incubation figures prominently in the theories of creativity as well as narrative accounts of creative breakthrough. The story-writing was conducted in English language. A test of measuring personal creativity by TPIT was used to obtain creativity scores of 37 subjects, who bifurcated into experimental group (19 subjects) and control group (18 subjects). After eight days instruction, the correlational analysis of the result was made. The findings reported high and positive effect of short story writing on development of creative potential through enhancement of incubating capacity of young students.

Patel (1988) had taken a study to know the effectiveness of brainstorming technique on the creative thinking of secondary school students in relation to their intelligence. The researcher used his own Brainstorming Technique Programme in the study. J.N. Patel's Creativity Test and Desai's Group Test of Intelligence were used as the means for obtaining creativity and intelligence measures. The experimental and control groups were randomly indentified. The experimental group was taught by Brainstorming Technique Programme, whereas, the control group was taught by traditional method. The 2x2 factorial design was followed in the study and the data were analysed by application of ANCOVA. The findings stated that the brainstorming technique proved successful for developing verbal and figural creativity, keeping positive relationship with intelligence. The gain scores in creativity of high IQ students of experimental group was found higher in comparison to the gain scores of low IQ students.

Sharma and Bhartiya (1988) in a 2x2x2 factorial design tried to establish the effectiveness of both linear strategy and branching style on creativity of secondary school students with relation to sex and intelligence. In total 80 students (40 boys and 40 girls) were taken as sample of the study. Pre-test and Post-test scores were analysed by unweighted mean analysis and by application of ANCOVA. The study reported that the linear strategy represents most convergent thinking and therefore creative students disliked the strategy. But in case of branching style, the creativity scores were found to be better predictors of post-test scores, because the branching model provided multi-tracks to think divergently.

Ekvall and Parnes (1989) compared the effects of four creative problem solving techniques-Brainstorming applied in classical manner, Brainstorming combined with analogical thinking, Morphological Analysis and Creative Group Leadership on the development of creative thoughts. The participants in the experiment were 30 product design engineers from Swedish Metalwork Companies. All were male and between 25 and 45 years of age, the mean age being 35. They were divided into five groups after being matched on creative potentials. Students were given a battery of psychological tests—two intelligence tests (one of verbal comprehension, one of logical reasoning), a creativity test (Produce Creativity Test) and a self-rating scale on creativity. After pre-tests, the groups (experimental and control) were exposed to different approaches of problem solving. The experimental groups were provided with leaders who directed the groups in various methods and procedures of attacking problems, whereas, the control groups were left leaderless. The experiment went on for three days and five product development problems were used during three days. The solutions produced by the groups were judged on three dimensions—usefulness, elegance and originality by a highly competent jury. The study reported that brainstorming combined with analogy brought better problem solution than all the other methods, including control condition.

Gill, Singh and Chauhan (1990) examined the effect of an intervention programme on some cognitive abilities of pre-schoolers. Taking 30 children from Ludhiana district, the researcher matched them on the basis of their parental education, income, birth order and intelligence. Pathak's Draw-a-Man Test was used as a measure of cognitive abilities of students. The result reported that the intervention programme was found to be effective in improving cognitive thoughts of students, which centered round familiarity with environment, sensori discrimination and sequential thinking.

Gupta (1990) experimented the effect of own Creative Training Programme (CTP) on the development of creative thinking of primary schoolers through a 2x3x2 factorial design. Intelligence and sex were studied as independent variables. Allthough the study was conducted on 357 samples, the data producing sample was 240. Mehdi's Verbal and Non-Verbal Tests of Creative Thinking, Jalota Group Test of Mental Ability and CTP Questionnaire were used as tools for the study. The CTP was designed to improve various creative thinking abilities—fluency, flexibility, originality and elaboration-in children through semantic and figural exercises unit classes and analysis of relations systems, transformations and implications. The programme consisted of 12 lessons having six each from semantic and figural content. For each unit three or four exercises were prepared. In total the programme had 42 exercises. Opinion was taken from experts on a rating scale for its face validation. The experimental group was exposed to the CTP intervention and the control group was taught through traditional method. Pre-Post test results were analysed by application of ANOVA which reported the successfulness of creativity training programme in developing creative thinking abilities in students. The experimental group was reported to be higher in their verbal and non-verbal creativity scores than the control group's creativity scores. High intelligent students were found to score higher in their verbal originality only. Sex showed no significant effect on CTP.

Burns and Reis (1991) stated five steps for developing thinking skill components in a gifted education programme. The steps included direct instruction on the development and use of lesson plan that defines, describes and models strategie skill; giving necessary training; planning schedule for teachers to develop units of instruction basing on practice of thinking skills;

observing the strategies by teacher and engaging students in guided practices. The investigators proved the significance of this programme to attain skill mastery and to transfer such to develop new thoughts in appropriate content area.

Buswell (1991) in an exploratory investigation used introspection as a methodology for developing creative products. A representative sample was selected for introspective focus and intellectual tools like introspection, imagination and intuition. Data gathered from the experimental and traditionally taught control groups were treated by cluster analysis, reliability analysis, correlational analysis and repeated measures tests. The analysis found the significant effect of introspection on development of creative abilities among students.

Ferrell (1991) studied the impact of teachers' questioning style on the improvement of students' critical thinking. Two control groups and two experimental groups were randomly selected for study. Wastson-Glaser Critical Thinking Appraisal Test was used as the measure of critical thinking ability. The experimental group was taught through asking question method by a well-trained teacher, whereas the control group was taught traditionally. The analysis of the result revealed a significant increase in Watson-Glaser Critical Thinking Test scores of students in treatment or experimental group. But no such increase was found in the students of control group.

Greer and Levine (1991) conducted a study on 85 data producing samples (100 initial sample) recruited from undergraduate courses in the College of Education situated at New Mexico State University. The purpose of the study was to investigate the relative effectiveness of a fantasy induction, intrinsic motivation induction and combined motivation induction upon creative writing performance. Three experimental groups were taught through three new treatment methods and control group was left to traditional method of teaching. Creativity on development of the Haiku style poems was used as dependent variable. Hence, the pre-post tests of the study were based on Haiku poems. Six judges rates the poems for creativity. The mean score for each condition was fantasy (M=42.91) intrinsic motivation (M=41.05) and conjuctive motivation (M=40.32) and control (M=32.70). The post-hoc analysis indicated that the experimental groups were significantly higher than the control groups in their creativity scores concerned to Haiku style poetry writing.

King (1991) studied the effect of training in strategic questioning on children's problem solving performance. Forty-six normally achieving fifth grade children (18 girls and 28 boys) at an elementary school in sub-urban southern California participated in the study. Students were randomly assigned to same-sex pairs for computer lab activities. It was resulted in 3 pairs of girls and 5 pairs of boys. But complete data were available from 7 pairs of guided peer questioning students, 8 pairs of unguided peer questioning students and 8 pairs control students. Hence, the study was based on three conditions related to computer-assisted problems. One group (guided questioning) used strategic questions to guide their cognitive and metacognitive activity during problem solving with partners engaging in a questioning-answering dialogue. A second group (unguided questioning) was simply instructed to ask and answer questions with their partners during problem-solving. A third group (control group) received no training or instructions in questioning. The problem-solving outcome was measured by a written test of problem-solving ability and by success on a novel computer assisted problem. Examination of verbal interaction between the partners during this task provided an assessment of problem-solving process and additional problem-solving outcomes. Analysis reported that guided questioners outperformed the unguided questioners and controlled both written test of problem solving and novel computer task. They also asked more strategic questions and gave more elaborated explanations during problem-solving than their untrained peers.

Singer (1992) developed and experimented the effect of "Teacher Consultation Programme" on the development of students' higher level thinking skills. Here, as reported by the investigator, the resoursefulness, competency and motivation of teacher are helpful for positive development of students' thinking capacity.

Coleman (1992) stressed on the effective use of Cognitive Map as metaphor for development of practical knowledge, logical thinking and critical judgement of students. He found positive and significant effect of such potentiality on the development of critical thinking ability or creative potentiality of gifted learners.

Shan (1992) experimented the effectiveness of brainstorming, problem solving, project and quiz in comparison to traditional method of teaching of science on the development of creative thinking ability. Two hundred sixty six ninth graders were administered the Verbal and Non-verbal creativity tests developed by the investigator, SES scale of Koul (1985) and Raven's Colour Progressive Matrices. The study was based on five groups Pre-Post Randomised Matched Design. After Pre-tests, the experiments on different methods were conducted followed by Post-test on creativity. Analysis of data through ANCOVA and 't' test found that the group of students who were taught science using various experimental methods: brainsterming, problem-solving, project and quiz gained significantly in their individual and composite creativity scores as compared to the group of students taught through traditional method. Brainstorming proved most effective in developing creative thinking in comparison to the use of project, quiz or problem solving activities in teaching.

Carson and Carson (1993) conducted an experimental study on 54 subjects to test the hypothesis—whether goal setting procedure and feedback increases creative potentiality. In the pre-test post-test design, data was analysed by application of ANCOVA. The study reported that subjects assigned a creativity goal with a quantity goal performed more creativity than the individuals assigned a goal for quantity only. Feedback dramatically improved creative performances among students when provided with creative goals. Hence, goal setting has taken one step in outlining a practical mechanism for creativity management which may ultimately enhance organisational productivity, showing a vital organisational effectiveness.

Grossman and Wiseman (1993) after a vivid research analysis stressed on seven cardinal principles for developing creative problem solving ability of chilidren through training. The principles were : 1. the future initiates or pulls creative thoughts, 2. initial fact finding is best postponed, 3. problem redefinition is often a retrospective event, 4. metaphors and analogies fuel the creative process, 5. forcing relationship is a key process factor, 6. convergence is highly creative process whose potential is often neglected, and 7. Work only on participants' real problem.

Jampole (1993) studied the effect of imagery training on creative writings of academically gifted students of elementary education level. One hundred twentysix academically gifted third and fourth graders were divided into imagery training group writing practice group and control group. After the pre-test, the two experimental groups were taught by imagery training procedure and writing practice method respectively, whereas, the control group was exposed to the traditional method. After intervention the post-test was administered. The analysis of pre-post test data showed that imagery training had significant effect on the enhancement of creative thinking potentialities among high IQ students.

Murdock, Isaksen and Lauer (1993) conducted a study on effectiveness of creative training and stability-*cum*-internal consistency of Kirton-Adaption Innovation Inventory on the creative talents. The subjects were 143 undergraduates enrolled in eight sections of an introductory course on creativity in a mideastern college and an additional group of 38 students from a general marketing class in the business department in the same campus. Pre-test post-test non-equivalent control group was used to measure the effects of creativity training in the classroom. Intervention period extended for 14 weeks. Kirtons measure was used for obtaining creativity measures. The creative method of teaching was to provide awareness and understanding of creativity in five major areas: creative process, creative person, creative press or environment, creative product and guidelines and techniques of creative problem-solving. The obtained data was analysed by application of Lindquist Type III Analysis of variance. The result reported no significant effect of training on the development of creative thinking. There was however a significant effect of gender by pre-post test interactions for the full KAI scale scores. The pretest and post-test means for men were 101.9 (SD=15.1) and 105.9 (SD=17.0) and pre-test and post-test means for women were 97.3 (SD=13.6) and 98.3 (SD=15.5), respectively.

Wesenberg (1994) advocated and tested the fruitful-ness of a new method of breeding individual-social drives for stimulating creative potentials. He, from his research analysis found that the creativity of workers in the organisations could be increased through observing and developing democratic and humanitarian managerial behaviours in the companies.

Gaekwad Nautial Pai and Paremu (1994) studied the effect of brainstorming on the creativity scores of institutionalized and non-institutionalized girls having age range 10-15 years. A 2x2 factorial design was adopted. The sample consisted of 26 institutionalized and non-institutionalized girls each divided equally into control and experimental groups. Six brainstorming sessions were conducted for two experimental groups over a period of 15 days. Scores obtained on Koul's Creativity Test before and after the intervention were compared by using the 't'-test. A significant elevation in creativity scores following brainstorming session was seen in the experimental group, particularly among the institutionalized subjects.

Mann (1994) in an experimental study, evaluated the effect of telecommunication, image processing and expert system on development of giftedness. He found a positive effect of these systems on enhancement of such abilities of students.

Moon and Feldhusen (1994) studied a programme for academic and creative enrichment. Taking a longitudinal and retrospective multi-case study design, the investigators tried to evaluate the accomplishment and future plans of elementary gifted students, who have undergone PACE programme since three years. The impression of students and family members on the effectiveness of PACE programme to develop students, talent was also obtained by the investigators. The analysed result supported both short-term and long-term effect of PACE in developing students' creative potentials.

Russel (1994) studied the effect of creative training on concept map complexity. The sample consisted of 120 students randomly selected from 5th, 6th and 7th classes and divided into experimental and control groups having 20 students in each group of learning disabled, regular education and mentally gifted students. The gain scores of pre-post test design were analysed by application of ANOVA. The results reported that the subjects who received creativity training developed significantly more complex concept maps than the subjects who received no such training.

Adaman and Blaney (1995) studied the effect of musical mood induction on creativity. Through a pre-test post-test experimental design they found that strong mood cultivated in either direction is associated with higher creativity scores. Their finding goes in favour of the study of Daubman and Nowicki (1987) who reported the positive effect of enduced mood on the development of creative thinking.

Ashnan, Write and Conway (1995) found the significant effect of a process-based instruction (PBI) teaching model applicable for all mainstream classrooms (containing students of diverse skills and abilities) on development of metacognitive skills of academically gifted students. A case study was conducted by the investigators to realise its great and tangible contribution for academic excellence.

Camp (1995), in a longitudinal divergent thinking study, collected data from 33 students (23 selected for treatment and 10 for non-treatment group), who had creative potentials. After six weeks treatment the effect on first to sixth grade treatment groups and fourth to sixth grade non-treatment groups the data were analysed. The study showed treatment effect up through the sixth grade with decline in divergent thinking scores occurring by ninth and 12th grades. It was suggested by the investigator that decline in divergent thinking after sixth grade was related to change in the enrichment programme in which students participation was less. But the causes of such less participation (which may indicate the less encouraging nature of treatment for students) was not revealed in the study, by the investigator,

Chislett (1995) compared the effectiveness of the creative problem solving (CPS) model on the schoolwide type III enrichment programme to enhance creative productivity of the students. Training in and use of the heuristic method with Type III enrichment was offered as an integrated approach. The findings of the study reported the authenticity of problem-solving activity in enhancing creative productivity of students concerned to school-wide enrichment programme.

Moukwa (1995) structured and experimented a training strategy for fostering creative talents in industrial and business organisations. The findings of the study stressed on principles of collaboration, cooperation, coalition, encouragement and establishment of suitable environment for developing creativity in industrial managements.

Klauer (1996) reported three experimental studies related to the effects of teaching of inductive reasoning on intelligence test performance, learning and problem-solving. In the third experiment, the investigator tried to examine the influence of inductive reasoning strategies and relevant knowledge about the system to be handled on the manysided problem solving capacity of the individual. Sixty eighth graders of a grammar school participated in the experiment. Most of the students were 13 years old. The subjects were randomly alloted to two conditions. In the rating condition the students were trained in the strategy of reasoning inductively for 10 hours. During that time, the control group students continued their classroom lessons. After the training sessions, both the groups were administered a post-test. The training was performed using the Inductive Reasoning Training Programme II (Klauer, 1991). The 10 training sessions were distributed over five different days and they took place in small groups of five students each. The pre-test post-test data were collected through a German Cognitive Abilities Test. The analysis showed that the training was successful. The training group had a mean total raw gain score of g=6.2, whereas, the control group had a loss in the mean score (g=6.5). An analysis of variance with the post-test as dependent variable and pre-test as covariate yielded a significant difference between trained and not-trained groups, $F(1,57)=35.55$, $P<0.01$. Thus, it was concluded that training showed a transfer effect to CAT programme.

Ritchie and Edwards (1996) evaluated the effect of general thinking skill programme and de Bono's CoRT (Cognitive Research Trust) programme, which features divergent and creative thinking. A repeated measures (i.e. pre-test, immediate post-test, delayed post-test) quasi-experimental design was chosen because it was not possible to assign randomly subjects to treatment and control groups. Forty aboriginal students from a total population of 125 children (age=7 yrs) were the focus of the study who were selected from sixth classes of the disadvantaged schools of North Queensland in Australia.

Five instruments were administered in the study. The tests were : Otis—Lennon School Ability Test—Intermediate Form R was used to measure scholastic aptitude; Torrance Tests of Creative Thinking (Verbal, 1990) was used to measure pre-test post-test creativity scores; Edwards's Thinking Approaches Questionnaire was used to assess the impact of the CoRT-1 programme on North Queensland Year 7 students; Self Concept As a Thinker (SCAT) Scale used to measure self concept; and the Intellectual Achievement Responsibility Questionnaire (IARQ) was used for achievement measure. The data were analysed by ANOVA, which supported the hypothesis that the creative thinking of urban aboriginal students was enhanced as a result of their participation in a twenty lesson CoRT programme.

CHAPTER 3

THE STUDY OF CMTE

3.1 Rationale

3.2 Statement of the Problem

3.3 Operational Definitions

3.4 Scope and Delimitation

3.5 Objectives

3.6 Hypotheses

3.7 Design

3.8 The Sample

3.9 Tools Used

CHAPTER 3

The Study of CMTE

3.1 RATIONALE

Creativity, now-a-days, has been regarded as the most commanding area of research. As a unique and higher order mental operation, though it has accomplished many definitional interpretations, methodological trends and approaches, separate dimensionality of creativity has still remained as a matter of great debate. A variety of relationships between creativity measures and other measures though have been explored, their findings posed conflicting contradictions and the results, in practice, are left inconclusive.

Getzels and Jackson's pioneering study which generated considerable interest among psychologists and educators around the world, dichotomised creativity and intelligence. The study described creativity as a separate entity showing its very low relationship with that of intelligence. Many reviewers (Merrifield, 1962; McNemar,1964) though tried to find out the linkages of Getzels and Jackson study, they failed to falsify the researches which established a low and non-significant relationship (Yamamoto, 1964; Thrope, 1965; Davis and Belcher, 1971; Weinstein and Bobko, 1980; Freeman, 1995) between creativity and intelligence. There are also a great number of research findings, which strongly support the positive and significant relationship between these two variables (Burt, 1962; Marsh, 1964; Mednick and Andrews, 1967; Cave, 1970; Dewing, 1970; Mishra, 1986; Chadha and Chandna, 1990; Runco and Nemiro, 1995).

The concept of creativity as a facilitator of achievement was considered as a field of research in the most recent time. For educators and parents, achievement and intelligence have proved their high concern as some sort of socio-individual aspirations are inherent in their closeness. Researchers, who established positive and significant relationship between creativity and scholastic achievement supported the impact of higher creative potentials to produce higher academic success and *vice-versa* (Bentley, 1966; Carey, 1996; Gilchrist, 1970; Richarson, 1989; Carroll and Howieson, 1992). Contrastically, there are research findings which reported low or negative proximity (Holland, 1961; Flescher, 1964; Dewing, 1970; Richardson, 1989; Toth and Baker, 1990). Torrance (1964) and Edward and Tylor (1965) showed negative relation between these two variables. But, the matter of great surprise is that, why do the creatives achieve low with no apparent learning handicaps, when, in another situation, they are recognised as high achievers. The answer is still conflicting as researchers demonstrated the interference of many socio-behavioural and learning variables (Dunn, 1983; Khatena, 1978; Whitemore, 1980; Torrance, 1970).

Similarly, the factors which manifest the individual's personality patterns in a societal condition, help the individual in developing his creativity. As a result, congenial socio-economic, cultural, educational and environmental support determine the trend and process of making an individual hydra-hearted and manysided in his behavioural dispositions. Research studies also found urban-rural background, high-low income range, race, attitude and awareness, status and style of living as the major determining factors of one's socio-economic status, which indirectly, to some extent, influences the thinking and activity of a person. Some researchers established positive relation between creativity and socio-economic status (SES) (Pandit, 1976; Sharma and Jarial, 1980; Sekhar, 1980; Chaudhury,

1983; Rao, 1988; Roy, 1993; Hussain, 1995). There are other studies which reported no significant relationship between creativity and SES (Seetharam and Vedrtayagam, 1979; Chadha and Sen, 1981). Though, some studies reported that, high creatives are from high SES, it is personally experienced by the investigator and reported by Khandelwal (1995) that many high creative persons of the world, e.g., Mark Twain, Alexander Fleming, Henery Fort, etc. were born and brought up in adverse and disadvantaged socio-economic conditions. Hence, the decision regarding relationship between creativity and SES remained in dilemma.

Although the modern world has recognized the status of women on par with men, the genetic discripancy and its impact on different behavioural dispositions of men and women is out of scientific control. Moreover, some orthodox social values and differentiations augment such diversity either by favouring a patriarchal or a matriarchal social setting. Some parental conservative preference to a particular sex also causes inferiority complex for the other. Some research findings supported the excellence of girls in creative thinking (Torrance, 1963; Naufield, 1965; Ogletree, 1968; Soloman, 1968; Anastasi and Schaefer, 1971; Ramkrishna, 1986; Patel, 1987; Behera, 1993), whereas, others found that boys have excelled girls (Kelly, 1965; Raina, 1969; Mari, 1973; Vora, 1984; Nayana, 1981; Lutzer, 1991; Kapoor, 1996). Most significant matter is that, there are studies showing no sex difference in creativity (Pogue, 1965; Mayhon, 1966; Raina, 1970; Pandey, 1981; Sharma and Bhartiya, 1988; Behera, 1993; Pandey and Rai, 1995). These differing research findings do not lead to any conclusive decision on the relationship of creativity with sex.

The individual may be male or female, he may be the bearer of high or low intelligence and may be brought up in high or moderate or low socio-economic status, but if he is creative we must regard him as most precious national-human resource. The talents which are stored in him or her should be progressively and productively channelized for excellence. There are researchers, who capitalized on genetic predominance of creativity, whereas, others on environmental support. Hereditarians stressed on the genetic transformation of creative tendencies from one generation to another, whereas, so-called behaviourists have laid emphasis on encouraging environment to foster creativity. By heredity Charls Darwin's grandfather was talented, Churchil's grandfather was a British Prime Minister, Roosevelt's causin was a president and on the other hand, Mark Twain, Alexander Fleming, Henery Ford were made creative even having no such higher genetic credibilities.

Now-a-days, psychologists and educationists around the world are thinking multidimensionally about the ways and means of increasing such exceptional attributes of the individual to uptimum. Besides natural environmental instigation, researchers have also devised the formal training strategies and packages to develop creative talents among people living in different sectors—education, business management, industrial organisations etc and among people having different levels of IQ—high, average and low. Many research, studies have also found different principles and means of enhancing creative capabilities of the individual through training (Torrance, 1965; Grossman and Wiseman, 1993; Davidow, 1995; Passi, 1996). Osborn's (1957) "Brainstorming", Gordon's (1961) "Synectics" and Taylor's (1961) 'PAKSA' were also some milestones in the history of creative training. Four sequential steps (Preparation, Incubation, Illumination and Verification) of Wallas (1945) and Davis's four techniques (Part-changing method, Checker Board, Checklist, Finding something similar) were also some guiding processes for effective training procedure to foster such extraordinary power. Seven operating principles for enhanced problem solving (Grossman and Wiseman, 1993), the five major ecological themes of creative intervention (Davidow, 1995, Passi's 1996), five instructional approaches, Albert Upton's "Strategic Reasoning", Feuerstein's "Instructional Enrichment", CoRT method of Edward de Bono (1992) based on Lateral Thinking are some spectacular methodological advancement for developing creative potentialities. Studies conducted by Prasad (1979), Golub and Hahn (1983), Katiyar and Jarial (1985), Singh (1985), Nandanpower (1986), Show and Cliat (1986), Torrance and Safter (1986), Burns (1988), Hennessey and Amabile (1988), Patel (1988), Gill, Singh and Chauhan (1990), Ferrel (1991), King (1991), Coleman (1992), Jampole (1993), Moon and Fledhusen (1994) and Camp (1995) reported the positive and significant effect of different types of training programmes on the development of creative potentiality. Most of the training programmes were conducted on creative problem-solving, imagery training, teacher consultation programme, use of cognitive map, brainstorming, questioning strategy, sensory discrimination, sequential thinking, story telling, foreign travel, VCDP, NCDP and on role playing. Only a single study was conducted on effect of language training on creativity (Nandanpower, 1986). There are also some studies which found 'no' or 'negative' impact of training on creativity development (Mitchell and Wilkens, 1986; Joseph, 1988; Murdock, Isaksen and Lauer, 1993). A very small number of studies showed the training effect on achievement and tried to establish the relationship between development of creativity with that of level of intelligence, as an effect of creative training programme.

On the method of the study, some researchers followed repeated measures design, whereas others adopted one group pre-test post-test design or Control and Experimental Groups Pre-post test Design. The samples were restricted or unrestricted, the number of which ranged from minimum ten students to maximum nearabout four hundreds in different studies. Different tests were used in different studies to obtain creativity, intelligence, SES and achievement measures. Accordingly, appropriate parametric and non-parametric statistical procedures were applied to analyse the data.

The review presented a striking feature that most of the correlational as well as training based studies were found to be conducted in the foreign lands. Specifically and comparatively, in India, the number of studies conducted on the effect of training on creativity development are very few, amidst which no study was available to the researcher relating to the effect of language training (specifically in English of secondary education level) on the development of creative thinking. Though some study attempted to find out the effect of intelligence on the development of creative thinking as a result of training programme, their findings were inconclusive. Not a single study had tried to findout the effect of language training on development of creative thinking with relation to sex, intelligence, SES and achievement combinedly. English, which has been accepted as the second language in India though has immense scope for generating new ideas, imaginary thoughts and creative products, has not yet been considered by the researchers as an important language for developing creative potentialities. Moreover, at the secondary level of Indian educational system, English has not received proper attention of the researchers as it needs. The prevailing traditional approaches of teaching English in secondary schools, though becoming suitable for students' scholastic achievements, in practice, are showing their incapabilities to develop meta-cognitive and higher order creative potentialities, which are within the secondary school students and are to be developed for our national reconstruction. Moreover, till now, our researchers have left this field of language uncultivated and the investiga or found not a single study which has tried to teach English in such a way that the creative potentiality of students has been developed to uptimum extent, keeping pace with achieveme1t of students in concerned subject.

Hence, here, the researcher has felt the exigency of devising and experimenting a new approach of teaching English for developing creativity of secondary school students. He has also realized the logistics of finding out the effect of the creative method of teaching English in the development of creative thinking of secondary school students in relation to their sex, SES, intelligence and achievement in English language.

3.2 STATEMENT OF THE PROBLEM

The research problem was to know the *'Effect of Creative Method of Teaching English (CMTE) on the Development of Creative Thinking of Secondary School Students'*.

3.3 OPERATIONAL DEFINITIONS

3.3.1 Creative Method of Teaching English

Creative Method of Teaching English is an instructional package designed to foster and develop creative thinking ability among students. Gordon (1961) believed that it was possible to train persons directly to develop their creative potentials by conscious analysis and effective training procedures. Walls and Practice (1960s) had identified four sequential steps such as preparation, incubation, illumination and verification for the development of creative thoughts. Likewise, Osborn's (1957) "Brainstorning" and Gordon's (1961) "Synectics" are some important creative methods through which creative thinking of students can be developed to excellence. Joice's "synectics model of Teaching" also aims to develop creative thinking ability.

Here, Creative Method of Teaching English (CMTE) is a new method of teaching developed by the author and it is different from any other traditional method related to teaching of English language. It has been developed as a new model of teaching specially designed for the teaching of English language. This model has syntax, the social system, the stage of reinforcement and the support system with specific principles and characteristics. This method of teaching is intended to develop creative thinking ability of students of secondary level through teaching of English language.

3.3.2 Creative Thinking

Creative Thinking is a term which possesses different connotations. Guilford (1959) accepted it as "divergent thinking, whereas Torrance (1975) defined it as "vertical". Ausubel (1960s) defined creative thinking as "the rare and unique talent in a particular field of endeavour."

Therefore, CREATIVE THINKING, here, is operationally defined as that, which is measured by the Mehdi's Verbal Test of Creative Thinking. This test is a part of the total battery which consists of both verbal and non-verbal Tests. As described by Mehdi (1987) "the verbal test of creativity includes four sub-tests, namely, consequence test, unusual uses test, similarity test and product improvement test" (p. 4). The theoretical frame-work of the test is based on Guilford's (1959) model of divergent thinking and in the preparation of the test, four major characteristics (such as : fluency, flexibility, originality and elaboration) out of six primary traits of Guilford's divergent thinking, are taken into consideration (p. 3). This verbal test includes following dimensions.

FLUENCY is defined as the number of relevent and unrepeated ideas which the tastee produces. Relevance is judged on the basis of the appropriateness of the response when considered in relation to the test problem. An unrepeated idea is one which has been expressed only once under a given problem. The more is the number of ideas produced by the individual to a given task, the greater is the possibility of some being creative.

FLEXIBILITY is represented by a person's ability to produce ideas which differ in class, approach or thought trend. All ideas which fall under one category of approach or thought trend are treated as one for purpose of flexibility. If five ideas produced and all belong to only one category of approach or thought trend, then the trends are treated as one for the purpose of flexibility. It is assumed that the greater is the variety of ideas, the more is the likelihood of them being creative.

ORIGINALITY is represented by uncommonness, novelity and cleverness of a given response. Responses given by less than 5% of the group are treated as original. It is assumed that the greater is the production of unusual ideas, the more is the possibility of those being creative.

3.3.3 Secondary School Students

Secondary School, so far as our Indian educational system is concerned, starts from Class IX and ends with Class XII including both Lower Secondary Stage (Classes IX and X) and Higher Secondary Stage (Classes XI and XII) under its preview (I.E.C.-1964-66; NPE-86). In this study, the Secondary School is defined as Lower Secondary Stage of Secondary Education.

"Secondary School Students is defined as both boys and girls reading in Class IX and X.

3.4 SCOPE AND DELIMITATIONS

3.4.1 Scope

The study was about developing creative thinking of Secondary School Students. It was related to teaching of English to Secondary School Students in India.

3.4.2 Delimitations

The following delimitations were made in this study:

(i) The study was restricted to ascertain the effectiveness of Creative Method of Teaching English (CMTE) on development of creative thinking ability.

(ii) The study was limited to students of class IX only.
(iii) It was limited to students of two Schools of urban area of Cuttack city of Orissa.

3.5 OBJECTIVES

The study had following objectives :

1. To find out relationship between creativity and intelligence.
2. To find out relationship between achievement and creativity.
3. To find out relationship between socio-economic status and creativity.
4. To find out difference in creativity of boys and girls.
5. To find out the effect of Creative Method of Teaching English (CMTE) on the development of creative thinking of students.
6. To find out the effect of Creative Method Teaching English (CMTE) on the development of language skills in English.
7. To find out the relationship between intelligence and development of creative thinking through Creative Method of Teaching English (CMTE).
8. To find out the relationship between change in creativity and change in achievement as a result of Creative Method of Teaching English (CMTE).

3.6 HYPOTHESES

To pave the way for easy realisation of objectives, the following null hypotheses (H_0) of the study were framed:

H_{01} : There is no significant relationship between creativity test score and intelligence test score.

H_{02} : There is no significant relationship between English achievement test score and creativity test scope.

H_{03} : There is no significant relationship between S.E.S. scale score and creativity test score.

H_{04} : (a) There is no significant difference between boys and girls in their mean creativity scores at the pretest stage.

(b) There is no significant difference between boys and girls in their mean creativity scores at post-test stage.

(c) There is no significant difference between boys and girls of the experimental group in their mean gain scores in creativity test.

H_{05}: (a) There is no significant difference between the experimental and control groups in their pre-test creativity mean scores.

(b) There is no significant difference between the experimental and control groups in their post-test creativity mean scores.

(c) There is no significant difference between the experimental and control groups in their mean gain scores in creativity test.

H_{06}: (a) There is no significant difference between the experimental and control groups in their pre-test mean achievement scores in English.

(b) There is no significant difference between the experimental and control groups in their post-test mean achievement test scores in English.

(c) There is no significant difference between the experimental and control groups in their mean gain scores in achievement test in English.

H_{07}: (a) There is no significant difference in creativity mean scores of high intelligence group and low intelligence group at pre-test stage of (i) Control Group and (ii) Experimental Group.

(b) There is no significant difference in creativity mean scores of high intelligence group and low intelligence group at post-test stage of (i) Control Group, and (ii) Experimental Group.

(c) There is no significant difference between high intelligence group and low intelligence group of control and experimental groups in their mean creativity gain scores.

H_{08}: (a) There is no significant difference in mean creativity gain scores of high achievers and low achievers in English achievement test scores of the experimental group.

(b) There is no significant different between mean achievement gain scores in English of high creative and low creative groups.

(c) There is no significant correlation between creativity gain scores and achievement gain scores.

3.7 DESIGN

Basically this research study was experimental by nature. The study had two research designs. First one was Pilot Study Design and second one was the Experimental Design.

3.7.1 Pilot Study Design

Before determining the final design for the experiment, the investigator had tried out the CMTE model. It was done with a view to study the real effectiveness and validity of the CMTE by eliminating its drawbacks and adding the necessary elements into the schemata of the model. For the pilot study, the investigator had followed One Group Pre-test Post-test Design which is presented in the Table 3.1.

TABLE 3.1
Paradigm of One Group Pre-test Post-test Design for Pilot Study

Test	*Variable*	*Test*
Pre-Test	Independent variable	Post-test
(T_1)	CMTE (X)	(T_2)

Here, the investigator had randomly taken a section of ninth graders from a school and had given pre-test on creativity. Mehdi's Verbal Test on Creative Thinking was used to measure the students' creative thinking ability (T_1). Then the same group was taught English language for eight weeks through CMTE (X). After the teaching period, post-test on creative thinking (T_2) was administered.

The collected data was analysed by the application of significance of difference between means (SE_D) and by using the 't test'. Table 3.2 shows the significance of difference between pre-test and post-test mean creativity scores. As the calculated result proved a significant difference (t=6.0518, P>0.01), the null hypothesis which stated, "There is no significant difference between the pre-test and post-test creativity mean scores as an impact of CMTE" was refuted. The investigator found the method effective for experiment and accordingly the experimental design was planned.

TABLE 3.2
Significance of Difference Between the Pre-test and Post-test Creativity Mean Scores in Pilot Study

Tests	*N*	*M*	*SD*	*t*
Pre-test	28	92.00	16.55	6.518
Post-test	28	124.00	22.56	

Significant at 0.01 level (P<0.01).

3.7.2 The Experimental Design

The study was experimental and intended to test the effecetiveness of Creative Method of Teaching English (CMTE) on development of creative thinking of secondary school students. The investigator, here, had followed Randomized Matched Groups Pre-test Post-test Design as indicated in the Table 3.3.

TABLE 3.3
Paradigm for Randomized Matched Groups Pre-test Post-test Design

Randomly assigned matched groups		*Pre-test*	*Independent variable*	*Post-test*
Control Group	C_1 C_2	T_{1C}	Teaching Through Traditional Method	T_{2C}
Experimental Group	E_1 E_2	T_{1E}	Teaching Through CMTE	T_{2E}

3.7.3 Description of the Design

Two schools were chosen for the study at random. From among those, four sections (C_1, C_2, E_1, and E_2) of class IX were selected and assignment of control group and experimental group were given to two sections each at random. Pre-tests on different variables were administered on both the control and experimental groups. Intelligence, creativity, socio-economic status, achievement and sex were the variables included in the study. Creative Method of Teaching English (CMTE) was accepted as independent variable in the study. After the pre-test, English language was taught to the experimental group through CMTE by the investigator himself and the same subject was taught to the control group through the traditional method by the concerned subject teacher. The experimental treatment continued for eight weeks. After the experimental period post-tests on creativity and achievement in English were administered to obtain measures of the dependent variables. Thenafter, the collected data were analysed by application of due statistical procedures to know the effectiveness of independent variable on dependent variables. The detail analysis is presented in Chapter IV.

3.8 THE SAMPLE

3.8.1 Area of Sample

The sample for the study was drawn from a leading urban city of Orissa, i.e. Cuttack. The sample consisted of ninth graders whose average age was 14 years. The mother tongue of the sample was Oriya and all were able to read, write and speak English, Oriya and Hindi. Some were also conversant with other regional Indian languages like Bengali and Urdu. The town had the status of municipality. From among the total number of government and aided schools of the city two schools were chosen at random having one in each type. Though, the nature of the sample was random, basically it was purposive.

3.8.2 Selection of Sections

Each school had several sections in the ninth class. Hence, the investigator had listed all the sections randomly and had given serial numbers to them. The combined listing was done.

By using the table of random numbers four sections were selected. Further, by following the similar procedure, assignment of control group and experimental group were given to different sections. At last, in the design, the investigator found two sections each in the control and experimental groups.

3.8.3 Recruitment of Sample

The selected sections were assigned control group and experimental group at random. Out of total 222 students, which included 103 boys and 119 girls, 176 students (Boys 79, Girls 97) were appeared in different tests. Out of 176 students those appeared in different tests, 140 students were recruited for the study with due attention to the presence of equal number of boys and girls in total groups. This selection was done at random. But the exclusion of many students from the study was due to the absence of students in different testing programmes, lack of necessary data required to be furnished by them in different tests and in the SES scale, non-availability of achievement records of some students and overall due to application of random methods to fulfil the necessity of equalizing the experimental and control groups with regard to the number of students. Students who had changed their sections during experimental period and those who were present in the pretest and also during experiment period, but found absent in either of post-tests, were not included in sample for the study. A groupwise sampling data is presented in Table 3.4 which is followed by a sampling framework of the study in Figure 3.1.

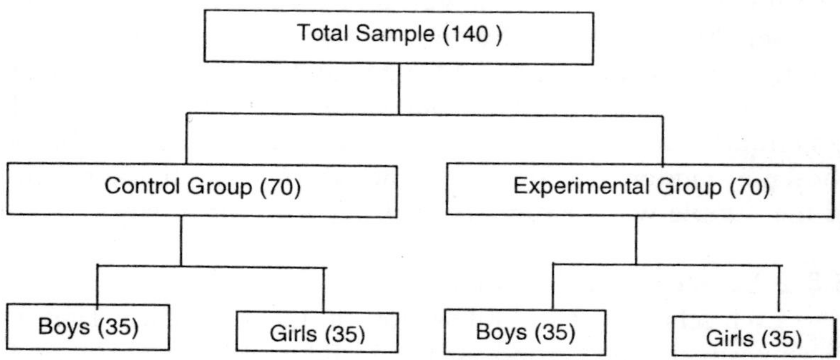

Fig. 3.1 : The Sampling Framework

TABLE 3.4
Data on the Sample of the Study

Group	*Total No. of students (Boys, Girls)*	*Appeared the test (Boys, Girls)*	*Recruited as sample (Boys, Girls)*
Control Group C_1	57 (B.35, G.22)	53 (B.33, G.20)	45 (B.28, G.17)
C_2	64 (B.20, G.44)	63 (B.11, G.32)	25 (B.7, G.18)
Total sample of Control group	121 (B.55, G.66)	96 (B.44, G.52)	70 (B.35, G.35)
Experiemental Group E_1	59 (B.36, G.23)	45 (B.28, G.17)	45 (B.28, G.17)
E_2	42 (B.12, G.30)	35 (B.7, G.282)	25 (B.7, G.18)
Total sample of Experimental group	111 (B.48, G.53)	80 (B.35, G.45)	70 (B.35, G.35)
Grand Total	222 (B.103, G.111)	176 (B.79, G.97)	140 (B.70, G.70)

The total distribution of the sample of the study is presented in Figure 3.1.

3.8.4 Matching of the Sample on Intelligence and Creativity

Intelligence and creative thinking ability of students were controlled at pre-test stage. Accordingly taking those two variables into consideration, at pre-test stage, the sample was matched groupwise.

(a) Matching on Intelligence

The intelligence of the students was measured by Tondon's Verbal Group Test of Intelligence. The obtained scores were analysed and schoolwise significance of difference was tested by application of SE and finding out the 't' value. Such significance testing was the base of matching different groups on intelligence.

(i) Difference in Mean Intelligence Scores of Control Group and Experimental Group of the First School (S_1)

The sample of S_1 consisted of 90 ninth graders, equally represented in control and experimental groups. Table 3.5 gives the data relating significance of difference between control and experimental groups of S_1 in mean intelligence scores.

TABLE 3.5

Significance of Difference between Control Group and Experimental Group of S_1 in Mean Intelligence Scores

Group	*N*	*M*	*SD*	*t*
Control	45	77.222	7.0675	1.6460 n.s
Experimental Group	45	74.6001	8.0148	

n.s. = not significant (P>0.05).

The data given in Table 3.5 stated a non-significant difference between the control group and experimental group of S_1 in mean intelligence scores (t=1.6460, P<0.05). It showed that in the first school both the control group and experimental group were more or less equal in their levels of intelligence.

(ii) Difference in Mean Intelligence Scores of Control Group and Experimental Group of the Second School (S_2)

The sample of S_2, consisted of 50 students. There were 25 students each in control group and in experimental group. Table 3.6 presents the data regarding significance of difference between control and experimental groups of S_2 in intelligence mean scores. It stated a non-significant difference between two

TABLE 3.6

Significance of Difference Between Control Group and Experimental Group of S_2 in Mean Intelligence Scores

Group	*N*	*M*	*SD*	*t*
Control	25	54.6	12.419	0.9479 n.s
Experimental Group	25	58.8	18.344	

n.s. = not significant (P>0.05).

groups in their mean intelligence scores. It revealed that in S_2 both the groups were found to be at equal level in their intelligence scores.

(iii) Difference in Intelligence Mean Scores of Control Group and Experimental Group of both the Schools (S_1+S_2)

There were 70 subjects each in the control group and in experimental group. Intelligence scores of the subjects were obtained by Tondon's verbal group test of intelligence and the significance of difference was tested by SE_D and t-test.

Table 3.7 shows the significance of difference between control group and experimental group in their intelligence scores. It showed a non-significant difference (t=0.0754, P>0.05) between control group and experimental group in their intelligence scores. This result confirmed that both the groups were same in their intelligence. Hence, the impact of intelligence was controlled here and both the groups were matched on intelligence.

TABLE 3.7
Significance of Difference Between Control Group and Experimental Group on Intelligence Mean Scores

Group	*N*	*M*	*SD*	*t*
Control	70	69.1427	14.3069	0.0754 n.s
Experimental Group	70	68.9572	14.7915	

n.s. = not significant at 0.05 level.

(b) Matching on Creativity

The creative thinking ability of students was measured by Mehdi's Verbal Test on Creative Thinking. The collected data was analysed by SE_D and t-tests to find out the significance of difference. The group-wise and total significance tests were presented in Chapter IV of this book. The result showed that the control group and experimental group of S_1 and S_2 did not differ significantly in their pre-test mean creativity scores being the 't'-values 1.2260 (P>0.05) and 0.4971 (P>0.05) respectively. The control group and experimental group of both the schools

(S_2 and S_2) also reported a non-significant difference being the 't'-value 0.4244 ($P>0.05$). These indicated that at pre-test stage all the groups were equal in their creativity mean scores. Hence, the students were matched in their creativity scores at pre-test stage.

Besides creativity and intelligence, socio-economic status and achievement of the sample were studied. But those were not experimentally controlled like creativity and intelligence. Those were measured to establish certain relationships and to study the impact of CMTE on some variables.

3.9 TOOLS USED

In this study, the investigator had used the Oriya version of Verbal Group Test of Intelligence developed by Tendon, Verbal Test of Creative Thinking of Baquer Mehdi, the Oriya version of SES scale for urban area developed by Kuppuswamy and the Listening-Speaking English Achievement Test I and II developed by the investigator. A brief description of these tools is presented as follows.

I. Verbal Test of Creative Thinking by Baquer Mehdi

Dr. Baquer Mehdi, Ex-Professor of Education, NCERT, New Delhi had developed this test battery for measurement of creative thinking ability. He had realized the importance of developing separate creativity tests specifically relevant to a given culture and attempted to solve this problem by preparing his creative test battery. Before it, Torrance, Guilford and Wallach & Kogan had brought out their creativity tests which are being extensively used not only in United States, but also in other countries including India either as such or with some Indian adaptations. But with consideration of Indian cultural ethos, Mehdi's test has a distinction. Mehdi's test was published first in 1973 by Mrs. Qamar Fatima under the sole distributorship of National Psychological Corporation (NPC), Agra. This test is meant for a wide range of sample starting from students of the middle school and going upto the graduate level.

This test has been used by different researchers at different times in various studies. Prasad (1979) and Singh (1984) had used this test to ascertain the effect of teaching methods like problem-solving and specially designed teaching strategy on creativity. Both the methods were found effective in developing creative thinking abilities of the children. Singh (1984) studied the relationship between creativity and other variables like adjustment, frustration and level of aspiration. Significant relationship was found between creativity and level of aspiration and adjustment. Insignificant relationship was found between creativity and frustration. Mehra and Singh (1982) found low correlation between creativity and intelligence. Agarwal and Sushila (1982) found relationship between creativity and risk-taking by using this creative thinking test. Oriya version of this test was first used by Miss Basanti Pradhan (1990) to measure the effect of teaching science by a creative method of teaching upon creative thinking.

The theoretical framework for the preparation of this test is based on Guilford's divergent thinking processes of the mental operation. It measures fluency, flexibility and originality aspects of creative thinking. It includes four sub-tests, namely, consequences test, unusual uses test, similarity test and product improvement test.

(i) Consequences Test

"The basis of this activity is Guilford's "Consequences Test" or Torrance's "Just Suppose Activity". The tasks included in this activity are based on familiar things but are presented in the form of hypothetical situations" (Mehdi, 1985). The consequences test consists of three hypothetical situations : (a) what would happen if man could fly like birds? (b) what would happen if our schools had wheels? and (c) what would happen if man does not have any need for food? These tasks confront the subject with a situation for which he can think of with a large number of possible consequences. This implies cause and effect thinking or stimulus-response activity of the individual's thinking process. The happenings may be usual or unusual, logical or illogical, but the subject is required to think as many consequences of these situations as he can and write them under each situation in the space provided. The test encourages free play of imagination and originality. The time allowed is four minutes for each of the three problems.

The number of relevant responses produced by the subject yields measure of his ideational fluency, the number of shifts in the thinking trends of consequences gives the measures of verbal flexibility and statistical infrequency of the response or the departure of thinking from the common place gives the measure of originality.

(ii) Unusual Uses Test

The basic idea of these tasks comes from Guilford's "Brick Uses Test" or Torrance's 'Tin Can Uses Test' or 'Cardboard Boxes Uses Test'. Common things like water, a wooden stick and a piece of stone are used as stimuli to let the subject's thinking go in different directions. The activity appears playful to the child, but quickly puts him on a train of thought which will yield many novel responses. This test presents the subject with the names of three common objects—a piece of stone, a wooden stick and water—and requires him to write as many novel, interesting and unusual uses of these objects as he may think of. The test measures the subject's ability to retrieve items of information from his personal information in storage. Total 15 minutes duration is allowed for the test with five minutes for each of the three objects. The number of relevant responses gives the measure of one's ideational fluency, the number of thought categories gives the measure of verbal flexibility and uncommonness of responses gives the measure of originality.

(iii) New Relationships or Similarity Test

Taking Mednick's word association definition of creativity and its remoteness into consideration, in this activity, articles of daily use with which the child is quite familiar are taken so as to enable him to think more naturally about relationships between two apparently dissimilar objects. This test presents the subject with three pairs of words apparently different—tree and house, chair and ladder, air and water and requires him to think and write as many novel relationships as possible between the two objects of each pair in the space provided. Here free play of imagination and originality of the subject is given utmost importance. For each pair of words five minutes time is allowed. The items of this activity provide possibilities for scoring responses for fluency, flexibility and originality in the same manner as for Unusual Uses Test.

(iv) Product Improvement Test

This test of verbal imagination has similarity with Torrance's Product Improvement Activity. But the difference is that Torrance used a picture of a toy monkey, whereas, here, Mehdi asked to imagine the figure of a toy horse and to give unusual responses regarding addition of new things by which he can make it more interesting and useful for the child to play with. The task puts the child in the state of imagination and spurs him to think in different directions. For this activity six minutes time is allowed. This test measures fluency, flexibility and originality.

Hence, the total time required for the test is 48 minutes besides the time for instruction, passing booklets to children and collecting those back. The test constructor gives the instruction to students to write the answer in mother tongue also. But the investigator used the English version of the test as the study intended to measure the development of students' creative thinking ability through teaching of English language. The respondents were also given freedom to answer in their mother tongue, if they required so. Mehdi's Verbal Test of Creative Thinking (English Version) is given in Appendix-A and the concerned scoring key in Appendix-B.

II. Socio-Econpmic Status Scale (Urban) By B. Kuppuswamy

A socio-economic status scale for urban area developed by B. Kuppuswamy, was used in the study. The scale was prepared by him and was first published by Manasayan in 1962. Since decades back researchers have experienced the status of SES as an independent variable for different criterion. Kuppuswamy (1962) "had stated that USA had a leading contribution in developing these indices related to urban industrial class structure of that country, with which a good deal of stratification had been made in the recent decades. But in India social prestige is dependent on the amount of income, source of income, education and occupation. A man who gets an income from his inherent property shows higher vanity than a person who has acquired his own property. 'Daily wage' of a person is associated with a lower social status than the monthly salary of a person. Similary, social prestige is dependent on occupation. The cooly, the ditch digger, sweepers and even the carpenters or plumbers and skilled workers are given low social prestige than an engineer or physician. Likewise a carpenter or a fitter who had completed his technical education never commands as much prestige as a person who has completed M.A. or B.A. degree. Now also, it has become the craze of every society to recognize people by looking at their titles, wealth, type of house in which a person lives, the area in which the house is situated, furniture of his house, presence of modern innovative articles at home, ownership of vehicle and the sphere of his social contact.

Looking at the existing social milleu and considering the attributes of some SES scales developed by Taussig (1928), who had built up a scale on the basis of income; Sims (1952) who first used 23 items and then 42 items like education of parents, occupation of parents, possession of telephone, books, etc. in the SES scale; Hollingshead (1958), who used three indications, viz. residential address, occupation and education in the scale; Kuppuswamy had developed and standardized his scale on urban area with three dimensions, such as education, occupation and income. Oriya version of this scale was prepared by the investigator and used in the study.

Description About the Scale

The scale had three dimensions and each dimension has seven items related to different aspects of the category.

(i) Education

Education, here, has been considered as an important factor of developing one's social prestige or status. With respect to education, categorization depends upon the length and type of education and accordingly weightage are given to respective category. Persons having some professional degree, M.A. or B.A. degree are ranked in top category. Persons having intermediate, post-high school diplomas, high school or middle school certificate are ranked in second category. The primary school certificate holders, literates and illiterates are ranked in third category.

(ii) Occupation

Here, looking at the standard of occupation categorization is made. The persons who are unemployed irrespective of their general and professional education or training are at lowest category. Then the categories are professional, semi-professional, skilled and semi-skilled with their specific characteristics. The semi-skilled group include those persons who receive some training to do their routining jobs efficiently, e.g., factory or workshop labourer library attendant, petty shop-assistant, etc. The skillet workers are those who have extensive training on complicated works, e.g., drivers, machine and telephone operators. The middle group includes the persons with some training in arithmetic and probably also in reading and writing. The work, here, generally is repeatitive by nature. The clerk, the typist, accountant, elementary school teacher also come into this group. The semi-professional group consists of occupations which involve post-high school or college education with lower grade professional training. The Junior Engineers, High School Teachers, Lecturers, Junior Administrators, Junior Medical Officers, Insurance Inspectors, Commission Agents, Musicians and Reseasrch Assistants, etc. are included into this group. Finally, the professional group includes the creative persons those involved in decision-making, policy-formation and execution. Doctors, Readers, Professors, Principals, Advocates, Engineers, etc. are coming under this category.

(iii) Income

Kuppuswamy has realized that to obtain accurate data on one's exact income is more difficult than obtaining exact information regarding education and occupation. On the other hand, the categories are very clear as they involve members. The only safety is that the categories have broad range of income and hence slight error does not affect the weightage of the variable and the final SES score.

The scale can be used for collection of information regarding the Socio-Economic Status of an individual or of his father. It is concerned with urban area only. There are two forms (Form A and Form B) separately formed to collect data either regarding the individual or regarding the father of the individual. Both the forms can be used as self-administering forms in the case of literate persons. Form A is meant for adults who are either earning or who are out of employment. It is a schedule to be completed by the investigator by asking questions especially in the case of illiterate persons. Form B is meant for students in schools and colleges to fill up the particulars regarding their parents or guardians. It is self-explanatory device. In both the forms information on education, occupation and income are sought. In this study, the reseasrcher had used the Form B1 as he wanted the SES of guardians or fathers of the concerned students. Before use, the scale was translated into Oriya version by the investigator himself.

A score card, prepared by the scale constructor indicates appropriate weightage score for each item of different categories. The scores may then be entered in the last column. Addition of these three scores gives the final score which determines the status category. Addition of scores of different categories gives the total score of the scale which are to be written in the relevant box, fixed on the top right hand side of the score-card. Realizing the impact of increasing economic condition, Kuppuswamy had brought two revisions in the weightage of income category in 1962 and 1976.

As nearly 20 years have passed away and our society has already realized an accelerated development in its economic standard, the researcher, in this study, has revised the range of income of the income category looking at the Index of our cost of living. The revision of the range category (for the year 1995) made by the investigator is given in the Table 3.8.

TABLE 3.8
Revised Weightage of the SES Scale Items Concerned to Income Category

	Range of Income per month	*Weightage*
1.	Above Rs. 7,000	12
2.	Between Rs. 4,000 to Rs. 6,999	10
3.	Between Rs. 2,500 to Rs. 3,999	6
4.	Between Rs. 1,500 to Rs. 2,499	4
5.	Between Rs. 1,000 to Rs. 1,499	3
6.	Between Rs. 500 to Rs. 999	2
7.	Below Rs. 500	1

A sample of this SES scale is given in Appendix C and the concerned scoring key is given in Appendix D.

III. Achievement Test in English

Two achievement tests were used in the study to measure the achievement of both control and experimental group students in four language skills, such as Listening, Speaking, Reading and Writing in English. First achievement test was given at pre-test stage and second was given at post-test stage. Students' eighth class annual examination marks in English and ninth class half-yearly examination marks in English were accepted as the pre-test achievement test scores and post-test achievement test scores respectively. These achievement tests were related to two language skills, such as Reading and Writing only. For the measurement of achievement of students in other two language skills such as Listening and Speaking, the investigator had prepared the Listening-Speaking English Achievement Test. For it a passage was selected for them from out of their course and that passage was read out before them by the investigator loudly with average speed and by following the necessary principles of reading. Then the passage was silently read by the students for five minutes. Thereafter, students were asked the questions related to the passage. Ten questions carrying four marks each were given on the passage. Each student was asked the questions and given only three seconds to start his answer. If within three seconds he/she fails to start the answer, then the concerned student is disqualified and the investigator has to ask questions to another students. During the time of asking questions the investigator had not asked questions to students serially with a view to test their mental alertness in the classroom, students from different directions were also asked the questions to test their presence of mind. Looking at the correctness of answer scores were given. At last, the scores obtained from listening-speaking achievement test were added to the scores obtained from classroom achievement tests on Reading and Writing both at pre-test and post-test stages. For it Listening-Speaking English Achievement Test I and II were prepared and administered both at pre-test and post-test stages respectively. Samples of such tests are given in Appendix G and H.

IV. Verbal Group Test of Intelligence (2/70) By R.K. Tondon

The verbal group test of intelligence (2/70) meant for secondary school students was developed by R.K. Tondon and was published by the National Psychological Association, Agra. The original Hindi test was first translated into Oriya by Miss Basanti Pradhan (1990) and here, the investigator had used that Oriya version of the test.

The test consists of 91 omnibus type of items like number series, co-relating relationship, hypothetical arguments, synonyms, antonyms, difference analysis and the like. The test is preceeded by some examples for practice and instructions. The students are to answer all the questions within 20 minutes and they are instructed to write the number of correct answer in the attached answer sheet. Each correct answer carries one mark and each wrong answer carries zero. The sample of this test and its scoring key are attached in Appendix E and F.

CHAPTER 4 : CREATIVE METHOD OF TEACHING ENGLISH (CMTE)

The Intervention Programme

Creative Method of Teaching English (CMTE)

The Intervention Programme

In this study, the researcher had used a new method of teaching of English. The method was called Creative Method of Teaching English, or shortly CMTE. This method is different from any other traditional method related to teaching of English at secondary level. The main features of this CMTE are as follows :

4.1 CMTE—IT'S AIMS AND OBJECTIVES

The principal aim of CMTE is to develop creative thinking ability among secondary school students. Creative ability includes the four dimensions of Guilford's divergent thinking, such as Fluency, Flexibility, Originality and Elaboration. Alongwith this aim, CMTE serves the other aims of teaching of English at secondary level; namely:

(a) to listen and understand spoken English,

(b) to understand what they read in English,
(c) to speak correctly in English, and
(d) to write correctly in English.

These four major aims are based on four language skills such as listening, speaking, reading and writing. Looking at the cognitive, affective and psycho-moter developmental characterstics of secondary school students, CMTE aims at developing specific language competencies among secondary school students in relation to above language skills. The objective-based competencies to be developed by CMTE are as follows :

General Objective 1

The students will develop the ability to read English with ease and comprehension.

Competence Specifications : To achieve this objective the student :

(i) grasps the words, phrases and sentences from the passage,
(ii) follows the sequenciality of ideas and facts,
(iii) acquires a reasonable speed in silent reading with ease and comprehension, and
(iv) interprets ideas, events and actions and identifies relationships between ideas and events with development of ability to draw inferences thereon.

General Objective 2

The student will develop the ability to understand English spoken in normal conversation speed.

Competence Specifications

To achieve this objective the student,
(i) understands the meaning of words, phrases and sentences spoken,
(ii) understands questions, comments, descriptions and follows the directions given orally,
(iii) follows the sequence of ideas and grasps the substance of central idea of spoken matter and understands the

matter presented to him/her with their many-sided uses and applicability.

General Objective 3

The student will develop the ability of writing correct English.

Competence Specifications

To achieve this objective the student—

(i) acquires the ability of writing correctly, legibly and neatly by using correct punctuation and spelling,

(ii) uses appropriate vocabulary and structures to express ideas and experiences clearly and organize those coherently,

(iii) displays personal imagination in writing semi-controlled compositions like stories and events which are original, and

(iv) elaborates an event or an idea or about the use of an object divergently.

General Objective 4

The student will develop the fluent speaking ability in English.

Competence Specification

To achieve this objective the student—

(i) speaks English intelligibly using correct, educated and indigenous English speech sounds, intonation patterns and with due stress on words and sentences,

(ii) uses appropriate vocabulary and structures to convey meaning while making statements, asking questions instructions, etc,

(iii) puts ideas in proper sequence and evokes required responses from the listeners, and

(iv) speaks fluently on different matters and topics with some original and divergent thoughts which are exceptional by nature.

Besides these general objectives or aims of teaching of English, CMTE has specific objectives which differ from topic to topic, basing on the nature and content of the topic. It may sometimes be found that though all the four teaching skills are possible to be developed through teaching a topic of CMTE, all the four dimensions of creative thinking may not be given equal emphasis in each topic. In this case, flexibility should be maintained as it is evident that neither a single class nor a single topic is enough for developing creative thinking among students.

Rather it is a longitudinal process and requires a wide drilling over an extended period of time and also through teaching a combination of different topics of a subject.

4.2 STEPS/PROCEDURES OF CMTE

The steps of CMTE are same for both prose and poetry teaching in English language. These steps are also applicable to teaching non-detailed study. The steps of CMTE are as follows:

(i) Introduction about the Topic and the Author

In the first step a brief introduction should be given to students about the topic that is to be taught to them. The introduction should be based on their previous knowledge and standard of their intellectual ability. Proper care must be taken in using appropriate standard of language and speed of speaking with correct pronunciation, both at the introduction and presentation stage. While introducing the topic, the teacher should inform the students regarding the area of the topic to be covered in the specific class. This introduction should be accompanied with the introduction of the writer or author, and his/her other literary works.

(ii) Model Loud Reading by the Teacher

After introducing the lesson the teacher shall ask the students to open their books where the concerned topic is written. Then he shall declare that all students should read silently while he reads the topic loudly. Here, both the activities will go on simultaneously. Hence, the teacher should not read the topic quickly. He shall read the topic slowly and with due care to pronunciation, punctuation and intonation, so that all students can read silently while listening to him and can comprehend the subject matter easily. Here, the teacher if requires so, may read out the topic loudly twice. But at both the times the students should be instructed to read silently. For students' better silent reading, the teacher should read the topic with minimum speed and proper care. Students should be instructed to recognise the difficult words and phrases.

(iii) Drilling of Language

Here, the teacher shall drill the difficult words, phrases, etc. The teacher may use different audio-visual aids to make the concepts more clear to students. The teacher shall also explain the meaning of the passage clearly to the students. All doubts and difficulties of students will be removed by the teacher.

(iv) Comprehension Test

Here some comprehension questions on the taught topic will be asked to students and answers will be collected. In case no correct answer is available from students, the teacher shall give the correct answer.

(v) Asking Divergent Questions

At this stage the teacher shall ask divergent questions on the topic with a view to develop creative thinking abilities (fluency, flexibility, originality and elaboration) of the students. The divergent questions should centre round metaphors (establishing relationship of likeness comparison of one idea or object to another idea or object by using one in place of other). Analogies (Personal analogy, direct analogy and compressed conflict), testing consequence of a happening unusual uses of a thing and improving the product by adding something unusual. These questions should be asked to students continuously and the teacher should create an encouraging environment to foster discussion and to encourage students to speak out the possible answers. One thing is to be kept in mind that, each and every response of the students should be accepted as correct. Whatever they speak would not be considered as wrong. This should be told to them and the teacher should encourage the discussion and answer by students by praising them and encouraging them through physical actions, postures acceptive facial reactions and by showing the magnanimity of a friend and guide for students. All divergent questions should be based on the subject matter of the topic and the words that are in the topic. But in crying need the teacher may lead the discussion or questioning process outside the topic if the sub-questions of the base question so require.

(vi) Application step and home task

At the application step one question from each type of divergent discussion may be asked to students. Under hometask some problems should be given and that should be checked in next class. Home task, in this teaching programme is an important aspect of utilizing the mental power of the individual child even in leisure time for some productive improvement.

A sample of a unit plan is attached in Appendix I.

4.3 TIME SCHEDULE FOR THE CMTE PLAN

A class having 40 minutes duration may be utilized for respective step of CMTE in following manner. It has been experimentally found suitable to reach the goal. But if necessary, the teacher should deviate from the time-limit looking at the ability of students, classroom environment and overall the nature and importance of the topic, as we have to correlate CMTE with students' achievement in English also. However, the time distribution to different steps of CMTE is given in Table 4.1.

TABLE 4.1
Distribution of Time of a Period for Different Activities under CMTE

	Steps	*Time Allotted*
(i)	Introduction About The Topic And The Author	3 minutes
(ii)	Model Loud Reading By Teacher	7 minutes
(iii)	Drilling Of Language	5 minutes
(iv)	Comprehension Questions	6 minutes
(v)	Asking Divergent Questions	14 minutes
(vi)	Application Step and Home Task	5 minutes
	Total	40 minutes

4.4 THE MODEL OF CMTE

The CMTE model possesses following characteristics.

4.4.1 Syntax

In the first phase, as discussed in the above theoretical concept of CMTE, the teacher is to introduce the lesson in advance and in brief. It is to acquaint students and to make them mentally alert to receive the forthcoming knowledge and instructions. In the second phase, the unit is to be presented before students by loud reading of teacher while students shall read the same silently. In third phase, difficult words and phrases are to be explained and comprehension is to be developed through question put to students at fourth step. In the fifth step divergent questions related to the topic are to be asked to students to develop creative thinking ability among them. Students are asked to state metaphors analogies consequences of happenings, unusual uses of things and improving the product by adding something unusual. And in last phase an evaluation of the developed thought is to be made.

4.4.2 Social System

It indicates teacher-taught relationship in the method. In CMTE, the teacher is the initiator of the divergent discussion. He just stimulates students' responses by asking many-sided questions. Students are also the active participants and their free-responses lead the method of teaching to success. The roles of both the teacher and the students are important. Hence, the model of CMTE is moderately structured.

4.4.3 Principles of Reaction

CMTE always instigates free and open ideas, non-rational and imaginative responses and divergent expressions. Here the teacher uses positive attitude for acceptance of views of all students. He should not use any comment which would hurt students' thought. He encourages them to express their personal ideas, thoughts and imaginations freely. Hence, here the teacher should accept all responses of all students with praise and approval.

4.4.4 Support System

In CMTE, audio-visual aids may be used at any stage if needed to develop comprehension and to elicit new thought processes among students. But its need is limited as we deal with divergent thinking. On the other hand necessary environment and support system to encourage active participation and free expression of students should be used.

4.4.5 Effects of CMTE Model

As instructional effects, the CMTE aims to develop creative thinking in English of the students. It also improves their comprehension in English.

As nuturant effects, the general creative thinking ability of the students is improved. Their achievement in English as well as in other subjects is also improved due to its nurtarant effet. Such impacts are diagrammatically shown in Figure 4.1.

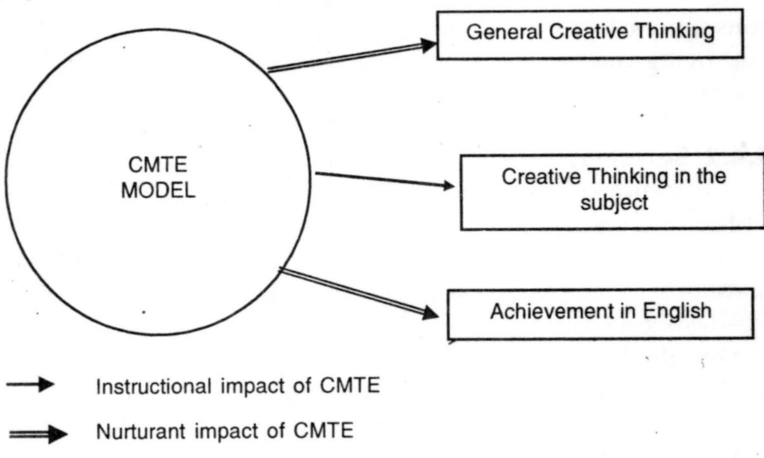

Fig. 4.1 : Effects of CMTE Model

4.5 A MODEL LESSON PLAN OF CMTE

Using all the principles, instructional procedures and systems of the CMTE model the researcher had developed each lesson plan for specific topic. Since it was a behavioural study, in the classroom situation some changes occur during teaching.

Bearing all changes and using the maximum possible audio-visual aids the researcher was able to elicit good response. However, a sample of the model lesson plan of CMTE is given in Appendix-I for reference of users of this model.

CHAPTER 5 : ANALYSIS AND INTERPRETATION

5.1 Intelligence-Creativity Relationship

5.2 Relation of Creativity and Achievement

5.3 Relation of Creativity and Socio-Economic Status

5.4 Sex Difference in Creativity

5.5 Impact of CMTE on Development of Creativity

5.6 Impact of CMTE on Development of Achievement

5.7 Levels of Intelligence and Development of Creativity

5.8 Development of Creativity and Achievement—An Impact Analysis of CMTE

CHAPTER 5

Analysis and Interpretation

There were different hypotheses to establish a variety of relationships between different variables of the study. Accordingly divergent statistical procedures scattergram correlation, 't' test, one-way and two-way analysis of variance were used to analyse the data and to verify the hypotheses of the study. The hypotheses were tested and the results were interpreted as follows. This study included five variables such as, 1. inelligence, 2. creativity, 3. achievement, 4. socio-economic status, and 5. sex.

5.1 INTELLIGENCE-CREATIVITY RELATIONSHIP

The first hypothesis of the study stated, "There is no significant relationship between creativity test score and intelligence test score".

The hypothesis was statistically tested by means of scatter diagram correlation method and the significance was verified by finding out the 't' value (Garrett, 1966). The coefficient of correlation was compared with 0.01 and 0.05 levels of significance. The table given in 'Appendix J' showed the correlation between creativity scores and intelligence measures calculated through scatter diagram procedure. The correlation was calculated by using the following formula.

$$r_{12} = \frac{\sum fxy - \frac{(\sum fx)(\sum fy)}{N}}{\sqrt{\sum fx^2 - \frac{(\sum fx)^2}{N}}\sqrt{\sum fy^2 - \frac{(\sum fy)^2}{N}}}$$

$$= \frac{463 - \frac{(-198)(-143)}{140}}{\sqrt{794 - \frac{(198)^2}{140}}\sqrt{627 - \frac{(-143)^2}{140}}}$$

$$= +0.5244$$

$$t = \frac{r}{\sqrt{1-r^2}} \times \sqrt{N-2}$$

$$= \frac{0.5244}{\sqrt{1-(0.5244)^2}} \times \sqrt{140-2}$$

$= 7.2351$ significant at 0.01 level.

The obtained result revealed a moderate positive correlation (r=+0.5244) between creativity and intelligence. Calculation of 't' value also established the high statistical significance of such relationship (t=7.2351) at 0.01 level of significance ($P<0.01$). The result showed that creativity is positively and significantly correlated with that of intelligence. Hence, the hypothesis which stated that creativity is not related to intelligence is rejected.

The finding of such analysis presupposed that a certain amount of intelligence was moderately helpful for creativity. These two variables can never be separated into two dimensions. Studies conducted by Yamamoto (1964), Wodtke (1964), Pogue (1965), Carey (1966), Mednick and Andrews (1967), Torrance (1968), Cave (1970), Dewing (1970), Anastasi and Schaefer (1971), Torrance (1984), McCabe (1991), Carroll and Howieson (1992), Runco and Nemiro (1995) and Mumford, Connelly, Baughman & Marks (1995) supported this finding, whereas studies of Getzels and Jackson (1962), Torrance and others (1962), McNemar (1964), Yamamoto (1964), Dudek (1976), Jershiled (1978), Milgram (1984), Mehdi (1973, 1977), Sharma (1979), Menon (1980) and Hota (1993) favoured a low correlation between creativity and intelligence.

5.1.1 Correlation Between Creativity and Intelligence by Partialling Out Achievement

The coefficient of correlation between creativity and intelligence was further verified by partialling out the impact of achievement. Method of partial correlation (Lindquist, 1953) was applied to find out the correlation value by partialling out achievement. The formula of finding out the relationship between creativity and intelligence by keeping the influence of achievement constant read as follows

$$r_{23} = \frac{r_{12} - (r_{13})(r_{23})}{\sqrt{(1 - r_{13}^2)(1 - r_{23}^2)}}$$

As per the requirement of the formula, r_{12} and r_{23} were already calculated and their correlation coefficient values were +0.5244 and +0.4659 respectively. The correlation coefficient between intelligence and achievement (r_{13}) was also calculated by taking the scattergram correlation values presented in Appendix-N and by applying the formula stated as follows:

$$r_{13} = \frac{\sum fxy - \frac{(\sum fx)(\sum fy)}{N}}{\sqrt{\sum fx^2 - \frac{(\sum fx)^2}{N}}\sqrt{\sum fy^2 - \frac{(\sum fy)^2}{N}}}$$

$$= \frac{596 - \frac{(-168)(-197)}{140}}{\sqrt{1030 - \frac{(-168)^2}{140}}\sqrt{793 - \frac{(-197)^2}{140}}}$$

$$= +0.5501$$

$$t = \frac{r}{\sqrt{1-r^2}} \times \sqrt{N-1}$$

$$= \frac{+0.5501}{\sqrt{1-(+0.5501)^2}} \times \sqrt{140-2}$$

= 7.7379 significant at 0.01 level.

The analysis showed a moderate, positive and significant correlation coefficient between intelligence and achievement (r_{13}=+0.5501, t=7.7379, P<0.01). Taking all the above values the $r_{12.3}$ was calculated as follows:

$$r_{12.3} = \frac{0.5244-(0.5501)(0.4659)}{\sqrt{[1-(0.5501)^2][1-(0.4659)^2]}}$$

= +0.3629

$$t = \frac{r}{\sqrt{1-r^2}} \times \sqrt{N-2}$$

$$= \frac{+0.3629}{\sqrt{1-(+0.3629)^2}} \times \sqrt{140-2}$$

= 4.5743 significant at 0.01 level.

The calculated value showed a low degree of positive correlation ($r_{12.3}$ = +0.3629) between creativity and intelligence when the impact of achievement was kept constant. Such relationship was found significant at 0.01 level of confidence (t=4.5743, P<0.01). This result showed that the relationship between creativity and intelligence which was found positive and significant (r=+0.5244, t=7.2351, P<0.01) was also found positive and significant when the impact of achievement was kept constant. From this analysis it was clear that achievement had not played any significant role to influence the relationship between creativity and intelligence.

5.1.2 Correlation Between Creativity and Intelligence By Partialling Out Socio-Economic Status

The coefficient of correlation between creativity and intelligence was still further verified by keeping the influence of socio-economic status constant. The intention of such analysis was to know whether socio-economic status influences such relationship. The formula of finding out the relationship between creativity and intelligence by partialling out socio-economic status read as follows.

$$r_{12.4} = \frac{r_{12} - (r_{14})(r_{24})}{\sqrt{(1 - r_{14}^2)(1 - r_{24}^2)}}$$

As per the requirement of the above formula, r_{12} and r_{24} were calculated and their correlation coefficient values were +0.5244 and +0.3289 respectively. The correlation coefficient between intelligence and socio-economic status (r_{14}) was also calculated by taking the scattergram correlation values presented in Appendix M and by applying the formula stated as follows:

$$r_{14} = \frac{\sum fxy - \frac{(\sum fx)(\sum fy)}{N}}{\sqrt{\sum fx^2 - \frac{(\sum fx)^2}{N}}\sqrt{\sum fy^2 - \frac{(\sum fy)^2}{N}}}$$

$$= \frac{537 - \frac{(-172)(-200)}{140}}{\sqrt{722 - \frac{(-172)^2}{140}}\sqrt{796 - \frac{(-200)^2}{140}}}$$

$$= +0.5706$$

$$t = \frac{r}{\sqrt{1-r^2}} \times \sqrt{N-2}$$

$$= \frac{+0.5706}{\sqrt{1-(+0.5706)^2}} \times \sqrt{140-2}$$

$= 8.1620$ significant at 0.01 level.

The analysis showed a moderate, positive and significant coefficient of correlation between intelligence and socio-economic status ($r_{14} = +0.5706$, $t=8.1620$, $P<0.01$). Taking the above values $r_{12.4}$ was calculated as follows:

$$r_{12.4} = \frac{0.5244-(0.5501)(0.3289)}{\sqrt{[1-(0.5506)^2][1-(0.3289)^2]}}$$

$$= +0.4343$$

$$t = \frac{r}{\sqrt{1-r^2}} \times \sqrt{N-2}$$

$$= \frac{+0.4343}{\sqrt{1-(+0.4343)^2}} \times \sqrt{140-2}$$

$$= 5.6633 \text{ significant at 0.01 level.}$$

The analysis gave a low, positive and significant coefficient of correlation (r=+0.4343, t=5.6633, P<0.01) between intelligence and creativity when the impact of socio-economic status was kept constant. It was more or less ,moderate, same to the positive and significant correlation coefficient that was found between creativity and intelligence. Such analysis showed a positive relationship between creativity and intelligence even after eliminating the effect of socio-economic status.

5.2 RELATION OF CREATIVITY AND ACHIEVEMENT

The second hypothesis of the study stated, "There is no significant relationship between English Achievement Test score and Creativity Test score".

The data obtained on students' creativity and achievement measures were analysed by the application of Scattergram correlation method and the significance of coefficient of correlation was tested by 't' test. Table given in Appendix K represents values relating scattergram correlation between creativity and achievement measures. The correlation was calculated as follows:

$$r_{23} = \frac{\sum fxy - \frac{(\sum fx)(\sum fy)}{N}}{\sqrt{\sum fx^2 - \frac{(\sum fx)^2}{N}}\sqrt{\sum fy^2 - \frac{(\sum fy)^2}{N}}}$$

$$= \frac{292 - \frac{(160)(-04)}{140}}{\sqrt{986 - \frac{(160)^2}{140}}\sqrt{474 - \frac{(04)^2}{140}}}$$

$$= +0.4659$$

$$t = \frac{r}{\sqrt{1-r^2}} \times \sqrt{N-2}$$

$$= \frac{+0.4659}{\sqrt{1-(+0.4659)^2}} \times \sqrt{140-2}$$

= 6.1849 significant at 0.01 level.

The calculated result showed a moderate and positive coefficient of correlation between creativity and achievement (r=+0.4659). The obtained t value was found significant at 0.01 level (t=6.1849, P<0.01). Hence, the hypothesis which stated that, creativity is not significantly related with achievement was refuted.

This finding was supported by the research studies conducted by Torrance (1959), Bentley (1966), Carely (1966), Gilchrist (1970), Khire (1971), Acharyulu (1977), Gupta (1979), Asha (1980), Joshi (1982), Brar (1986), Hota (1993), and Padhi (1995). But studies conducted by Holland (1961), Pathak (1962), Flescher (1964), Edward and Tylor (1965), Bruininks and Feldman (1970), Sharma (1981), Dey (1984), Richardson (1989), Chadha and Chandna (1990) and Freeman (1995) opposed such finding.

5.2.1 Correlation Between Creativity and Achievement by Partialling Out Intelligence

Further analysis was made to know the relation between creativity and achievement by partialling out the influence of intelligence ($r_{23.1}$). Such partial coefficient of correlation was calculated by using the formula stated as follows:

$$r_{23.1} = \frac{r_{23} - (r_{12})(r_{13})}{\sqrt{(1-r_{12}^2)(1-r_{13}^2)}}$$

All the correlation coefficients of r_{12}, r_{13} and r_{23} required by above formula, were calculated as +0.5244, +0.5271 and +0.4659 respectively. Hence, the partial correlation coefficient was found out as follows:

$$r_{12.4} = \frac{0.4659-(0.5244)(0.5501)}{\sqrt{[1-(0.5244)^2][1-(0.5501)^2]}}$$

$$= +0.2496$$

$$t = \frac{r}{\sqrt{1-r^2}} \times \sqrt{N-2}$$

$$= \frac{+0.2496}{\sqrt{1-(+0.2496)^2}} \times \sqrt{140-2}$$

= 3.0272 significant at 0.01 level.

The calculated value showed a low degree of positive correlation coefficient that existed between creativity and achievement (r_{23}=+0.2496, t=3.0272, P<0.01) by keeping the impact of intelligence constant. The coefficient of correlation between creativity and achievement which was found significant (r=+0.4659, t=6.1849, P<0.01) was also reported as significant when intelligence was kept constant. It showed that creativity had significant and positive relationship with achievement even after eliminating the effect of intelligence.

5.3 RELATION OF CREATIVITY AND SOCIO-ECONOMIC STATUS

The third hypothesis of the study stated, "There is no significant relationship between Socio-Economic Status scale score and creativity test score."

This hypothesis was verified by application of Scattergram correlation method and by finding out the 't' value for significance testing of correlation coefficient. Table given in Appendix L gives the values related to scatter diagram correlation between creativity measure and Socio-Economic Status scale score.

The correlation coefficient was calculated by using the following formula:

$$r_{24} = \frac{\sum fxy - \frac{(\sum fx)(\sum fy)}{N}}{\sqrt{\sum fx^2 - \frac{(\sum fx)^2}{N}}\sqrt{\sum fy^2 - \frac{(\sum fy)^2}{N}}}$$

$$= \frac{332 - \frac{(-166)(-142)}{140}}{\sqrt{708 - \frac{(166)^2}{140}}\sqrt{628 - \frac{(-142)^2}{140}}}$$

$$= +0.3289$$

$$t = \frac{r}{\sqrt{1-r^2}} \times \sqrt{N-2}$$

$$= \frac{+0.3289}{\sqrt{1-(+0.3289)^2}} \times \sqrt{140-2}$$

= 4.7153 significant at 0.01 level.

The analysis revealed that creativity was positively and significantly correlated with that of socio-economic status. The calculated correlation coefficient indicated a low degree of positive relationship (r_{24}=+0.3289) of creativity with that of socio-economic status which was found significant at 0.01 level of significance (t=4.7153, P<0.01). Therefore, the hypothesis which conjectured significant relationship between creativity and SES, was rejected. The analysis ascertained that socio-economic status had a low degree of positive influence on creativity. Such finding was supported by Pandit (1976), Sharma (1979), Sharma and Jarial (1980), Sekhar (1980), Pandey (1981), Srivastav (1982), Chaudhary (1983), Ramakrishna (1986), Rao (1988), Pandey (1990), Kumar (1992), Kaur (1993) and Hussain (1995). Studies conducted by Seetharam and Vednayagam (1979), Jarial (1979), Chadha and Sen (1981) and Patwardhan (1995) reported non-significant relationship between SES and creativity which went against the finding of this study.

5.3.1 Correlation Between Creativity and Socio-Economic Status by Partialling Out Intelligence

The correlation coefficient that existed between creativity and socio-economic status was verified by keeping the impact of intelligence constant. Such partial correlation ($r_{24.1}$) was calculated by the formula stated as follows:

$$r_{24.1} = \frac{r_{24} - (r_{12})(r_{14})}{\sqrt{(1-r_{12}^2)(1-r_{14}^2)}}$$

The calculated values of r_{12}, r_{14} and r_{24} were +0.5244, +0.5706 and +0.3289 respectively. These values were used in the above formula to find out partial correlation coefficient as follows:

$$r_{12.4} = \frac{0.3289-(0.5244)(0.5706)}{\sqrt{[1-(0.5244)^2][1-(0.5706)^2]}}$$

$$= +0.0424$$

$$t = \frac{r}{\sqrt{1-r^2}} \times \sqrt{N-2}$$

$$= \frac{+0.0424}{\sqrt{1-(+0.0424)^2}} \times \sqrt{140-2}$$

= 0.4980 significant at 0.01 level.

The calculated coefficient of partial correlation was very negligible and found non-significant at 0.05 level of significance ($r_{24,1}$=+0.0424, t=0.4980, $P>0.05$). The correlation between creativity and socio-economic status which was found low, positive and significant (r_{24}=+0.3289, t=4.7153, $P<0.01$), came down to +0.0424 when the impact of intelligence was partialled out. From such analysis it was evident that the relationship which was found significant between creativity and SES was only due to intelligence. So, when the impact of intelligence was partialled out that relationship between creativity and SES came to zero and found non-significant. Hence, whatever relationship had the creativity with SES was only due to relationship with intelligence.

5.4 SEX DIFFERENCE IN CREATIVITY

The fourth hypothesis of the study had three sub-hypotheses. All the hypotheses conjectured no sex differences in the students' creativity scores of different testing stages and also between different groups included in the experiment. All the three sub-hypotheses were tested by the application of SE_D (Standard Error of Different Between Means) and their significance were verified by finding out respective 't' values. The formulae applied for SE_D and 't' value were as follows.

$$SE_D = \sqrt{\frac{\sigma^2 1}{N1}} + \sqrt{\frac{\sigma^2 2}{N2}} \quad \text{...(Garrett, 1966)}$$

$$t = \frac{M_1 \sim M_2}{SE_D} \quad \text{...(Garrett, 1966)}$$

5.4(a) Testing of First Sub-Hypothesis [$H_{04(a)}$]

The first sub-hypothesis stated, "There is no significant difference between boys and girls in their mean creativity scores at the pre-test stage."

The total sample (N=140) had an equal representation of boys and girls (boys=70 and girls=70). Mehdi's Verbal Test of Creative Thinking gave the creativity scores of boys and girls. The raw scores of the creativity test were transferred to grouped data as the sample was found quite large and ungrouped method was not found convenient for analysis. The range of the class interval was 10 (i=10) for both the sex groups. Means and SDs of both the groups of boys and girls were calculated by using the formulas mentioned as follows:

$$M = AM + \frac{\sum fd}{n} \times i \quad \text{.....(Aggarwal, 1990)}$$

$$SD = i\sqrt{\frac{\sum fd^2}{N} - \left(\frac{\sum ed}{N}\right)^2} \quad \text{.....(Aggarwal, 1990)}$$

Obtained means and SDs were used in the formulae related to SE_D the 't' value. Table 5.1 shows the significance of difference between boys and girls in creativity scores at pre-test stage.

TABLE 5.1
Significance of Sex difference in Pre-test Creativity Score

Group	*N*	*M*	*SD*	*'t'*
Boys	70	119.0715	28.407	2.3915*
Girls	70	106.50	33.577	

* (P>0.05) significant at 0.05 level).

In the Table 5.1, the calculated 't' value had shown a significant difference (t=2.3915) at 0.05 level of confidence. It indicated that the boys and girls differed significantly in their creativity mean scores at pre-test stage. The mean creativity score of boys (M=119.0715, SD= 28.407) was found to be higher than the creativity mean score of girls (M=106.50, SD=33.577). It showed that boys were superior to girls in their creativity scores at pre-test stage. On this basis, the first sub-hypothesis which stated "no significant relationship between boys and girls in their pre-test creativity scores" was refuted at 0.05 level of confidence and retained at 0.01 level of confidence.

This finding was supported by the studies conducted by Kelly (1965), Straus and Straus (1968), Raina (1969), Bar'l (1971), Mari (1973), Nayana (1981), Sajid (1984), Lutzer (1991), Gelade (1995), and Kapoor (1996). The research findings of Torrance (1961), Klausmeier and Wiersma (1964), Naufield (1965), Ogletree (1968), Soloman (1968), Richmond (1971), Singh (1978), Patel (1987), and Behera (1993) went against this finding.

5.4(b) Testing of Second Sub-Hypothesis [$H_{04(b)}$]

The second sub-hypothesis stated, "There is no significant difference between boys and girls in their mean creativity scores at post-test stage."

Such significance was tested by using the formula of significance of difference between means (SE_D) and by finding out the "t" value. At the post-test stage the total sample was 140. Boys and girls were equally represented in the sample (70 in each group). The creativity raw scores obtained through Mehdi's Verbal Test of Creative Thinking was transferred to grouped data. The range of the class interval was 15 for boys group and 20 for girls group. Means and SDs of both the groups were calculated by applying respective formulae mentioned earlier. Table 5.2 presents the data relating significance of difference between boys and girls on their post-test creativity scores.

TABLE 5.2
Significance of Sex Difference in Post-test Creativity Score

Group	*N*	*M*	*SD*	*'t'*
Boys	70	146.50	40.4355	0.4194 n.s
Girls	70	149.784	51.546	

(ns = not significant, P< 0.05).

Data presented in Table 5.2 showed that the calculated 't' ratio found no significant difference in the creativity mean scores of boys and girls at post-test stage (t = 0.4196, P>0.05). But in creativity mean score, the girls were found at higher level than the boys having mean creativity scores 149.784 and 146.50 respectively. Hence, the hypothesis which stated that boys and girls were not significantly different from each other in their post-test creativity scores was retained. Such finding was supported by the research findings of Pathak (1962), Pogue (1965), Raina (1970), Pandey (1981), Katiyar and Jarial (1985), Rao (1988), Sharma and Bhartiya (1988), Behera (1993) and Pandey and Rai (1995).

5.4(c) Testing of Third Sub-Hypothesis [$H_{04(c)}$]

The third sub-hypothesis read as, "There is no significant difference between boys and girls of the experimental group in their mean gain scores in creativity test".

The experimental group consisted of 70 students including 35 each from boys and girls. Mehdi's Test on Creative Thinking (Verbal) was used to obtain their pre-test and post-test creativity scores. The gain scores in their creativity scores were obtained by subtracting the pre-test creativity scores from the post-test creativity scores of each participant. The obtained creativity gain score of each student was treated as raw score. The raw scores were grouped into class intervals. The range of the class interval for boys and girls groups were 10 and 15 respectively. Means,

SDs and 't' values were calculated by using specific formulae. Table 5.3 represents the data relating significance of sex difference in the mean creativity gain scores of the experimental group.

TABLE 5.3
Significance of Sex Difference in Creativity Gain Scores of the Experimental Group

Group	*N*	*M*	*SD*	*t*
Boys	35	53.786	22.05	
Girls	35	76.2855	33.311	3.2636**

**P>0.01, significant at 0.01 level.

Table 5.3 gives the 't' value regarding significance of sex difference in creativity gain scores of experimental group. The analysis of data found that gain scores of boys and girls of experimental group differed significantly (t=3.2636, P<0.01) at 0.01 level of confidence. A view on the mean gain scores in creativity test showed superiority of girls over boys bearing mean creativity gain scores 76.2855 and 53.786 respectively. Therefore, the hypothesis which stated; boys and girls of experimental group do not differ significantly in their gain scores in creativity test was refuted and the girls were found more benefitted from the creative method of teaching English by scoring more than the boys. This finding was substantiated by Torrance (1961, 1963), Kalusmeier and Wiersma (1964), Motlagh (1968), Ogletree (1968), Soloman (1968), Bower (1969), Hussain and Hussain (1975), Maccoby and Jacklin (1975), Patel (1987) and Richardson (1986). But Kelly (1965), Harold (1968), Vora (1984), Dharmangadan (1981) and Lutzer (1991), in their studies reported that boys were superior to girls in their creativity.

An overall analysis of the fourth hypothesis of the study showed that, at pre-test stage, sex difference was found significant having 't' ratio 2.3915 (P<0.05) with superiority of boys (M=119.0715, SD=28.407) over girls (M=106.50, SD=33.577). Constrastically, such sex difference was not significantly noticed at post-test stage. The mean creativity scores of boys (M=146.50, SD=40.4355) was, in actual sense, lower than those of girls (M=149.784, SD=51,546). But that difference was not found statistically significant. A comparative analysis could explain that the development and increment of creativity scores of girls from pre-test stage to the post-test stage was more spectacular and more upward than the increment of mean creativity scores of boys from pre-test to post-test. The difference between mean creativity scores of pre-post test stages for girls was 43, whereas, the difference of such mean creativity scores for boys was 27. It was further substantiated by the testing of third hypothesis which found a significant difference in their creativity mean gain scores in favour of girls. From this analysis it was evident that girls had been benefitted more by CMTE model than the boys. Figure 3 shows the differential progress of mean creativity scores of boys and girls from pre-test stage to post-test stage. The analysis of mean gain scores in creativity test of boys and girls of experimental group showed a significant sex difference in favour of girls also. It substantiated the result presented in Figure 3.

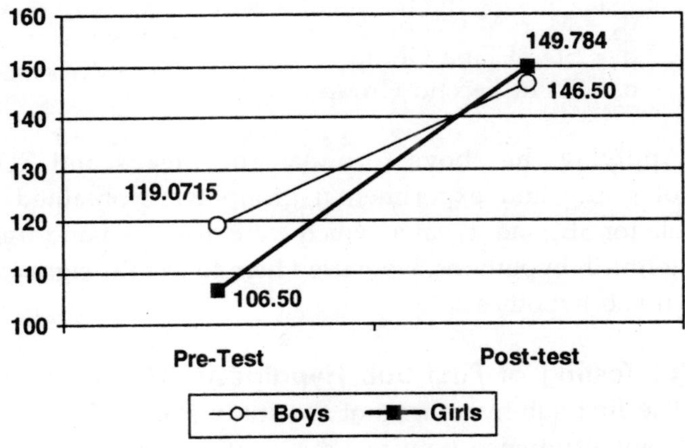

Fig. 5.1 : Mean Creativity Scores of Boys and Girls at Pre-test and post-test stages

5.5 IMPACT OF CMTE ON DEVELOPMENT OF CREATIVITY

The fifth hypothesis of the study had three sub-hypotheses. All the three sub-hypotheses were tested by using the SE_D and the significance was tested by finding out 't' values. The fifth hypothesis entirely attempted to measure the differences in mean creativity scores of experimental group and control group at various testing stages (such as: Pre-test and Post-test stages) and in their creativity gain scores. Both experimental and control groups as described in the sample section of chapter III had two sub-groups each. Means and SDs were calculated for each sub-group by applying the formulae mentioned earlier. Combined Means (M comb) and Combined Standard Deviations (σ comb) were obtained by using the respective formulae as follows:

$$\text{M comb.} = \frac{M_1N_1 + M_2N_2}{N_1N_2} \qquad \text{...(Garrett, 1966)}$$

$$\sigma\,\text{comb.} = \frac{N_1\left(\sigma_1^2 + d_1^2\right) + N_2\left(\sigma_2^2 + d_2^2\right)}{N_1 + N_2} \qquad \text{...(Garrett, 1966)}$$

where

$d_1 = M_1 - \text{M comb.}$

$d_2 = M_2 - \text{M comb.}$

σ_1 = SD of First Group

σ_2 = SD of Second Group

Applying the above formulae the Means and SDs of control group and experimental group were obtained. The formula for SE_D and 't' value which were discussed and used in testing fourth hypothesis, were used here to test the significance of each sub-hypothesis.

5.5 (a) Testing of First Sub-Hypothesis [$H_{05(a)}$]

The first sub-hypothesis of the study stated, "There is no significant difference between the experimental and control groups in their pre-test creativity mean scores". Before determining the significance of such difference, intra-school difference in pre-test creativity scores was calculated. The hypothesis was tested by application of SE_D and finding out 't' value. The significance was compared with 0.05 and 0.01 levels of confidence.

(i) Difference in Pre-test Creativity Mean Scores of Control Group (C_1), and Experimental Group (E_1,) of the first school (S_1)

The total number of sample in the S_1 was 90 with equal representation in control group (45) and experimental group (45). Mehdi's Verbal Test of Creative Thinking gave the pre-test creativity score. Table 5.4 gives the data relating significance of difference in pre-test creativity mean scores of control group and experimental group of S_1.

TABLE 5.4

Significance of Difference Between Control Group (C_1) and Experimental Group (E_1) of S_1 in Pre-test Creavitity Scores

Group	*N*	*M*	*SD*	*'t'*
Control Group	45	121.944	21.666	1.2260 n.s
Experimental Group	45	127.833	23.851	

n.s. = not significant at 0.05 level.

Table 5.4 showed no significant difference between control group and experimental group of the first school (S_1) in their pre-test creativity mean scores. The calculated 't' value (t=1.2260) was found to be lower than the table value at 0.05 level of confidence. It showed that both the control and experimental groups of S_1, had performed equally in their creativity measures at pre-test stage.

(ii) Difference in Pre-test Creativity Mean Scores of Control group (C_2) and Experimental Group (E_2) of the Second School (S_2)

The total number of sample in the S_2 was 50 with equal representation in the control and experimental groups. Table 5.5 gives the data relating significance of difference in Pre-test creativity mean scores of control group and experimental group of S_2. The table showed that control group and experimental group of the second school did not differ significantly in their pre-test creativity scores. The calculated 't' value (t=0.4971, P>0.05) was found to be lower than the table value. It showed that both the groups of S_2 had performed equally in their creativity measures at pre-test stage.

TABLE 5.5
Significance of Difference Between Control Group (C_2) and Experimental Group (E_2) of S_2 in Pre-test Creativity Mean Scores

Group	*N*	*M*	*SD*	*t*
Control Group	25	93.7	26.369	0.4971 n.s
Experimental Group	25	89.3	35.543	

n.s. = not significant at 0.05 level.

(iii) Difference in Pre-test creativity scores of control group and experimental group of S_1 and S_2 as a whole

Mehdi's Verbal Test of Creative Thinking was administered as pre-test and the creativity raw scores of 140 students (70 of experimental group and 70 of control group) were obtained. As four sub-groups of S_1 and S_2 (two sub-groups each in experimental and control group) constituted the total sample, the means and SDs were calculated separately for each sub-group. The combined Means and SDs were also calculated for experimental and control groups from which SE_D and 't' value were obtained to verify the hypothesis. Table 5.6 gives the data relating significance of difference between control group and experimental group in their pre-test mean creativity scores.

TABLE 5.6
Significance of Difference between Control Group and Experimental Group in Pre-test Creativity Scores of the combined sample of both schools

Group	*N*	*M*	*SD*	*'t'*
Control Group	70	111.8568	27.0785	0.4244 n.s
Experimental Group	70	114.0692	34.0261	

n.s. = not significant at 0.05 level.

Table 5.6 showed no significant difference between the control group and experimental group in their pre-test mean creativity scores. The calculated 't' value (t=0.4244) was found to be lower than the table value at 0.05 level of confidence ($P>0.05$). Hence the sub-hypothesis which stated "no significant difference between experimental and control groups in their pre-test creativity mean scores" was retained at 0.05 level of confidence.

5.5(b) Testing of Second Sub-Hypothesis [$H_{05(b)}$]

The second sub-hypothesis of the study stated, "There is no significant difference between experimental group and control group in their post-test creativity mean scores. After intervention programme, the creativity scores of the sample were obtained through administration of Mehdi's verbal test on creative thinking. Sub-groupwise means and SDs were calculated to find out the significance of difference between the sample of different groups of S_1 and S_2 separately, before verifying the above hypothesis.

(i) Difference in Post-test Creativity Mean Scores of Control Group (C_1) and Experimental Group (E_1) of First School (S_1)

The total number of sample in S_2 was 90. In the experimental and control group, there was equal representation of the sample. Table 5.7 presents the data relating significance of difference in post-test creativity mean scores of control group and experimental group of S_1.

TABLE 5.7
Significance of Difference Between Control Group (C_1) and Experimental Group (E_1) of S, in Post-test Creativity Mean Scores

Group	*N*	*M*	*SD*	*'t'*
Control Group	45	129.611	22.961	9.2468**
Experimental Group	45	181.055	29.422	

** Significant at 0.01 level.

The data presented in Table 5.7 showed a significant difference between control group and experimental group ($t=9.2468$, $P<0.01$). The mean value of experimental group

(M=181.055, SD=29.422) was found to be at higher level than the mean value of control group (M=129.611, SD=22.961). It was already verified that, at pre-test stage, these two groups proved no significant difference in their creativity scores. But such post-test difference which went in favour of experimental group supported the intervention programme, i.e. CMTE. It was also evident that the mean value of creativity gain scores of control group of S_1 (M=3.8444, SD=9.1727) was far lower than the mean value of creativity gain scores of the experimental group (M=54.722, SD=22.753) of the same school. The gain of control group may be attributed to maturation, time-factor, teacher effectiveness or students' intéraction. But the excessive and significant gain of the experimental group (t=9.2468, P<0.01), no doubt, was due to the CMTE, through which the students were taught. Therefore, the experimental group of S_1, was found benefitted significantly from CMTE.

(ii) Difference in Post-test Creativity Mean Scores of Control Group (C_2) and Experimental Group (E_2) of the Second School (S_2)

The total number of sample in S_2 was 50 with equal representation in the control group and in experimental group. Table 5.8 presents the data relating significance of difference in post-test creativity mean scores of control group and experimental group of S_2. The table showed that the control group and experimental group of S_2 differed significantly in their post-test creativity mean scores (t = 5.9821, P<0.01). The calculated mean value of the experimental group (M=167.9, SD=54.88) was found to be higher than the mean value of the control group (M=94.5, SD=27.422). It indicated that the experimental group had performed better in post-test creativity measures than that of control group. The further analysis of the mean gain scores in creativity test showed that control group was at lower level in mean value in post-test creativity measures (M=3.8444, SD=9.1727) than the mean value of post-test creativity gain scores of the experimental group (M=83.7, SD=37.127). Such gain of the control group may be due to the psycho-environmental influence or for some testing fluctuations, but the significant gain of experimental group (t=10.4405, P<0.01) was only because of the creative method of teaching English. Therefore, it can be accounted that, CMTE had proved more beneficial for the experimental group of S_2 in increasing creativity scores of their students in comparison to the traditional method through which the control group was taught.

Table 5.8
Significance of Difference Between Control Group (C_2) and Experimental Group (E_2) of S_2 in Post-test Creativity Mean Scores

Group	*N*	*M*	*SD*	*'t'*
Control Group	25	94.5	27.422	5.9821**
Experimental Group	25	167.9	54.88	

** Significant at 0.01 level.

(iii) Difference in Post-test Creativity Scores of Control Group and Experimental Group of Both the Schools (S_1 + S_2)

After the intervention programme (teaching English language through CMTE), the creativity scores of both experimental and control groups were obtained through administration of Mehdi's Verbal test of creative thinking. Sub-groupwise means and SDs were obtained for experimental and control groups. At final stage, SE_D was calculated and the significance was tested by finding out 't' value. Table 5.9 presents the data relating the significance of difference in post-test creativity mean scores of control group and experimental group.

Table 5.9
Significance of Difference Between Control Group and Experimental Group in Post-test Creativity Mean Scores of both the schools

Group	*N*	*M*	*SD*	*'t'*
Control Group	70	117.0713	29.9690	9.777**
Experimental Group	70	176.3567	40.9297	

**Significant at 0.01 level.

Table 5.9 showed a significant difference between control group and experimental group in their post-test creativity mean scores at 0.01 level of confidence (t=9.7779, P<0.01). The experimental group was found to be at higher level in its mean value (M=176.3567, SD=40.9297) than that of the control group (M=117.0713, SD=29.9690). The result showed a favourable increase of creativity scores of experimental group. Hence, the sub-hypothesis which stated "no significant difference in post-test creativity mean scores of control and experimental group" was refuted. From this analysis, it was assumed that, it was Creative Method of Teaching English (CMTE) which caused such increase in creativity scores of students belonging to experimental group. On the other hand, the students of control group who had been taught through traditional method did not show any significant change in their creativity scores. Hence, it may, here, be concluded that CMTE was an effective method of developing creative thinking ability of secondary school students. In contrast, traditional method of teaching English was not found congenial to develop such talent among students.

5.5(c) Testing of Third Sub-Hypothesis [$H_{05(C)}$]

The third sub-hypothesis of the fifth hypothesis of the study stated, "There is no significant difference between the experimental and control groups in their mean gain scores in creativity test".

Mehdi's verbal test of creative thinking was adopted and administered both for pre-post test creativity measures. The creativity gain score of each student was obtained by subtracting the post-test creativity raw score from the pre-test creativity raw score of the concerned student. Schoolwise significance of differences in creativity gain scores were calculated by application of SE_D and 't' value. Sub-groupwise means and SDs were calculated and taking those values combined mean and combined SD formulae were applied to calculate the significance of difference. After schoolwise analyses the total analysis made between the experimental and control groups of the study, as required by the major hypothesis.

(i) Difference Between Control Group and Experimental Group of the First School (S_1) their Creativity Gain Scores

The total sample of the first school (S_1) was 90 with equal representation in control and experimental groups. Table 5.10 gives the data relating the significance of difference between control group and experimental group of S_1 in creativity gain scores. The result showed that the control group and experimental group differed significantly from each other in their gain scores in creativity test ($t=13.9123$, $P<0.01$). The experimental group was found to be at higher degree in the mean value ($M=54.722$, $SD=22.753$) than the control group of S_1 ($M=3.8444$, $SD=9.1727$). It showed that the experimental group had gained significantly more in creativity measures than the control group. Such analysis confirmed that the CMTE, through which the experimental groups were taught, proved more effective in developing the creativity of students than the traditional method, which was followed to teach English to the control groups of the study.

TABLE 5.10

Significance of Difference between Control and Experimental Groups of S_1 in Creativity Gain Scores

Group	*N*	*M*	*SD*	*'t'*
Control Group	45	3.8444	9.1727	13.9123**
Experimental Group	45	54.722	22.753	

**Significant at 0.01 level.

(ii) Difference Between Control Group and Experimental Group of the Second School (S_2) in their Creativity Gain Scores

The S_2 had 50 students with equal representation in control group and experimental group. Table 5.11 represents data relating the significance of difference in gain scores in creativity test of control group and experimental group of the S_2. The result showed that control group and experimental group of S_2 differed significantly in their creativity gain scores ($t=10.1527$, $P<0.01$). Further analysis reported that the experimental group was at higher degree in its mean value (M=83.70, SD=37.127) than the control group of S_2 (M = 6.000, SD = 9.2735). It explained that, the experimental group of S_2 had gained more in creativity measure than the control group. Such data further confirmed that the Creative Method of Teaching English (CMTE), through which the experimental group was taught English language, had proved more beneficial than the traditional method, through which the control group was taught the same subject, in developing creative thinking ability of secondary school students. The result showed that it was CMTE, which caused difference in students' gain scores in creativity test.

TABLE 5.11

Significance of Difference Between Control Group and Experimental Group of S_2 in Creativity Gain Scores

Group	*N*	*M*	*SD*	*'t'*
Control Group	25	6.000	9.2735	10.1527**
Experimental Group	25	83.70	37.127	

**Significant at 0.01 level.

(iii) Difference Between Control Group and Experimental Group of both the Schools (S_1+S_2) in Creativity Gain Scores

The total sample of the study was 140. The experimental and control groups had 70 subjects each. Table 5.12 gives the data pertaining significance of difference in mean creativity gain scores of control group and experimental group.

TABLE 5.12

Significance of Difference in Mean Creativity Gain Scores of Control and Experimental Groups of both the Schools

Group	*N*	*M*	*SD*	*'t'*
Control Group	70	4.6142	9.1726	15.2369**
Experimental Group	70	65.0712	31.9048	

** P>0.0l, Significant at 0.01 level of confidence.

Table 5.12 showed that there were 70 students each in control group and experimental group. Analysis of data showed a significant difference between control group and experimental group in their creativity mean gain scores. The calculated 't' value was found higher than the table value (t=15.2369, P<0.01). The experimental group showed a higher mean value (M=65.0712, SD=31.9048) than that of the control group mean value in creativity gain scores (M=4.6142, SD = 9.1726). It showed that the experimental group had gained more in creativity scores than the control group. Hence, the sub-hypothesis which stated, no significant difference in creativity mean gain scores of experimental and control group was refuted.

This finding of the study confirmed that students belonging to the experimental group were exposed to intervention programme based on CMTE. Only for such new method of teaching English the students of experimental group scored more in their post-test creativity measures. An overall discussion stated that, at pre-test stage, no significant difference was found between the experimental and control group in their creativity mean scores (t=0.4244, P>0.05). After intervention, the post-test creativity scores were obtained. The second sub-hypothesis showed a significant difference between experimental and control groups in their post-test mean creativity scores (t=9.7779, P<0.01). The third sub-hypothesis also found a significant difference between experimental and control groups in their mean gain scores in creativity test (t=15.2369, P<0.01). In post-test creativity scores and in mean creativity gain scores the experimental group was found to have scored higher mean values than control group. It showed that, the intervention programme or CMTE had influenced the creativity scores of the students belonging to experimental group. The traditional method was not found so effective in developing students' creative talents as the students of control group were found at lower degree in their post-test mean creativity scores and also in their mean creativity gain scores. From it, the conclusion may be drawn that CMTE is an effective method in increasing creative talents of secondary schoolers.

This finding was substantiated by the research studies of Prasad (1979), who used discovery method and found significant result in increasing students' creative talent; Golub and Hahn (1983), who found open classroom as an effective means of increasing creativity of students; Hooda and Jarial (1983), who found role playing as an instigating means of creativity. Vora's (1984) "divergent thinking programme", Gupta's (1985) Creative Training Programme (CTP), Katiyar and Jarial's (1985) veral and non-verbal creativity development programme, Singh's (1985) creative method of teaching mathematics, Sharma's (1986) Creative Instructional Package, Buyer's (1988) experiment on criteria cued, Brainstorming and Standard instructions on development of students' creative potentiality; Gill, Singh and Chauhan's (1990) intervention programme and Shan's (1992) brainstorming procedure were also found significant and positive on the development of creativity among students. Studies conducted by Murdock, Isaksen and Lauer (1993), Joseph (1988), Mitchell and Welkens (1986) gave a contrastic finding that, training has 'no' or 'negative' impact on creativity

5.6 IMPACT OF CMTE ON DEVELOPMENT OF ACHIEVEMENT

The sixth hypothesis had three sub-hypotheses. All the three sub-hypotheses attempted to measure the significance of difference in the achievement in English language of the experimental group and control group at pre-test stage, post-test stage and in their gain scores in achievement test. The significance of each of the three sub-hypotheses was tested by applying SE_D and finding out 't' values. Both experimental and control groups had two classes or sub-groups each and were obtained from two schools (S_1 and S_2). Means and SDs were separately calculated for each group. The means and SDs of the control and experimental group in total were obtained by applying the combined mean and combined SD methods as discussed in testing of fifth hypothesis. SE_D was calculated and the significance was tested by findings out 't' values and comparing the 't' value with the table values at 0.01 and 0.05 levels of confidence.

5.6(a) Testing of First Sub-Hypothesis [$H_{06(a)}$]

The first sub-hypothesis stated, "There is no significant difference between the experimental and control groups in their pre-test mean achievement scores."

School marks in English obtained by the students in their annual class VIII examination were collected as the achievement scores on reading and writing. That score was added to the scores obtained by the students on Listening-Speaking English Achievement Test-I to represent the total achievement score. Before determining the significance of difference in pre-test achievement scores of control group and experimental group of S_1 and S_2 the "intra-school difference was tested to determine the impact of school on students' achievement".

(i) Difference in Pre-test Achievement Test Scores of Control Group and Experimental Group of the First School (S_1)

The total number of sample in the S_1 was 90 with equal representation in the control group (45) and experimental group (45). Table 5.13 gives the data relating significance of difference in pre-test achievement scores of control group and experimental group of S_1.

TABLE 5.13
Significance of Difference Between Control Group and Experimental Group of S_1 in Pre-test Achievement Scores

Group	*N*	*M*	*SD*	*'t'*
Control Group	45	42.111	11.3275	2.1051*
Experimental Group	45	36.667	13.14	

*Significant at 0.05 level.

The data presented in Table 5.13 showed a significant difference between control group and experimental group of S_1 in their pre-test achievement scores ($t=2.1051$, $P<0.05$). The mean achievement value of control group was found to be higher ($M=42.111$, $SD=11.3275$) than the mean achievement value of the experimental group ($M=36.667$, $SD=13.14$). Such higher achievement scores of control group may be due to the presence of higher intelligent students or due to some other educational variables.

(ii) Difference in Pre-test Achievement Test Scores of Control group and Experimental Group of the Second School (S_2)

The total number of sample present in the second school was 50 with equal representation in control group and experimental group. Table 5.14 presents the data relating significance of difference in pre-test achievement scores of control group and experimental group of the second school (S_2).

TABLE 5.14

Significance of Difference Between Control Group and Experimental Group of S_2 in the Pre-test Achievement Scores

Group	*N*	*M*	*SD*	*'t'*
Control Group	25	30.00	14.9665	1.2089 n.s
Experimental Group	25	25.40	11.747 .	

n.s. = not significant at 0.05 level.

The data presented in the Table 5.14 showed that the control group and experimental group of S_2 did not differ significantly in their pre-test achievement scores (t=1.2089, P>0.01). It indicated that the students of control and experimental group had performed more or less equally in the pre-test achievement measure.

(iii) Difference in Pre-test Achievement Scores of Control Group and Experimental Group of Both the Schools (S_1+S_2)

The experimental group and control group of the study were consisted of 70 students each. Combined means and SDs were calculated for both the groups. SE_D and t values were calculated to verify the first sub-hypothesis [$H_{05(a)}$]. Table 5.15 represents the data relating the significance of difference between experimental and control groups of both S_1 and S_2 in their pre-test mean achievement scores.

TABLE 5.15
Significance of Difference in Pre-test Mean Achievement Score of Control Group and Experimental Group of both the Schools

Group	*N*	*M*	*SD*	*'t'*
Control Group	70	37.7856	14.0057	2.1912 *
Experimental Group	70	32.6430	13.7631	

*Significant at 0.05 level.

Table 5.15 revealed a significant difference in the mean achievement scores of control group and experimental group at pre-test stage. The calculated 't' value (t=2.1912) was found to be higher than the table value at 0.05 level of confidence (P<0.05). The control group was found to be at higher level in its mean achievement scores (M=37.7856, SD=14.0057) than that of the experimental group (M=32.6430, SD=13.7631). Such difference was only due to the impact of school as was found in previous analysis. However, the hypothesis which stated that the experimental group and control group do not differ significantly from each other in their pre-test mean achievement scores was rejected. The difference was found significant and that difference went in favour of control group.

5.6(b) Testing of Second Sub-Hypothesis [$H_{06(b)}$]

The second sub-hypothesis of the sixth hypothesis read, "There is no significant difference between the experimental and control groups in their post-test mean achievement test scores in English." Before testing this sub-hypothesis the intra-school difference in post-test achievement scores were verified by finding out significance of mean difference.

Students' school marks in English obtained from Class IX half-yearly examination were taken as the marks on reading and writing. Achievement scores obtained from Listening-Speaking English Achievement Test-II were added to the school marks to find out total post-test achievement score of each student. The significance of difference was tested by SE_D and 't' test.

(i) Difference in Post-test Mean Achievement Scores of Control Group and Experimental Group of the First School (S_1)

The control group and experimental group of S_1, had 45 students each. Table 5.16 gives the data relating the significance of difference in the post-test mean achievement of scores of control group and experimental group of S_1.

TABLE 5.16
Significance of Difference in Post-test Mean Achievement Scores of Control Group and Experimental Group of S_1

Group	*N*	*M*	*SD*	*t*
Control Group	45	43.8885	11.9855	0.2464 n.s
Experimental Group	45	44.556	13.6555	

n.s. = not significant at 0.05 level.

The data presented in Table 5.16 showed a no significant difference in the post-test mean achievement scores of control group and experimental group of S_1. Though it indicated no significant difference, a comparison between the pre-test and post-test mean achievement scores of the control group and experimental group of the S_1 proved more mean gain score for experimental group in achievement test (M=8.5999, SD=4.4541) than the control group (M=1.4222, SD=4.6767). It showed that the experimental group was more benefitted by the creative method of teaching English than the control group in increasing the achievement score significantly.

(ii) Difference in Post-test Mean Achievement Scores of Control Group and Experimental Group of the Second School (S_2)

The total sample of S_1 was 50 with equal representation in control group and experimental group. Table 5.17 presents the data regarding significance of difference in post-test mean achievement scores of control group and experimental group of S_2.

TABLE 5.17

Significance of Difference in Post-test Mean Achievement Scores of Control Group and Experimental Group of S_2

Group	*N*	*M*	*SD*	*'t'*
Control Group	25	30.00	14.9665	2.0962*
Experimental Group	25	37.80	11.0525	

*Significant at 0.05 level.

Data presented in Table 5.17 indicated a significant difference between control group and experimental group of S_2 in post-test mean achievement score ($t=2.0962$, $P<0.05$). The calculated mean value of experimental group was found to be higher ($M=37.80$, $SD=11.0525$) than the post-test mean achievement value of control group. It confirmed that the CMTE through which the experimental group of S_1 was taught, was proved to be more beneficial in increasing students' achievement than the traditional method, through which the control group of S_2 was taught.

(iii) Difference Between Control Group and Experimental Group of Both the Schools (S_1+S_2) in Post-test Mean Achievement Scores

The S_1 and S_2 each had an experimental group and a control group. Out of total 140 subjects, 70 were in experimental group and 70 were in the control group. Means and SDs on post-test achievement scores were calculated separately for each sub-group. Combined Means and SDs were also calculated for experimental group and control group separately to facilitate the application of SE_D and to find out 't'-value for significance testing. Table 5.18 gives the data relating significance of difference in post-test mean achievement scores of experimental group and control group.

Table 5.18 showed that both the experimental and control groups had 70 students each. The calculated 't' value found a non-significant difference in the post-test mean achievement scores of control and experimental groups ($t=1.2481$, $P>0.05$). Hence the second hypothesis, which stated that the control group and experimental group do not differ significantly from

TABLE 5.18
Significance of Difference in Post-test Mean Achievement Scores of Control Group and Experimental Group of both Schools

Group	*N*	*M*	*SD*	*t*
Control Group	70	39.2854	13.8918	14.2481 n.s
Experimental Group	70	42.1431	3.1902	

n.s. = not significant at 0.05 level.

each other in their post-test mean achievement scores was retained.

5.6(c) Testing of Third Sub-Hypothesis [$H_{06(c)}$)

The third sub-hypothesis of sixth hypothesis of the study stated, "There is no significant difference between the experimental and control groups in their mean gain scores in achievement test in English."

The annual school marks in English of class VIII examination were added to the scores of Listening-Speaking English Achievement Test-I to obtain pre-test achievement scores in English. Likewise the English marks of students in class IX half-yearly examination were added to the scores of Listening-Speaking English Achievement Test-II to obtain post-test achievement scores in English. The gain scores in achievement in English was found out by subtracting the post-test achievement scores from that of the pre-test achievement scores of each participant. The sub-groupwise means and SDs on achievement gain scores were calculated by applying necessary statistical procedures. Schoolwise difference were analysed with total difference between control and experimental groups in their achievement gain scores. Significance was tested by application of SE_D and 't' ratio and combined means and SDs were calculated for each group for this purpose.

(i) Difference Between Control Group and Experimental Group of the First School (S_1) in Achievement Gain Scores

The S_1 consisted of 90 students having 45 students each in control group and experimental group. Table 5.19 shows the data pertaining significance of difference between control group and experimental group in their achievement gain scores. The data showed a significant difference that existed between the control group and experimental group of S_1 (t=7.4558, P<0.01). The mean value of the analysis showed that the experimental group was at higher level (M=8.5999, SD=4.4541) than the control group (M=1.4222, SD=4.6767). It showed that in S_1 the experimental group had gained more in achievement than the control group. Such gain in achievement of experimental group went against the post-test analysis of significance of S_1, where both the groups did not differ significantly. It was because, at pre-test stage the control group had more achievement mean score which was overlapped by experimental group at post-test stage. Such analysis confirmed that the experimental group of S_1 gained more than control group in scores of achievement in English. This was due to the creative method of teaching English. It was the CMTE which made such difference. Hence, it was confirmed that CMTE had positive and significant influence on the development of students' academic achievement in English.

TABLE 5.19

Significance of Difference Between Control Group and Experimental Group of S_1 in Achievement Gain Scores

Group	*N*	*M*	*SD*	*'t'*
Control Group	45	1.4222	4.6767	7.4558**
Experimental Group	45	8.5999	4.4541	

**Significant at 0.01 level.

(ii) Difference Between Control Group and Experimental Group of Second School (S_2) in Achievement Gain Scores

The S_2 had 50 subjects having 25 each in control and experimental groups. Table 5.20 shows the data relating significance of difference between control and experimental groups of S_2 in their achievement gain scores.

TABLE 5.20

Significance of Difference Between Control Group and Experimental Group of S_2 in Achievement Gain Scores

Group	*N*	*M*	*SD*	*T*
Control Group	25	0.56	1.5252	12.6471**
Experimental Group	25	13.45	4.8627	

**Significant at 0.01 level.

Table 5.20 showed a significant difference that existed between control group and experimental group of S_2 in their achievement gain scores (t=12.6471, (P<0.01). The mean value of experimental group was found to be at higher level (M=13.45, SD=4.8627) than the mean value of control group (M=0.56, SD=1.5252) in achievement gain scores. Such higher gain in achievement of experimental group was only due to the CMTE, through which the concerned group was taught. In contrast the control group which was taught by traditional method showed no such significant difference in gain scores in achievement test. This data was also substantiated by the analysis of post-test achievement mean scores of S_2 where the difference was found significant (t=2.0962, P<0.05) and the mean value of experimental group was higher (M=37.8) than control group (M=30.00). From these analyses, it was clear that the higher gain in achievement of the experimental group was only due to CMTE. Creative Method of Teaching English (CMTE) proved more beneficial to increase students' achievement in comparison to the traditional method.

(iii) Difference Between Control Group and Experimental Group of Both the Schools (S_1+S_2) in Achievement Gain Scores

The hypothesis, "there is no significant difference in achievement gain scores of control group and experimental group" was tested by SE_D and 't' ratio. The total sample of the study was 140 having 70 each in control group and experimental group. Table 5.21 shows the data relating significance of difference in mean gain scores in achievement test of experimental and control groups.

TABLE 5.21
Significance of Difference in Mean Gain Scores in Achievement of Control Group and Experimental Group of both the Schools

Group	*N*	*M*	*SD*	*'t'*
Control Group	70	1.1142	3.8809	11.9509**
Experimental Group	70	10.3320	5.1574	

**Significant at 0.01 level (P<0.01).

Table 5.21 showed that experimental group and control group differed significantly from each other in their mean gain scores in English achievement test. The calculated 't' value (t=11.9509) was found to be significant statistically at 0.01 level of confidence (P<0.01). The table also revealed that the experimental group had shown its superiority in mean value (M=10.3320, SD=5.1574) over the control group (M=1.1142, SD=3.8809). Therefore, the sub-hypothesis which stated that the control and experimental groups do not differ significantly from each other in their mean gain scores in English achievement test was rejected.

An overall verification of all the three sub-hypotheses of sixth major hypothesis showed that the difference in mean achievement scores of control group and experimental group which was found significant at pre-test stage (t=2.1912, P<0.05), was not visible at post-test stage (t=1.2481, P>0.05). But a striking feature was visible when the mean values of those groups were compared at pre-post test stages comparatively. At pre-test stage, the control group was at higher level in its mean value (M=37.7856) than the experimental group (M=32.6430). But at post-test stage, although the experimental group was at higher level in its mean value (M=42.1431) than the control group (M=39.2854), the difference was not found significant statistically. A critical view on the range of increment of achievement score from pre-test stage to post-test stage kept the experimental group at higher order with a range of mean value increment of 9.5001 than that of control group, the range of mean value increment of which was 1.4998. From this analysis it may be proved that the experimental group had achieved significantly more in mean achievement test scores in English than that of control group, although the difference at post-test stage was found non-significant. Such finding is substantiated by the third sub-hypothesis which found a significant difference ($t=11.9509$, $P<0.01$) in mean gain scores in achievement test scores of control group and experimental group. Figure 5.2 diagramatically distinguished the differences lies in the pre-post test achievement mean values of both experimental and control groups. It clearly indicated higher rate of increment of the achievement scores of experimental group over the control group.

From Figure 5.2, it is clear that such increment in achievement scores of experimental group was due to the impact of the Creative Method of Teaching English (CMTE). On the other hand, the control group which was taught the English language through traditional method had achieved comparatively lower gain in achievement scores in English. The slight increment of achievement scores of control group from pre-test stage to post-test stage could be due to the impact of time, subject-interaction and students' personal labour. But, the spectacular increase of achievement scores in English of the experimental group was obviously due to the creative method of teaching English. Hence, it showed that the Creative Method of Teaching English (CMTE) was more effective for increasing students' achievement in English than the traditional method.

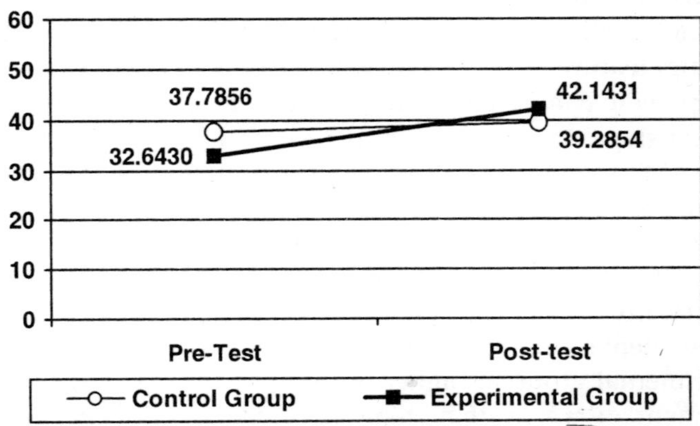

Fig. 5.2 : Mean Achievement Scores of Experimental and Control Groups at Pre-test and Post-test Stages

5.7 LEVELS OF INTELLIGENCE AND DEVELOPMENT OF CREATIVITY

The seventh hypothesis of the study had three sub-hypotheses intended to verify the relationship between levels of intelligence and creativity scores. The intelligence was bifurcated into high and low levels by eliminating the average group. Quartile Deviation Method was used to find out the students bearing high and low levels of intelligence. Q_1 was fixed as the point (25th Percentile approximately) below which the students were considered as low intelligent and Q_3 was fixed as the 75th percentile above which the students were considered highly intelligent. The Quartile Deviation formulae used in the analysis were as follows.

$$Q_1 = 1 + \frac{N/4 - F}{fq} \times i$$ ... (Garrett,1966)

$$Q_3 = 1 + \frac{3N/4 - F}{fq} \times i$$ ... (Garrett,1966)

The creativity scores of the students of both the groups were analysed by application of ANOVA as per the need of respective hypothesis.

5.7(a) Testing of First Sub-Hypothesis [$H_{07(a)}$]

The first sub-hypothesis stated, "There is no significant difference in creativity mean scores of high intelligence group and low intelligence group at pre-test stage of—(1) control group, and (2) experimental group". Two-way analysis of variance (2×2 ANOVA) was used to test the significance of the hypothesis.

Mehdi's Verbal Test of Creative Thinking and Tondon's Group Test of Intelligence (Verbal, 2/70) were used for obtaining creativity and intelligence scores of the participants. The total sample was 140. The intelligence raw scores were converted into grouped data for both the control and experimental groups separately. The range of the class interval for both the groups was five. The quartile deviation method was applied to find out the Q_1 (25th percentile) and Q_3 (75th percentile) of the distributions. Students those scored above Q_3 or 75th percentile were included in high-intelligence group and students scored below Q_1 or 25th percentile were included in low intelligence group. Following such procedure the Q_1 and Q_1 obtained from the intelligence scores of control group were 58 and 80 (approximately) respectively. Accordingly, the Q_1 and Q_1 obtained from the intelligence scores of experimental group were 58 and 78 (approximately) respectively. The high-intelligence groups and low-intelligence groups were formed both from control group and experimental group. In total, four groups were formed as follows:

- High-intelligence Control Group
- High-intelligence Experimental Group
- Low-intelligence Control Group
- Low-intelligence Experimental Group

Equal cell method of 2×2 ANOVA was followed in the analysis. There were 15 subjects in each cell (n=15) and the total number of subjects was 60 (N=60). For such equalization of number of subjects in each cell some subjects were randomly eliminated. These procedures were same for testing the three sub-hypotheses of the seventh hypothesis.

As per the requirement of the first sub-hypothesis stated above, the pre-test creativity scores of high-intelligence and low-intelligence groups of control group and experimental group were entered into the respective cells. Then the Raw Score Method was applied to findout F ratio through two-way analysis of variance and to test the significance of the first sub-hypothesis. Table 5.22 gives the data relating summary of 2×2

TABLE 5.22

Summary of 2x2 ANOVA on Pre-test Creativity Mean Scores of High Intelligence and Low-Intelligence Groups of Control and Experimental Groups

Source	*df*	*SSv*	*MSv*	*F*
Group	1	516.26	516.26	0.6767 n.s
Level of Intelligence	1	36605.4	36605.4	47.9852 **
Interaction	1	187.27	187.27	0.2454 n.s
Within	156	42719.47	762.8476	

n.s. = not significant at 0.05 level, ** significant at 0.01 level.

ANOVA on pre-test creativity mean scores of high-intelligence group and low intelligence group of control group and experimental group.

Table 5.22 represented the data relating to summary of ANOVA on pre-test mean creativity scores of students of different level of intelligence of control and experimental group. The data showed a non-significant effect of groups on the creativity mean scores of high and low intelligence groups (F=0.6767, df=l, P>0.05). The interaction effect was also found non-significant (F=0.2454, df=l, P>0.05). But there was a significant effect of levels of intelligence on the students' creativity mean scores (F=47.9852, df=l, P>0.0l). The analysis of the creativity mean values of different groups showed that the high-intelligence group of experimental group was at higher degree (M=136.8) than the low-intelligence group of the same group (M=83.8666). Similarly, the high-intelligence group of control group was at higher degree in creativity mean value (M=127.4) than the mean value of low-intelligence group of the control group (M=81.5333). The analysis confirmed that, levels of intelligence had significant effect to cause difference in pre-test creativity mean scores. The high-intelligence group scored more in pre-test creativity measures than the low-intelligence group.

5.7(b) Testing of Second Sub-Hypothesis ($H_{07(b)}$)

The second sub-hypothesis of the seventh hypothesis conjectured, "There is no significant difference in creativity mean scores of high intelligence group and low intelligence group at post-test stage of: (i) control group, and (ii) experimental group". Two-way analysis of variance (2×2 ANOVA) was used as the means of verifying the sub-hypothesis. The same procedure which was followed in finding different groups of students required by the first sub-hypothesis was also followed here in testing the second sub-hypothesis. As per the requirement, the post-test creativity scores of high intelligence group and low intelligence group of control and experimental groups were entered into the respective cells. Then the raw score method was applied to find out the F ratio and to test the second sub-hypothesis. Table 5.23 gives the data relating summary of 2×2 ANOVA on post-test creativity mean scores of high intelligence and low intelligence groups of control and experimental groups.

TABLE 5.23
Summary of 2x2 ANOVA on Post-Test Creativity Mean Scores of High-Intelligence and Low-Intelligence Groups of Control and Experimental Groups

Source	*df*	*SSv*	*MSv*	*F*
Group	1	65670.40	65670.40	44.5468**
Level of Intelligence	1	20203.30	20203.30	13.7047**
Interaction	1	220.50	220.50	0.1495
Within	56	82554.40	1474.1857	

**Significant at 0.01 level.
n.s. = not significant at 0.05 level.

Table 5.23 represented the data relating summary of ANOVA on post-test mean creativity scores of different levels of intelligence (high and low) and different groups (control and experimental). The 2×2 ANOVA showed that the main effect of different levels of intelligence and different groups were significant. The main effect of different groups on the creativity mean scores was found significant (F=44.5468, df=l, P<0.0l). It indicated that the experimental group had, significantly higher mean value in creativity measures than the control group. The F value of different levels of intelligence also gave a significant difference (F=13.7047, df=l, P<0.0l) in mean creativity scores. It showed that high intelligence group scored significantly more in post-test creativity test than the low intelligence group.

The mean value of high-intelligence experimental group (M=190.6) was found to be higher than the mean value of low-intelligence experimental group (M=157.7333). Similarly, high-intelligence control group scored more in mean creativity score (M=128.2666) than low-intelligence control group's mean creativity value (M=87.7333). Such difference was analogous to the difference that existed between the pre-test mean creativity scores of high-intelligence and low intelligence groups. The table showed no significant interacting effect on the creativity mean scores of students at post-test stage (F=0.1495, df=l, p>0.05). Such results showed that level of intelligence was a factor that influenced creativity. Specifically, CMTE had proved more effective for high-intelligence students than for low-intelligence students. The experimental group also found to have fared better than the control group in post-test creativity scores. It confirmed that, it was CMTE which had caused such significant difference by helping the experimental groups to score better than their counterparts. Such finding was also supported by the analysis of second sub-hypothesis of fifth hypothesis of the study, which showed a significant difference in post-test creativity score of experimental group and control group (t=9.7779, P>0.0l) in favour of experimental group. Such finding was supported by Carroll and Howieson (1992), Runco and Nemiro (1995), Sharma (1974), Badrinath and Satyanarayan (1979), Mishra (1986), Sharma and Bhartiya (1988), Padhi (1990) and Mishra and Mishra (1993).

5.7(c) Testing of Third Sub-Hypothesis [$H_{07(c)}$]

The third sub-hypothesis of the seventh hypothesis stated, "There is no significant difference in the creativity gain scores of high-intelligence group and low intelligence group of: (i) control group, and (ii) experimental group.

The hypothesis was tested by 2x2 ANOVA. After finding out the groups, the creativity gain scores of high-intelligence and low-intelligence students of control and experimental group were entered into respective cells. The raw score method was applied to find out F ratio to test the hypothesis. Table 5.24 represents the data relating summary of 2×2 ANOVA on

TABLE 5.24

Summary of 2×2 ANOVA on Creativity Gain Scores of High-Intelligence and Low-Intelligence Groups of Control and Experimental Groups

Source	*df*	*SSv*	*MSv*	*F*
Group	1	62081.67	62081.67	81.4955**
Level of Intelligence	1	920.5	920.5	1.2083 n.s.
Interaction	1	356.5	356.5	0.4679 n.s.
Within	56	42659.67	761.7798	

**Significant at 0.01 level, n.s. = not significant 0.05 level.

creativity gain scores of high-intelligence and low-intelligence students of control and experimental groups.

The data of Table 5.24 showed a significant effect of groups on the creativity gain scores (F=81.4955, df=1, P<0.01).

The analysis of mean value stated that the experimental group was at higher level (M=68) than the control group (M=3.7333) in their creativity gain scores. It confirmed that the experimental group had gained more in creativity measures and that was due to the impact of CMTE. Hence it could be assumed that, CMTE had proved its effectiveness in enabling the experimental group in securing more gain scores in creativity test. There was no significant effect of level of intelligence and the combined effect of groups and levels of intelligence on the students creativity gain scores. This showed that there was no significant difference in the creativity gain scores of high intelligence and low intelligence groups. Both high intelligence and low intelligence groups gained equally in creativity score as a result of intervention.

5.8 DEVELOPMENT OF CREATIVITY AND ACHIEVEMENT—AN IMPACT ANALYSIS OF CMTE

The eighth hypothesis of the study had three sub-hypotheses. The hypotheses tried to establish relationship between creativity gain scores and levels of achievement; achievement gain scores and levels of creativity and the correlation between creativity gain scores and achievement gain scores. One-way ANOVA method was used to test the first two sub-hypotheses, whereas the third sub-hypothesis was tested by Scatterrgram Correlation Method.

5.8(a) Testing of First Sub-Hypothesis [$H_{08(a)}$]

The first sub-hypothesis stated, "there is no significant difference in mean creativity gain scores of high achievers and low achievers in English achievement test scores of the experimental group". One-Way ANOVA was used to verify the first sub-hypothesis.

The total sample of the experimental group was 70. Mehdi's Verbal Test of Creative Thinking was administered both at pre-test and post-test stages. The creativity gain scores were obtained by subtracting the pre-test creativity scores from the post-test creativity scores. Students' English marks in Class VIII annual examination were added to the Listening-Speaking English Achievement Test-I scores to produce pre-test achievement scores in English. The pre-test achievement scores of students were taken to dichotomise them into high-low achievers.

To find out the high and low achievers of the experimental group, the raw scores of achievement test were transferred into grouped data keeping range of the class interval fixed at five. The quartile deviation method was applied to find out the Q_1 (25th Percentile) and Q_3 (75th percentile). Students who secured above Q_3, were considered as high achievers and students who secured below Q_1 were considered as low achievers in English achievement test. The calculated Q_1 was 21 and Q_3 was 43 approximately. Accordingly the high and low achievers were found out of the experimental group. There were 17 students each in high achiever's group and low achiever's group. Hence, the two cells were found equal in their subject number. As per the need of the hypothesis the gain scores in creativity test were obtained for each student of high and low achiever groups. Then, the Deviation Score Method of ANOVA was applied to findout F ratio to test the sub-hypothesis. Table 5.25 gives the data relating the difference in mean creativity gain scores of high achievers and low achievers in English achievement test of experimental group calculated by one-way ANOVA.

TABLE 5.25

ANOVA Summary on Mean Creativity Gain Scores of High-Achievers and Low-Achievers of Experimental Group

Source	*df*	*SSv*	*MSv*	*f*
SS_B	116.73	1	116.73	0.1598(ns)
SSW	23364.01	32	730.1253	

(ns) = not significant (p<0.05).

Table 5.25 showed the data on the mean creativity gain scores of high achievers and low-achievers of experimental group. The calculated F ratio indicated non-significant difference (F=0.1598, df=1, P<0.05) in the mean creativity gain scores of high achievers and low achievers. It showed that, both the groups were found more or less equal in their mean creativity gain scores. It also explained that the intervention programme (CMTE) was proved equally useful for both high and low achievers in increasing their creative potentialities. The hypothesis which stated no significant difference in creativity gain scores of high and low achievers of experimental group was retained.

5.8 (b) Testing of Second Sub-Hypothesis [$H_{08(b)}$]

The second sub-hypothesis stated, "There is no significant difference between mean achievement gain scores in English of high creative and low creative groups". The difference was tested by application of One-Way ANOVA.

Mehdi's Verbal Test on Creative Thinking administered at pre-test stage was taken into consideration to find out high creative and low creative students. Quartile deviation formula was applied to find out Q_1 and Q_3 to determine the point below and above which the low and high creative students were identified. The calculated Q_1 was 100 and Q_3 was 134 approximately. Pre-test achievement scores were subtracted from post-test achievement scores to obtain achievement gain scores. Students' English marks obtained from class VIII annual examination were added to Listening-Speaking English Achievement Test-I scores to produce pre-test achievement scores in English. Similarly, students' English marks obtained from Class-IX half-yearly examination were added to the Listening-Speaking English Achievement Test-II scores to produce post-test English achievement scores.

Taking the Q_1 and Q_3 values of pre-test creativity scores the high-creative and low-creative groups were formed. Some subjects were randomly eliminated to equalize the ANOVA cells. There were 30 subjects in each cell. The achievement gain scores of the high and low creative students were obtained and Deviation Score Method was utilized to find out the F ratio for significance testing. Table 5.26 gives data regarding mean achievement gain scores of high creatives and low creatives.

TABLE 5.26
ANOVA Summary on Mean Achievement Gain Scores of High Creatives and Low Creatives

Source	*df*	*SSv*	*MSv*	*F*
SS_B	28.0167	1	28.0167	0.8233 ns
SSW	1973.5667	1	58	34.0270

ns = Not Significant, (P<0.05).

Table 5.26 showed the ANOVA summary on the mean achievement gain scores of high creative and low creatives. The calculated F ratio showed a non-significant difference between high creatives and low creatives in their mean achievement gain scores (F=0.8233, df=l, P>0.05). It indicated that the high creative students and low creative students did not differ significantly in their mean achievement gain score. Their achievement was found to be more or less equal to each other. Hence, the hypothesis, which stated "no significant difference between high creatives and low creatives in their mean achievement gain scores was retained. This analysis further stated that, though CMTE helped in developing students' achievement, it favours neither high-creatives nor low-creatives for such development. Hence, CMTE is found equally beneficial for high and low creative students in developing their academic achievement in English

5.8(c) Testing of Third Sub-Hypothesis [$H_{08(c)}$]

The third sub-hypothesis stated: "There is no significant correlation between creativity gain scores and achievement gain scores." The significance of such relationship was verified by application scattergram correlation and finding out "t" value.

Table given in Appendix '0' showed the correlation between creativity gain scores and achievement gain scores through scatter diagram. Different values obtained from scattergram table were posted in the coefficient correlation formula as follows:

$$r = \frac{\sum fxy - \frac{(\sum fx)(\sum fy)}{N}}{\sqrt{\sum fx^2 - \frac{(\sum fx)^2}{N}}\sqrt{\sum fy^2 - \frac{(\sum fy)^2}{N}}}$$

$$= \frac{373 - \frac{(74)(270)}{140}}{\sqrt{242 - \frac{(74)^2}{140}}\sqrt{1440 - \frac{(270)^2}{140}}}$$

$$= +0.5332$$

$$= \frac{+0.5332}{\sqrt{1-(+0.5332)^2}} \times \sqrt{140-2}$$

= 9.1675 significant at 0.01 level

The calculated coefficient of correlation gave a moderate and positive result. Further the 't' value proved its significance at 0.01 level of confidence ($t=9.1765$, $p<0.01$). The analysis reported a positive and significant correlation between creativity gain scores and achievement gain scores. Hence, the hypothesis which stated that, creativity gain score is not significantly correlated with achievement gain score, was rejected. It confirmed that the growth of creativity as a result of CMTE is moderately related to the growth of students' achievement.

CHAPTER 6

CONCLUSIONS

6.1 A Brief Description

6.2 Findings

6.3 Recommendations

6.4 Implications for further Research

CHAPTER

6

Conclusions

The investigator realized the contradictions of several research studies on the creativity and its relationship with those of intelligence, achievement SES and sex. Though some foreign studies established positive effect of training on development of creative potentials, those were opposed by a number of other research studies. Moreover, the studies were divergent by nature, in their methods, sample, tools and in statistical interpretations. The research findings based on foreign environmental conditions may not be applicable under Indian conditions. On the other hand, in India, we lack such studies to resolve the research conflicts. Not a single research study was found on using the creative method of teaching English to develop creative thinking of secondary school students. Hence, the investigator undertook this study.

6.1 A BRIEF DESCRIPTION

The research problem reads as "Effect of Creative Method of Teaching English (CMTE) on Development of Creative Thinking of Secondary School Students."

The study was experimental in nature and was based on Randomized Groups Pre-test Post-test Design. The sample of the study consisted of 140 ninth graders (70 boys, 70 girls) drawn from four sections of two Secondary Schools of Cuttack city of Orissa. Each school had a control group and an experimental group. The experimental groups were taught the English language by Creative Method of Teaching English (CMTE) by the investigator and the control groups were taught by the traditional method by the respective subject teachers. The duration of intervention extended for eight weeks. Before the experiment, the CMTE model was prepared and tried out by the investigator by . pilot study using One Group Pre-test Post-test Design, which indicated positive effect of CMTE on development of creativity. In the main study the investigator tried to findout the relationship of creativity with intelligence, SES, achievement and sex. Specifically the study was intended to know the effectiveness of CMTE on the development of students' Creative Thinking. Mehdi's Verbal Test on Creative Thinking, Tandon's Verbal Group Test of Intelligence (Oriya) and Kuppuswamy's Socio-Economic-Status Scale (Oriya/ Urban, Form B) were used to obtain scores on creativity, intelligence and socio-economic-status respectively. Students' class VIII annual examination's English marks and half-yearly examination's English marks of class IX were added to the scores of Listening-Speaking English Achievement Test I and II respectively to obtain pre-test and post-test achievement scores in English.

The tests were administered and scored by following specific scoring procedures. The obtained data were tabulated and analysed through application of scattergram correlation, Standard Error of Difference Between Means (SE_D) and analysis of variance. All the hypotheses were verified and the significance of the result was tested at 0.01 and 0.05 levels of confidence. The analysis and interpretation of data were made hypothesiswise from which the following major findings were drawn.

6.2 FINDINGS

1. There existed a moderate, positive and significant

correlation between creativity and intelligence (r=+0.5244, t=7.2351, p<0.01). Such relationship became low and positive, but significant when the effect of achievement was made constant (r=+0.3629, t=4.5743, P<0.01) and also when the effect of SES was kept constant (r=+0.2618, t=3.1858, p>0.01). These findings showed that even after eliminating the effect of achievement and SES creativity is significantly and positively correlated with intelligence.

2. Achievement had a moderate, positive and significant relationship with that of creativity (r=+0.4659, t=6.1849, P<0.01). Such relationship became low and positive but significant when the impact of intelligence was made constant (r=+0.2496, t=3.0272, P<0.01).
3. There existed a low, positive and significant correlation (r=+0.3289, t=4.7153, p<0.01) between creativity and socio-economic status. Such relationship lowered to near about zero and was non-significant when the impact of intelligence was partialled out (r=+0.0424, t=0.4980, P<0.05). It explained that whatever relationship SES had with that of creativity was only because of intelligence.
4. There was significant difference between the boys and girls in their creativity mean scores at pre-test stage (t=2.3915, p<0.05). Boys scored more than the girls in mean creativity value (Boys' mean = 119.0715, Girls' mean = 106.50).
5. There was a non-significant difference in the post-test mean creativity scores of boys and girls (t=0.4194, P>0.05).
6. There existed a significant difference in the creativity gain scores of boys and girls (t=3.2636, P<0.01). Girls were found to have gained more in creativity measures (M=76.2855, SD=33.311) than the boys (M=53.786, SD=22.05). Girls were found to be more benefited from CMTE than boys in respect of development of their creative thinking abilities.
7. There was a non-significant difference in the pre-test creativity scores of control and experimental group of school no. 1 (S_1) (t=1.2260, P>0.05).

8. There was a non-significant difference in the pre-test creativity scores of control group and experimental group of school no. 2 (S_2) (t=0.4971, P>0.05).
9. The control and experimental groups of both the S_1 and S_2 showed a non-significant difference in their pre-test creativity mean scores (t=0.4244, p>0.05).
10. There were significant differences in the post-test creativity mean scores of control group and experimental group of S_1 (t=9.2468, P<0.0l), of S_2 (t=5.9821, P<0.0l) and of both S_1 and S_2 (t=9.7779, p<0.01). In both the schools the experimental group was found to have scored more in creativity mean scores than the control group.
11. The experimental group and control group of the first school (S_1) differed significantly in their creativity gain scores (t=13.9123, P<0.0l). The experimental group scored higher mean value (M=54.722, SD=22.753) than the control group (M=3.8444, SD=9.1727).
12. The experimental group and control group of the second school (S_2) differed significantly in their creativity gain scores (t=10.1527, p<0.0l). The experimental group scored more mean value (M=83.70, SD=37.127) than the control group (M=6.0000, SD=9.2735).
13. The control group and experimental group of both S_1 and S_2 differed significantly from each other in their creativity gain scores (t=15.2369, p<0.01). The experimental group was found to have gained more in creativity mean value (M=65.0712, SD=31.9048) than the control group (M=4.6142, SD=9.1726).

    All these analyses—pre-test, post-test and gain scores in creativity test showed the effectiveness of CMTE on the development of students' creative thinking. The Creative Method of Teaching English (CMTE), through which the experimental groups were taught was found effective in increasing the creative thinking of secondary school students.
14. There was significant difference between control and experimental groups of the first school (S_1) in pre-test achievement scores (t=2.1051, p<0.05). The control

group had more achievement mean value (M=42.111, SD=11.3275) than the experimental group (M=36.667, SD=13.14).

15. There was no significant difference in the pre-test mean achievement scores of control and experimental groups of the second school (S_2) (t=1.2089, P>0.05).
16. The experimental and control groups of both S_1 and S_2 differed significantly from each other in their pre-test achievement scores (t=2.1912, P<0.05). The control group was found to have more mean value in achievement measures (M=37.7856, SD=14.0057) than the experimental group (M=32.6430, SD = 13.7631).
17. The control and experimental groups of the first school (S_1) showed a non-significant difference in their post-test achievement mean scores (t=0.2464, P>0.05).
18. The control and experimental groups of the second school (S_2) differed significantly from each other in post-test achievement mean scores (t=2.0962, p<0.05). The experimental group was found to have scored more mean value (M=37.80, SD=11.0525) than the control group (M=30.00, SD=14.9665).
19. The experimental and control groups of both S_1 and S_2 showed a non-significant difference between their post-test achievement mean scores (t=1.2481, P>0.05).
20. The control group and experimental group of the first school (S_1) differed significantly in their achievement gain scores (t=7.4558, p<0.0l). The experimental group was found to have gained more in achievement (M=8.5999, SD=4.4541) than the control group (M=1.4222, SD=4.6767).
21. The control group and experimental group of the second school (S_2) differed significantly in their achievement gain scores (t=12.6471, P<0.01). The experimental group had higher gain in achievement (M=13.45, SD=4.8627) than the control group (M=0.56, SD=1.5252).
22. The control group and experimental group of both S_1 and S_2 differed significantly in their achievement gain scores (t=11.9509, P<0.01). The experimental group obtained higher gain in achievement (M=10.3320,

SD=5.1574) than the control group (M=1.1142, SD=3.8809).

The overall analyses—pre-test, post-test and gain score analysis of achievement measures showed that, the experimental groups had gained more in achievement from the intervention programme, i.e., CMTE. Hence, it was proved that CMTE was found to be beneficial in increasing the achievement of secondary school students in English.

23. Level of intelligence exerted significant effect on the pre-test creativity scores (F=47.9852, df=l, P<0.01), which was also found significant in post-test creativity scores (F=13.7047, df=1, P<0.01). At both times, the high intelligence groups obtained higher mean creativity scores than low-intelligence groups.
24. There was significant group effect in the post-test creativity mean scores of high-intelligence and low intelligence groups (F=44.5468, df=1, P<0.01) and also in creativity gain scores of high-intelligence and low-intelligence group. The subjects of experimental group always scored more in creativity scores (in post-test scores and in gain scores) than the control group. It showed that due to the effectiveness of CMTE, such higher scores of experimental group were observed.
25. The levels of achievement exerted no significant effect on the creativity gain scores of the secondary schoolers (F=0.1598, df=1, P>0.05). It explained that Creative Method of Teaching English (CMTE) was equally beneficial for high-achievers and low achievers to enhance their creative abilities.
26. Levels of creativity had no such significant effect on the achievement gain scores (F=0.8233, df=l, P>0.05). It explained that CMTE had proved equally beneficial both for high creatives and low creatives in developing their achievement.
27. There existed a moderate, positive and significant correlation (r=+0.5332, t=9.1675, P>0.01) between creativity gain score and achievement gain score. It showed that due to the impact of CMTE, students'

achievement was developed keeping pace with their creativity.

6.3 RECOMMENDATIONS

Although effect of heredity on creativity remained inconclusive, effect of environment on development of creativity is widely accepted. Training was proved to be the most effective means to increase such extraordinary talent.

Creative Method of Teaching English (CMTE) was found to be an effective training strategy, which facilitated the development of creative thinking. It was found profitable for students who were reading in urban secondary schools. English, taught through CMTE, was found effective to enhance students' divergent thinking abilities. Side by side, the CMTE increased the achievement of students in English language, Considering the above-stated major findings of the study the following recommendations were made:

(1) The secondary school teachers, the administrators and educational planners should try for the wide application of this method for teaching English in secondary schools.

(2) Teachers' Training Institutes, Institutes of Advanced Studies in Education (IASEs), Regional Institutes of Education should develop due training packages on CMTE for teacher trainees, so that they may be able to transact the curriculum for attainment of such objective.

(3) Innovative learning materials should be used to increase the effectiveness of such method.

(4) As high-intelligence students are found to be more benefitted by CMTE than the low-intelligence students, teachers in the classroom should never try to demoralize the low-intelligent students. Rather, free, encouraging, playful and failure-bearing teaching-learning environment should be made available for students in the learning situation.

(5) Teacher-taught relationship should be cordial and democratic. Students are to be given immence freedom

for expressing their open-ended thoughts. Teachers are to guide their ill-organized thoughts to structured one.

(6) No discrimination should be made between boys and girls while the teacher is transacting a curricular task in the classroom through this method. They should be given equal importance during creative teaching for the development of their creative thinking.

6.4 IMPLICATIONS FOR FURTHER RESEARCH

The following studies are recommended for further research.

1. The present study may be replicated in different subject areas, such as Modern Indian languages and in social studies to know the effectiveness of such approach on the development of creativity and achievement of students.
2. CMTE may be tried out at different levels of education—primary and higher secondary level.
3. Effectiveness of CMTE may be studied outside India and on different subjects taught at various levels of their educational systems.

APPENDICES

A. Mehdi's Verbal Test on Creative Thinking
B. Scoring Key of Mehdi's Verbal Test on Creative Thinking
C. Socio-Economic Status Scale (Oriya) by Kuppuswamy
D. Scoring Key of SES Scale by Kuppuswamy
E. Group Test of Intelligence (Verbal, 2/70) by R.K.Tondon
F. Scoring Key of Verbal Group Test of Intelligence by R.K.Tondon
G. Listening-Speaking English Achievement Test-I
H. Listening-Speaking English Achievement Test-II
I. The CMTE Lesson Plan Model

APPENDIX A

Confidential

Dr. BAQER MEHDI

M.A. (Columbia), Ph.D. (Aligarh)

Professor of Education

N.C.E.R.T., New Delhi-110016

No. 458715

TCW

Name:	Age :
Class:	School/College :
Father's/Guaridan's Name:	Occupation:
Home Address:	Date :

GENERAL INTURCTION

In this booklet you will find mentioned some interesting problems which will require the use of your thinking ability and imagination to solve them. The purpose is to see how quickly and imaginatively you can think under situations which require novel ways of dealing with them. Read each problem carefully and apply your bethinking in giving the responses. Write your responses either in English or in your mother tongue. Responses have to be given briefly but clearly in the space provided under each problem. Give a serial number to each of your responses. There are no right or wrong responses to any of these problems. Therefore, use your imagination to think of as many responses as you can.

The problems are divided into Four Activities. Each Activity is separately timed. Within the time-limit for each Activity you may work on the different problems according to your speed. When you finish one problem, go to the next. If necessary, you may return to the previous one again for any addition you would like to make. Remember that you have not to go the next activity until the time for the first activity is over and you are told to proceed further.

At the end you will be given 5 minutes extra time. Which you may use at any problem of any Activity in which you want to do additional work.

Please do not omit any problem.

Activity : 1

NOVEL USES OF THINGS

DIRECTIONS

1. On this and the next pave, you have been given names of certain things which could be used in many different ways. You have to think in how many different and new ways the things may be used.
2. Write as many uses as you can, but do try to think also those which are novel, that is those which you think no one else might have thought of.
3. You will be given 12 MINUTES for this activity. . After every four minutes you will be told the time so that you may move on to the next item in the activity.

Below is given an example which will help you to know what you have to do.

Example : Newspaper,

Uses : (i) To read the news.

(ii) To make paper toys.

(iii) To get protection from the sun.

(iv) To wrap something.

(v) To cover a dirty place; etc.

PROBLEMS

1. Piece of Stone.

____

____

2. Wooden stick

____

____

3. Water

____

____

Activity : 2

SIMILARITIES

DIRECTIONS

1. On this and the next page, you have been given pairs of words which can be related to each other in many different ways, You have to think in how many different and new ways are they related.
2. Write as many relationships as you can, but also try to think these which are novel, that is those which you think no one else might have thought of.
3. You will be given 15 MINUTES for this activity. After every 5 minutes you will be told the time so that you may move on to the next item in the activity.

Below is given an example which will help you to know what you have to do.

Example : Man and animal
Uses : (i) Both have life.
(ii) Both need food and water.
(iii) Both can fall ill.
(iv) Both are afraid of enemy.
(v) Both have the experience of feeling cold and hot, etc.

PROBLEMS

1. Tree and House.

 ____

 ____

2. Chair and Ladder

 ____

 ____

3. Air and Water

 ____

 ____

Activity : 3

MAKING THINGS MORE INTERESTING AND USEFUL

DIRECTIONS

Just keep in mind a simple model of a horse. You have to imagine in what ways you can change this simple model into an interesting and novel one for children to play with. You may think of adding any number of parts or accessories in order to make it really interesting and fascinating for children. Do not bother about the cost of the new parts or accessories that you would like to use in order to make the toy model interesting and fascinating for children.

Write all the ideas which come to you mind in a serial order in the space given below.

You will give 6 minutes for this activity.

APPENDIX B

TCW

SCORING SHEET

ACTIVITY I

	Fluency	Flexibility	Originality
Item 1.	.....	.....	.....
Item 2.	.....	.....	.....
Item 3.	.....	.....	.....
Total	.....	.....	.....

ACTIVITY II

	Fluency	Flexibility	Originality
Item 1.	.....	.....	.....
Item 2.	.....	.....	.....
Item 3.	.....	.....	.....
Total	.....	.....	.....

ACTIVITY III

	Fluency	Flexibility	Originality
Item 1.	.....	.....	.....
Item 2.	.....	.....	.....
Item 3.	.....	.....	.....
Total	.....	.....	.....

ACTIVITY IV

	Fluency	Flexibility	Originality
Item 1.	.....	.....	.....

SCORE SUMMARY

	Fluency	Flexibility	Originality
Activity I	.....	.....	.....
Activity II	.....	.....	.....
Activity III	.....	.....	.....
Activity IV	.....	.....	.....
Grand Total	.....	.....	.....

ORIGINALITY SCORING FOR RESPONSES NOT MENTIONED IN THE RESPONSE LIST

For any novel response for mentioned in the responses list given in the manual, first of all briefly note it down in the space provided below giving the number of the activity and the item to which it belongs. Then, after you have scored all the test scripts, give it a score according to the scheme given in the manual and note the score in the appropriate column in the scoring sheet. In all probability, there will be very few such responses.

Activity	*Item*	*Response*	*Originality Score*

C.E.P. Agra

APPENDIX C

INFORMATION BLANK
SOCIO-ECONOMIC STATUS SCALE (URBAN)
B. KUPUSWAMY

SESS
Class

FORM-B

Please answer the following questions carefully regarding your father. If your father is not alive then give the particulars regarding your guardian.

Name : ______________________ Age ______________
Address (Institutional) : ______________________
Address (Home) : ______________________

A. Education of Father/Guardian

School or College Examination Passed	*Year if known*	*Technical or Professional Examinations passed*	*Year if known*

B. Occupation of Father/Guardian

1. (a) In which organization he does his work ?

   ____

   (b) Who controls the organization ?

   ____

2. (a) What is the exact designation ?

   ____

   (b) What is the nature of work ?

   ____

C. Income of Your Father/Guardian

1. What is the monthly salary or weekly wage of your father or guardian ?

   ____

   ____

2. What are the Allowances or bonus he gets.

   ____

   ____

3. Any other sources of Income? Monthly Income ______

   (a) ______________ ______________

   (b) ______________ ______________

   (c) ______________ ______________

   (d) ______________ ______________

APPENDIX D

B. KUPUSWAMY
SOCIO-ECONOMIC STATUS SALE (URBAN)
(SCORE CARD)

Code No. : Name :

Age : Address :

Check below by putting a cross in the appropriate item box on the basis of information Blank, Put the weights (Scores) in last column.

Items	*Eight Score*
A. Education	
1. Professional degree or Hons M.A. & Above	7 ☐
2. B.A. or B.Sc. Degree	6 ☐
3. Intermediate of Post-High Scholl Dimplomas	5 ☐
4. High School Certificate	4 ☐
5. Middle School completion	3 ☐
6. Primary School or literate	2 ☐
7. Illiterate	1 ☐
	A..........
B. Occupation	
1. Profession	10 ☐
2. Semi-Profession	6 ☐
3. Clerical, Shop owners. Farm owners, etc.	5 ☐
4. Skilled worker	4 ☐
5. Semi-skilled worker	3 ☐
6. Unskilled worker	2 ☐
7. Unemployed	1 ☐
	B..........
C. Income	
1. Above Rs. 1000 per month	12 ☐
2. Between Rs. 750 and Rs. 999	10 ☐
3. Between Rs. 500 and Rs. 749	6 ☐
4. Between Rs. 300 and Rs. 499	4 ☐

5. Between Rs. 101 and Rs. 299 3 ☐
6. Between Rs. 51 and Rs. 100 2 ☐
7. Below Rs. 50. 1 ☐

C..........

Total Score
(Add A.B.C.)

	Total Score	SESS Class
S	26 – 29	I
C	16 – 25	II
A	11 – 15	III
L	5 – 15	IV
E	Below 6	V

APPENDIX E

Confidential

VERBAL GROUP TEST OF INTELLIGENCE (2/70)
(By Dr. R.K. Tondon)

Do not write and mark anything on this test. All answers are to be written in the answer paper attached at the end of the test.

XXX XXX XXX XXX

INSTRUCTION

It is a is a simple mental ability test. There are 91 questions in five pages which are to be answered within twenty minutes. All questions are written in simple language. You are to find out the correct answer and write the number of answers in the answer paper. Likewise answer of all questions are to be given in numbers. So writing is less very less. In each question there is a correct answer and every answer has a number or numeral. As there is less time it may not be possible for a person to answer all questions. So answer the questions as quick as possible. If any questions seems more difficult, it is better to switch over to another question without wasting time in that.

You will start answering when instruction will be given to do so and will try to answer as quick as possible.

Writing or marking on the test is not allowed.

Now turn over the page and read the questions given for practice.

EXAMPLE FOR PRACTICE

Answers are given in Answer sheet (See the Practice column).

The following questions are like the questions given in the test. Answers of these practice questions are given in the answer sheet. Now we will try to answer those questions.

1. 1, 2, 3, 4, 5, 6,..... write the next number in serial
   (1) 8, (2) 9, (3) 6, (4) 10, (5) 7
2. 5, 10, 15, 20, ... Write next number in serial
   (1) 7, (2) 25, (3) 35, (4) 30, (5) 4
3. Fan is useful for us, because—
   (1) It is costly, (2) It given us air, (3) It looks nice, (4) Everyone can use it easily
4. Mouse is dangerous, because—
   (1) It spreads plague, (2) It frightens right, (3) They are found in houses (4) It looks ugly
5. Meaning of the word "Rich" is—
   (1) Kindness, (2) Healthy, (3) Big, (4) Welwisher, (4) Wealthy
6. Meaning of word "Mother" is—
   (1) Friend, (2) Enemy, (3) Relative, (4) Brother, (5) 'Ma'
7. Opposite of Black colour is—
   (1) Dark, (2) Day, (3) White (4) Night, (5) Light
8. Opposite of the word "Life" is—
   (1) End, (2) Death (3) Pessimism (4) Pleasure (5) Soil
9. Cow : Calf :: Goat :
   (1) Horse, (2) Sheep (3) Citten, (4) Kid (5) Dog
10. Lion : Lioness : : King :
    (1) Owner, (2) Maid servant, (3) Queen, (4) Palace, (5) State
11. Ram is sitting in right side of Mahesh and Ramesh in left side of Mahesh. So who is in the middle?
    (1) Ram, (3) Ramesh, (3) Mahesh.
12. If Rita is taller than Rama, Prava is shorter than Sita and Rita is taller than Prava, so who is shortest among all?
    (1) Rama, (2) Rita, (3) Sita, (4) Prava.
13. Which word is different from others ?
    (1) Dog, (2) Cat, (3) Monkey, (4) Cow, (5) Rat
14. Which word is different from others?
    (1) Wool, (2) cotoon, (3) gum, (4) silk, (5) velvet

(If you have any doubt on above questions, you can ask and clear your doubts)

(Do not turn over the Page Until you are told to do so)

QUESTIONS FOR THE TEST

(Write the answers of questions of this page in column-01 of Page-1.

1. What is the meaning of millionnaire
(1) Big, (2) Healthy, (3) Rich, (4) Full, (5) Old
2. We wear cotton dresses, because—
(1)If looks beautiful, (2) It is produced in India in large numbers (3) It is colourful (4) It protects the body.
3. Ram is Thiner than Mohan. Kamala is thiner than Rama. Who is the thinnest one—
(1) Ram, (2) Mohan, (3) Kamala
4. Meaning of flower is—
(1) Tree, (2) wasp, (3) bud, (4) Sunshine, (5) Dust
5. We drink milk because—
(1) It is tasteful, (2) It is white, (3) Sugar is easily mixed in it (4) It is useful for health.
6. Opposite of word cold is—
(1) Hot, (2) Cold, (3) Ice, (4) Water, (5) Fire
7. Tree is helpful for us, because—
(1) It has leaves, (2) It is dense, (3) It gives us wood, (4) Birds live here.
8. 16, 17, 18, 19, 20, ... Write the next number
(1) 22, (2) 25, (3) 14, (4) 21, (5) 23.
9. The meaning of Labourious means—
(1) Good, (2) Industrious, (3) Lazy, (4) Happy, (5) cleaver
10. Air us useful. Because—
(1) It is found in atmosphere, (2) It protects from heat, (3) Cold air is comefortable, (4) It helps in making live.
11. Opposite of word "Friend" is—
(1) Brother, (2) Relation, (34) Enemy, (4) Own family member, (5) Distance relation
12. Eye : See : : Ear :
(1) Speak, (2) Smell (3) Cut, (4) listen, (5) walk
13. Water is useful for us, because—
(1) It helps in washing, (2) We drink it, (3) It is easily available, (3) mix easily with milk.
14. 6, 7, 12, 13, 18, ... Which is the next serial number?

(1) 14, (2) 10, (3) 15, (4) 19, (5) 25

15. Meaning of word powerless is—
(1) Sick, (2) patient, (3) strong, (4) weak (5) sorrowful
16. Rakesh borns before Ramesh, Krushna born before Rakesh, so who is youngest?
(1) Ramesh, (2) Rakesh, (3) Krushna
17. Which word is different from others?
(1) Bird, (2) Parrot, (3) Mayna, (4) Pigeon, (5) Rabbit
18. Meaning of shouting is—
(1) Regulation, (2) Loadn, (3) Utter loudly, (4) Jump.
19. 14, 13, 12, 11, 10, ... Write the next number.
(1) 15, (2) 16, (3) 8, (4) 11, (5) 9
20. Cat : Mew : : Dog : ?
(1) Mother (2) Bark, (3) Brite, (4) Cat
21. The opposite of word "Sportive"is—
(1) Running, (2) work, (3) Happy, (4) Quick, (5) Sorrowful
22. Playing is necessary for children, because—
(1) It keeps healthy, (2) It gives new friends, (3) Time will not available in future, (4) It helps in reading.
23. Which word is different?
(1) Lemon, (2) Banana, (3) Home, (4) Mango, (5) Papaya.
24. Ram is infront of Prema, Shyam is after prem, who is in last ?
(1) Ram, (2) Prem, (3) Shyam
25. We have stove, because—
(1) It makes dark, (2) It is made of iron, (3) It looks nice (4) It gives heat
26. Meaning of Season is—
(1) Hot, (2) Saint, (3) Rain, (4) Fruit, (5) Weather
27. Opposite of Nectar is—
(1) Hot, (2) Sour, (3) Sweet (4) Speed, (5) Poison.
28. 5, 8, 11, 14, 17, ... write next number in serial.
(1) 18, (2) 16, (3) 20, (4) 22, (5) 21.
29. Electricity is profitable because—
(1) It gives light, (2) It constructs river bond, (3) It is available everywhere. (4) People use it.
30. Which word is different from others?
(1) Table, (2) Gitar, (3) Flute, (4) Carrom Board, (5) Sitar

31. Puspa runs faster than Asha, Nirmala runs faster than puspa. Who runs fastest.
(1) Asha, (2) Puspa, (3) Nirmala.
32. Tree : Green : : Slate :?
(1) Red, (2) Yellow, (3) Black, (4) White, (5) Blue
33. Opposite of Pure is—
(1) Impure, (2) Unholy, (3) Pious, (4) Opaque
34. Meaning of brave is
(1) win, (2) strength, (3) fight, (4) coward, (5) Powerful
35. 32, 30, 28, 26, 24,.... Write the next serial number
(1) 25, (2) 23, (3) 22, (4) 33, (5) 35
36. Which word is different from others?
(1) Black, (2) yellow, (3) Blue, (4) Dark, (5) white
37. We watch cinema, because—
(1) We meet people there, (2) For use of money, (3) It makes study easy, (4) It is entertaining
38. Ram is shorter than Mohan, Mohan is shorter than Krushna, Who is tallest?
(1) Ram,. (2) Mohan, (3) Krushna
39. Man : Face : : Bird :?
(1) Feather (2) Head, (3) Beak, (4) Fly, (5) Eat
40. Opposite of the word Power is—
(1) Patient, (2) Powerless, (3) Sorrow, (4) Soft, (5) Pain
41. Meaning of word "citizen" means—
(1) villagers, (2) residents of a capital, (3) Hill dwellers (4) Voters live in a state, (5) Turban
42. 4, 14, 22, 31, 40.... Write the next serial number
(1) 46, (2) 8, (3) 49, (4) 30 (5) 58
43. Which word is different from others?
(1) Table, (2) chiar, (3) Stove, (4) cot, (5) wife
44. If Cricket is more expensive than hockey, hockey is less expensive than Badminton and cricket is more expensive than badminton, so which play is most expensive?
(1) cricket, (2) Hockey, (3) Badminton.
45. One should not take wine, because
(1) Taking wine is sin, (2) It destroyes the heart, (3) person get intoxicated, (4) It smells bad
46. Opposite of word "optimistic"—
(1) pleasure, (2) success, (3) sorry, (4) future, (5) pessimistic

47. Dog : Goat : : Puppy : ?
(1) Kid, (2) Pegeon, (3) Rabbit, (4) Rat, (5) Puppy
48. Meaning of word "Pradhan"—
(1) Man, (2) Rich, (3) Road, (4) Head, (5) Right
49. 1, 3, 5, 7, 9, ... write next number in serial
(1) 10, (2) 11, (3) 13, (4) 12, (5) 8
50. Which word is different from others?
(1) Gomati (2) Godabari, (3) Ganga, (4) Sarojini, (5) Jamuna
51. Rama is more intelligent than Prava, Sita is more intelligent than Rama, who is most intelligent?
(1) Prava, (2) Sita, (3) Rama
52. Farmer cultivates, because—
(1) He has plaugh, (2) It makes soil fertile, (3) He has seeds, (4) He is proficient in if—
53. Opposite of the word hospitality is—
(1) Ideal, (2) Desobey, (3) False, (4) Disrespectful, (5) Respect
54. Head : Cap : : Leg :
(1) Cloth, (2) Body, (3) Tape, (4) Shoe, (5) Trouser
55. The organ through which we smell is—
(1) Tongue, (2) Nose, (3) Ear, (4) Eyes, (5) Hand
56. 2, 4, 6, 8, 10, ... write the next number in serial
(1) 11, (2) 9, (3) 01, (4) 12, (5) 14
57. Which word is different from others?
(1) Jump, (2) Bind, (3) go, (4) walk, (5) stand
58. If 'R' is in right of 'C' and to left of 'T', which letter is in the middle?
(1)R, (2) C, (3) T
59. Children should go to school, because—
(1) They quarrel at home (2) They can play new games in school, (3) It can change their behaviour (4) They can read well.
60. Opposite of word male is—
(1) Son, (2) youth, (3) girl, (4) female, (5) man
61. Orange : Fruit : : Potato :
(1) Cabbage, (2) Tamato, (3) Beans, (4) Vegetable
62. Meaning of word similar is—
(1) Colour, (2) same, (3) nice, (4) plain, (5) size

63. 23, 21, 19, 17, 15,... write the next number in serial
(1) 14, (2) 13, (3) 22, (4) 23, (5) 32
64. Which word is different from others?
(1) Sea, (2) stream, (3) pond, (4) Mountain, (5) River
65. Rama's name comes before Shyam, Shyam's name comes before Krishna, Hari's names comes before Krishna, so which name comes last?
(1) Rama, (2) Shyam, (3) Hari, (4) Krishna
66. We travel in train, because—
(1) It is comfortable, (2) It runs on track, (3) It has Engine, (4) Scenic environment available to see.
67. Opposite of "introduction" is—
(1) Real, (2) Discussion, (3) Beautiful, (4) Conclusion, (5) End.
68. Eating : Water : : Hungry : ?
(1) Lemon, (2) Less, (3) Thirsty, (4) Milk, (5) Fasting
69. Meaning of the word "quarrel" is—
(1) Straight, (2) Tossle, (3) Enviousness (4) Enemy (5) Friend.
70. 186, 62, 54, 18, 6, ... write the next number.
(1) 7, (2) 5, (3) 2, (4) 16
71. Which word is different from others?
(1) Fish, (2) Crocodile, (3) Lion, (4) Crab, (5) Tortoise
72. Shyam is more handsome than Suresh, Prem is more handsome than Shyam, Prem is less handsome than Ramesh, so who is least handsome?
(1) Shyam, (2) Suresh, (3) Prem, (4) Ramesh
73. Opposite of Word Ugly is—
(1) Black, (2) Beautiful, (3) White (4) Young (5) Attraction
74. Poet : Poetry : : Artist : ?
(1) Heart, (2) colour, (3) Brush, (4) Art, (5) Scene
75. Meaning of the word "Surprise" is—
(1) Astonisment, (2) Experience, (3) Wasty, (4) Faithless, (5) Happy.
76. 1, 3, 9, 27, 81, ...write the next number
(1) 82, (2) 102, (3), 243, (4) 100, (5) 150
77. Which word is different from others?
(1) Sweet, (2) salty, (3) yellow, (4) sour, (5) Pritter

78. Mannu's name comes before Chunnu, Puspa's name comes before mannu, Tunnu's name comes before Puspa, so whose name is in last?
(1) Munnu, (2) Chunnu, (3) Tunnu, (4) Puspa.
79. Opposite of the word "Conscious" is—
(1) Dream, (2) Unconscious, (3) work, (4) Boat, (5) Sleep
80. Cloud : Thunder : : Rain ?
(1) Water, (2) Storm, (3) Lightning, (4) Sound, (5) Difficult.
81. 45, 42, 39, 36, 33, ... write the next number.
(1) 32, (2) 31, (3) 34, (4) 29, (5) 30
82. Which is different from other words?
(1) Tea, (2) Coffee, (3) Roti, (4) Milk, (5) Lassi
83. Om is lighter than Hari, Satish is heavier than Rama but lighter than Hari, Shyam is heavier than Om, but lighter than Rama. Who is lightest among all.
(1) Satish, (2) Rama, (3) Hari, (4) Shyam, (5) Om.
84. Cycle : Pedal : : Boat : ?
(1) Sea, (2) Traveler, (3) Driver, (5) Sand, (6) Oar
85. 1, 3, 6, 10, 15, ... write the next number
(1) 21, (2) 16, (3) 18, (4) 14, (5) 20
86. Which one is different from other words?
(1) Temple, (2) Mosque, (3) Church, (4) Gurudwara, (5) Dharamasala
87. Pear's Dictionary is smaller than Oxford Dictionary, Chamber's Dictionary is smaller than Bhargava Dictionary, Nalanda Dictionary is bigger than Bhargava. Both Oxford and Chambers are same. Which dictionary is the biggest one?
(1) Nalanda Dictionary, (2) Oxford Dictionary, (3) Bhargava Dictionary, (4) Chambers Dictionary, (5) Pear's Dictionary
88. Diwali : Light :: Holi :?
(1) Dusserah, (2) Colour, (3) Sports, (4) Festival, (5) Holiday
89. Which word is different from others?
(1) India, (2) China, (3) Japan, (4) Delhi, (5) America
90. Sunday : March : : Monday
(1) Old, (2) April, (3) Month, (4) May, (5) February
91. Day : Night : : Word :
(1) Unfaithful, (2) Labour, (3) Comfort, (4) Slumber, (5) Conscious.

VERBAL GROUP TEST OF INTELLIGENCE (2170)

ANSWER SHEET

Name :

Class :

Date :

School/College :

Age :

Profession of father :

Annual income of Family :

Your birth order in family :

Example Practice	
Q.	*A.*
1	5
2	
3	2
4	
5	4
6	
7	3
8	
9	4
10	
11	3
12	
13	5
14	

Page–1		*Page–2*		*Page–3*		*Page–4*		*Page–5*	
Q.	*A.*	*Q.*	*A.*	*Q.*	*A.*	*Q.*	*A.*	*Q.*	*A.*
1		21		41		61		81	
2		22		42		62		82	
3		23		43		63		83	
4		24		44		64		84	
5		25		45		65		85	
6		26		46		66		86	
7		27		47		67		87	
8		28		48		68		88	
9		29		49		69		89	
10		30		50		70		90	
11		31		51		71		91	
12		32		52		72			
13		33		53		73			
14		34		54		74			
15		35		55		75			
16		36		56		76			
17		37		57		77			
18		38		58		78			
19		39		59		79			
20		40		60		80			

APPENDIX F

VERBAL GROUP TEST OF INTELLIGENCE (2170)

Scoring Key

Name : Class :

Date : School/College :

Age : Profession of father :

Annual income of Family : Your birth order in family :

Example Practice	
Q.	A.
1	5
2	2
3	2
4	1
5	4
6	5
7	3
8	2
9	4
10	3
11	3
12	4
13	5
14	3

Page–1		*Page–2*		*Page–3*		*Page–4*		*Page–5*	
Q.	A.	Q.	A.	Q.	A.	Q.	A.	Q.	A.
1	3	21	5	41	5	61	4	81	5
2	4	22	1	42	3	62	1	82	3
3	3	23	3	43	5	63	2	83	5
4	3	24	3	44	1	64	4	84	2
5	4	25	4	45	3	65	2	85	1
6	1	26	5	46	5	66	1	86	5
7	3	27	5	47	1	67	4	87	1
8	4	28	3	48	4	68	3	88	2
9	2	29	4	49	2	69	2	89	4
10	4	30	4	50	3	70	3	90	4
11	3	31	3	51	3	71	3	91	3
12	4	32	3	52	2	72	1		
13	2	33	2	53	4	73	2		
14	4	34	2	54	4	74	4		
15	5	35	3	55	2	75	1		
16	1	36	4	56	4	76	3		
17	5	37	4	57	2	77	3		
18	3	38	2	58	2	78	3		
19	5	39	3	59	4	79	3		
20	2	40	2	60	3	80	3		

APPENDIX G

LISTENING-SPEAKING ENGLISH ACHIEVEMENT TEST-I

Instruction

The following passage is to be read out by the teacher loudly and perfectly before the students. After completion of teacher's loud reading, students are to be given five minutes for silent reading for easy understanding of the passage. Then, the students have to answer the questions orally, which are written at the end of the passage. These questions are to be asked by the teacher. Each question carries four marks.

The Passage

Many birds do not stay in the same country all round the year. In summer, they lay their eggs and bring up their young in places which are not too hot. But these places become very cold in winter. So, when winter sets in, they fly to warmer lands.

Birds which lay their eggs and bring up their young ones in the northern half of the globe, fly south in winter. Some go only a few hundred kilometers to where the climate is warmer. Others go right across the equator. For the same reason, birds in the south fly north.

This is called migration. Migrating birds may fly great distances, sometimes more than 10,000 kilometers (6,000 miles). The Arctic tern makes the longest journey of all. Each year it flies from the Arctic region right down to the Antarctic and back.

Birds which usually live on land like to migrate over land. In this way they can stop and rest on their journey. Sea birds are happier over the oceans and seas.

QUESTIONS

1. When do the birds lay their eggs ?
2. Why do the birds fly to warmer lands ?
3. To which area do the birds of northern half of the globe fly in winter ?
4. Why do the birds of south fly to north ?
5. What does migration mean?

6. How long do the migrating birds fly ?
7. Which bird makes the longest journey ?
8. Do the birds stop and rest during their journey ?
9. Why are the sea birds happier ?
10. Where does the 'Arctic tern' fly to every year ?

APPENDIX H
LISTENING-SPEAKING ENGLISH ACHIEYEMENT TEST-II

Instruction

The following passage is to be read out by the teacher loudly and perfectly before the students. After completion of teacher's loud reading, students are to be given five minutes for silent reading for easy understanding of the passage. Then, the students have to answer the questions orally, which are written at the end of the passage. These questions are to be asked by the teacher. Each question carried four marks.

The Passage

"That seller was rude, but this seller looks gentle. It is likely that he will take the bowl," the girl said.

Seeing her grand daughter's eagerness, the old woman called Serivan in. So he came into the house and they put the bowl in his hands. He was surprised to see that it was made of gold.

"Do you really want to exchange this, old mother?" he asked with hesitation. Encouraged by it, the young girl asked, "Will you exchange it for a plate?"

"Old mother, your bowl is made of pure gold and is worth a lot of money. I haven't so much money with me.

Both the women were astonished to hear this. "My son, a seller, who came yesterday, said the bowl was worth less and threw it on the ground. It must be your touch which has turned it into gold. Take it! Give us anything you please in exchange and go away."

QUESTIONS

1. Who was Serivan?
2. How did he look like?
3. Why was Serivan surprised?
4. Why was the seller unwilling to buy the bowl from the old woman?
5. Why were both the women stonished? What did Serivan ask to the old woman?

6. What does the golden bowl tell us?
7. What does the golden bowl tell us about the past life of the two women?
8. What differences do you find between two sellers?
9. There is a word in the passage which is the opposite of "rude" in meaning. Find it out and use it in a sentence of your own.
10. Make a sentence by using the verb form of the word "hesitation".

APPENDIX I

THE CMTE LESSON PLAN MODEL

A Model of CMTE lesson plan, through which students of Class IX were taught the topic : "The Owl Who was God" was as follows:

Class-IX

Topic : The Owl Who was God Time – 40 minutes

Through teaching this topic I intended to :

(i) Make students conversant with the story relating animals and birds,

(ii) Enable students to know why the animals and birds considered the Owl as the greatest and wisest among all, and

(iii) Develop students' divergent thinking abilities through discussion of the topic.

Introduction

Teacher : 'Can you identify the birds which you see in this picture ?' (Showing the picture of some birds with the picture of an Owl).

Student : 'Yes, Sir.'

Teacher : 'Tell me their names.'

Student 1 : 'Parrot, Hen.'

Student 2 : 'Peacock.'

Student 3 : 'Hen, Owl.'

Teacher : 'Yes, these birds have their kingdom—their association or group, where they live, discuss and solve their different problem like us.'

Student 1 : 'Sir, likewise there is animal kingdom. Do you discuss and solve their problems?'

Teacher : 'Yes, there is also animal kingdom where they live, discuss and solve their problems. Today we shall read a topic relating to these creatures. It is written by James Grover Thurber, an eminent story writer. He, here, explained how the animals and birds and misunderstood the owl and how their foolishness led them to destruction.'

Then, I read out the topic in a loud voice with proper pronunciation and information. The students were told to read silently when my loud reading was going on. I read the topic twice for their easy comprehension.

Drilling of Language

Student : 'Sir, What does 'slip by' mean?'

Teacher : 'Slip by' refers to 'get away quicly.'
The thief tried to slip quietly by tacking the ornaments.
Then I asked to frame similar sentences by using "slip by".

Student 1 : 'I was frightended as the snake slipped by me'.

Student 2 : 'The pick pocketer slipped away by taking the money from Rambabu's pocket.'

Teacher : 'Very Good. Have you any other difficulties?'

Student : 'Yes Sir, please explain the word 'unnoticed'.

Teacher : Unnoticed means 'without being seen by anyone'. Hari left his village unnoticed.'
Then I asked to frame similar sentences by using the word unnoticed and students responded as follows :

Student 1 : 'Girish went out of the class unnoticed.'

2 : 'Great men of the world like to live unnoticed.'

3 : 'The beggar died unnoticed.'

Teacher : 'Many many thanks for your good responses'. Do you know the meaning of the phrase 'Call on'?

Student : 'No Sir, Please explain us.'

Teacher : 'Call on' is a phrase which means "to visit".
The Inspector of Schools called on our school yesterday.
'Dear students, try to frame similar sentences by using it.'

Students : (i) 'The Chief Minister of Orissa called on the flood affected area.'
(ii) 'I don't know why the lawyer calls on Hari frequently.'

Teacher : 'Thanks. Have you any other difficult word in this topic.'

Students : 'No, Sir.'
Giving thanks, I explained the intent meaning of the topic. Then I asked the following comprehension questions.

Comprehension type Questions

Teacher : 'Did the moles want to meet the owl? Why?'

Student : (i) 'No. The moles did not went to meet the owl. Because they wanted to pass by quickly not being seen by any body.'
(ii) 'The moles wanted to slip by unnoticed. It seemed that they did not want to meet the owl.'

Teacher : 'Very Good. Why did the moles feel scared and astonished ?'

Students : (i) 'The moles tried to get away quickly being unnoticed by others. But the owl saw them in such a deep dark night. So, they felt scared and astonished.'
(ii) 'It was deep dark night, when the moles were getting away. They thought that nobody could see them in such dark night. But the owl recognised them. Hence, they felt scared and astonished.'

Teacher : 'Thank you. What made the two moles think that the owl was wisest and of all greatest animals?'

Student : 'There for which two moles were causes thought the owl as the greatest and wisest of all. They were: (i) the owl could see in dark, and (ii) he Could answer to any question.

Teacher : 'Why did the secretary bird went to meet the owl?'

Students : (i) 'The secretary bird wanted to meet the owl to know whether the owl could see in the dark and whether he could really answer any question he was asked to.'
(ii) 'The secretary bird wanted to meet the owl to establish the truthfulness of the statements given by two moles regarding the owl his greatness and wisdom.'

Teacher : 'When and Why did the secretary bird call on the owl?'

Students : (i) 'The secretary bird called on the owl in a dark night because he wanted to know whether the owl could see in the dark.'

(ii) 'To verify the statement of two moles, that the owl could see in the dark, the secretary bird visited the owl in a dark night.'

Teacher : 'What was the third question of the secretary bird to the owl?'

Students : 'Why does a lover call on his love,? 'was the third question asked by secretary bird to the owl'.

Teacher : 'What was the answer of the owl to the third question asked by the secretary bird?'

Students : "To Woo", 'was the answer of the owl to the third question asked by the secretary bird.'

Teacher : 'Many many thanks to all of you. Now, we will switch over to another type of question-answer session.

Here each question has several possible answers. The interesting you think thing is, whatever over the question, Your answer will is right only never be wrong, Are imagine, You and to think of as new and many ideas on a question as possible. You have to express your answer diver gently. Hence, try to exercise your brain power with utmost interest.'

For example, I asked, 'What would happen if man could fly like birds?' Your answer may be of different types as follows:

(i) He could go to heaven and talk to God.

(ii) He would require any vehicle.

(iii) Transport and communication difficulties would be eliminated.

(iv) Friendship with birds would be established.

(v) There would be need of fuel. Petrol and Diesel rate would be diminished.

(vi) Easy escape from the attack of enemies and so on.

Here, totally individuals based on answers are imagination. So, you have to activate your imaginary capacity and produce new "things as far as possible. One thing you should in your mind is wrong. That Whatever you imagine and speak out is correct and carried Keep no answer certain values. Likewise, answer the following questions.

Divergent Thinking Questions

Teacher : 'How does a dark night look like?'
Students : (i) 'Like a black-cloud.'
(ii) 'As a confusing essay.'
Teacher : 'What does confusing essay mean?'
Students : 'Its meaning explanation is and unclear and ambiguous.'
Students : 'Dark night with person's compared be a may sorrowful mind.'
Student : 'It looks like a new-moon night.'
Student : 'Cloudy night.'
Student : 'The dark age in history.'
Teacher : What does dark age mean?
Student : 'A paper coloured with black.'
Student : 'Unfortunate Person.'
Students : 'Gloomy future.'
Teacher : What is the opposite of 'gloomy future'?
Student : - 'Bright future'
- 'Enlightened future'
- 'Brilliant future'
- Progressed life'
Teacher : Find out similarities between brilliant future and full-moon night.
Student : - 'Both possess optimum development.'
- 'Both have bright achievement.'
- 'As moon the brilliant person takes the credit.'
- 'As stars around the moon, there are many admirers around the brilliant person.'
- 'Both help others.'
- 'Both possess good character.'
- 'Both have their area for movement.'
Teacher : What will happen if sun is not found in the sky.
Students : 'There will be energy crisis.'
- 'There will be no rain.'

- 'World will be full of darkness'.
- Thieves will be very active and our life will be in danger.'
- Evaporation will be stopped.'
- 'I will go to the sun to request him to back.'
- 'Small herbs, grass and plants will be destroyed'.

Teacher : What will you do if you are at heaven?

Students : - 'I will talk with God.'
- 'I will bring the wealth from heaven for our neighbours'.
- 'I will invite my friend to heaven.'
- 'I will say to Lord Indra to construct a bridge from heaven to earth.'
- 'I will drive my bi-cycle there.'
- 'I will open a book-shop there for Gods and Goddess. '
- 'I will ride the horse of Lord Indra.'
- 'I will meet Lord Ganesh and pray for intelligence and knowledge.'
- 'I wll1 complain to the God against my elder brother who beats me.'
- 'I will enjoy the beauty of heaven.'
- 'I will pray God to stop power-cut and heat from our state.'

Teacher : I told, "many many thanks to you. You are using your mental power and imagination divergently. Try to do so in a better manner".
Then I showed them the picture of a tree and asked about different uses of the tree. The students answered as follows:

Students : 'Used for the purpose of making paper.'
'Resting place for birds.'
'Essential for rain.'
'Tree is life.'
'Prepares coal.'
'Some trees produce oil.'
'Maintains ecological balance.'

Teacher : 'Many many thanks for your good responses. Now you find out the similarities lies between tree and house.

Students : 'Both are made of wood.'
'Both are living places for creatures.'
'Both give shade.'
'Tired persons take under both tree and rest house'.

Teacher : "You can say that both can be destroyed."

Students : Yes Sir. 'Both can also be maintained.'
'Flood may damage both tree and house.'
'We play hide and seek at both places'.

Teacher : State the similarities between a fox and a dog.

Students : 'Both have life.'
Both have four legs, one tail, two one nose, eyes, two years.'
'Both can be called hunting animals.'
'Both are helpful for society.'
'Both are cleaver.'
'Both have flesh and bone in their bodies.'
'Both are faithful.'

Teacher : I showed the mode of a Car and asked, "try to think of the addition of different things, parts to it so that the model will be more interesting and useful."

Students : 'Seats of the Car will be made of Silver.'
'I will make it bullet-proved.'
'I will fit A.C. for my easy journey.'
'I will fit an engine to use water for its fuel.'
'I will make it a flying car to reach different places with no accident.
'I will make it as big as a train for transportation of goods.'
'I will decorate it with good and pearls.'
'I will decorate it will dazzling light.'
'I will engage my Dog for its driving.'

Teacher : 'Very Good. Now you say, what will happen if animals start speaking like man?'

student : 'They will surplus us in intelligence.'
'There will be good friendship between animal and man.'
'I will understand the difficulties of my pet dot 'Ramu'.
'It may happen that the animals will administer us.'

'The world will be changed into a different type of society.'
'Cooperative bring national life will development'.
'Animals will with will read and become us doctors and mechanics.'

Teacher : "Many many thanks for your divergent answers. Try to exercise your mental power and imagine as different exceptional and thinks new as possible."

Application Type Questions

'Dear students, now, asking some questions I am, related to your topic. Try to answer the questions.'

Teacher : 'What was the natural condition, when two moles came across the owl?'

Student : 'It was a dark night when the two moles came across; the own.'

Teacher : 'Why did the moles get astonished?'

Student : 'The two moles wanted to get away quickly being unnoticed by anybody in the dark night. Still, the owl recognised them. So they get astonished.'

Teacher : 'Why did the moles call the owl as the greatest and wisest among all animals?'

Students : 'It was because the owl could see in dark and could answer any question he was asked.'

Teacher : 'Think and express different uses of a piece of wood. '

Students : 'For fuel.'
'For furniture.'
'Doors and windows.'
'Construction of body of vehicles.'
'Wooden stick for driving away animals and snakes.'
'Wooden stick to beat the drum.'
'A stick to rest the door or window.'
'Wooden ball.'

Teacher : After getting above answers from the students, I gave them the following home-tasks and left the class giving them thanks and encouraging them to think of different things in divergent manner.

Home-Tasks

Write the answer of the following questions. Try to give as many new answers as you can:

1. What will happen if an animal becomes our king?
2. What similarities exist between a Cat and an Eagle?
3. Add different things in the model of a horse to make it more interesting to play.

Bibliography

Abney, C.W. (1970). A Comparative Study of Creative Thinking Ability in three Student Groups at the University Arkansas as Measured by the Remote Associates Test. Dissertation Abstracts International, 30, 7, 2717-A.

Acharyulu, S.T.V.G. (1977). A Study of the Relationship among Creative Thinking, Intelligence and School Achievement. Unpublished Doctoral Dissertation, Utkal University, Orissa.

Adaman, J.E and Blaney, P.H. (1995) The Effects of Musical Mood Induction on Creativity. *The Journal of Creative Behavior*, 29 (2), 95-108.

Aggarwal, Y.P. (1990). Statistical Methods: Concepts, Applications and Computation. New Delhi : Sterling Publishers Pvt. Ltd.

Anastasi, A. and Schaefer, C.S. (1971). Note on the Concepts of Creativity and Intelligence. *The Journal of Creative Behavior*, 5 (2), 113-16.

Andal, M., Krishnan, S.S. and Thomas, M. (1995). Critique on Creative Thinking. *The Educational Review*, C-7, 101-05.

Andal, M. and Krishnan, S.S. (1996). A Study of Creative Thinking in Relation to Sex and Locale. *The Educational Review*, C-11, 5-6, 104-07.

Alter, J.B. (1991). Experiencing Creating and Creativity in Classroom. *The Journal of Creative Behavior*, 25, 2, 162-68.

Arieti, S. (1976). Creativity : The Magic Synthesis. New York : Basic Books.

Asha, C.B. (1980). Creativity and Academic Achievement among Secondary School Children. *Asian Journal of Psychology and Education*, 6, 1-4.

Ashman, A.F., Write, S.K. and Conway, R.N.F. (1995). Developing the Metacognitive Skills of Academically Gifted Students in Mainstream Classroom. *Psychological Abstracts*, 81, 8, 3795.

Ausubel, D.P. (1963). Psychology of Meaningful Verbal Learning : An Introduction to School Learning. New York : Grune and Stratton Inc.

Barlett, F.C. (1958). Thinking : An Experimental and Social Study. New York : Basic Books.

Behera, A.P. (1993). Sex difference in Creativity : A Study in Navodaya Vidyalayas. *Journal of Indian Education*, 19(2), 46-48.

Behera, A.P. (1996). Rural-urban differences in Creativity : A Study in Navodaya Vidyalaya in Orissa. *Journal of Educational Research and Extension*, 32, 3, 149-54.

Berdyaev, N. (1962). The Meaning of Creative Act. New York : Collier Books.

Best, J.W. and Khan, J.V. (1991). Research in Education. New Delhi : Prentice-Hall of India Pvt. Ltd.

Bleedoan, B.D. (1986). Creativity : Number one Leadership Talent for Global Futures. *The Journal of Creative Behaviour*, 20, 4, 276-82.

Bloom, B.S. (1956). Taxonomy of Educational Objectives; Cognitive domain Book I. New York : Me Kay.

Boersma, F.J. and O'Blryan, K. (1968). An Investigation of the Relationship between Creativity and Intelligence under two Conditions of Testing. *Journal of Personality*, 36(3).

Bono, E.D. (1986). Cort Thinking Teacher's notes 1-6, Oxford : Pergamon Press.

Borg, W.R. and Gall, M.D. (1989). Educational Research: An Introduction. New Delhi : Longman.

Bower, G.H. and Hilgard, E.R. (1986). Theories of Learning. New Jersy : Prentice-Hall International Inc.

Brandt, R. (1984). Overview : Teaching of Thinking, for Thinking, about Thinking. *Educational Leadership*, 42(1), 3.

Bruce J. and Weil, M. (4th ed.) (1992). Models of Teaching. New Delhi : Prentice-Hall of India Pvt. Ltd.

Bruch, C.B. (1988). Metacreativity : Awareness of thoughts and Feelings during Creative Experiences. *The Journal of Creative Behaviour,* 2(2), 112-21.

Bruininks, R.H. and Feldman, D.H. (1970). Creativity, Intelligence and Achievement among Disadvantaged Children. *Psychology in the Schools,* VII, 3.

Buch, M.B. (ed.). (1985). Third all India Survey on Educational Research. New Delhi : National Council of Educational Research and Training.

Buch, M.B. (ed.). (1993). Fourth all India Survey on Educational Research. New Delhi; National Council of Educational Research and Training.

Burns, D.E. and Reis, S.M. (1991). Developing a Thinking Skills Component in the Gifted Education Programme. *Roeper Review,* 24(2), 72-79.

Burns, M.T. (1988). Music as a tool for Enhancing Creativity. *The Journal of Creative Behavior,* 22(1), 62-69.

Burt, C. (1962). Critical Notice : The Psychology of Creative Ability. *The British Journal of Educational Psychology,* XXXII, 292-2W.

Buswell, H.R. (1991). Introspection as a Possible Methodology for Creative Thinking. Unpublished Doctoral Dissertation in Education. University of Georgia.

Buyer, L.S. (1988). Creative Problem Solving : A Comparison of Performance under different Instructions. *The Journal of Creative Behavior,* 22 (I), 55-61.

Cameron, L. (1968). Intelligence, Creativity and English Examinations. *Scottish-Educational Studies,* 1, 55-60.

Camp, G.C. (1995). A Longitudinal Study of Correlates of Creativity. *Psychological Abstracts,* 82(3), 1417.

Carroll, J. and Howieson, N. (1992). Recognizing Creative Thinking Talent in the Classroom. *Roeper Review,* 14 (4), 209-12.

Carson, P.P. and Carson, K.D. (1993). Managing Creative Enhancement through Goal Setting and Feedback. *The Journal of Creative Behavior,* 27(1), 36-45.

Cave, R.L. (1970). A Combined Factor Analysis of Creativity and Intelligence. *Multivariate Behavioral Research,* 5, 2.

Chadha, N.K. and Chandna, S. (1990). Creativity, iIntelligence and Scholastic Achievement : A Residual Study. *Indian Educational Review,* 25 (3), 81-85.

Chakraborty, B.D. (1992). Education of the Creative Children. New Delhi : Konark Publishers Pvt. Ltd.

Chislett, L.M. (1995). Integrating the CPS and Schoolwise Enrichment Models to Enhance Creative Productivity. *Psychological Abstracts*, 82 (3), 1417.

Clark, C.M., Veldman, D.J. and Thorpe, J.S. (1965). Convergent and Divergent Thinking Abilities of Talented Adolescents. *Journal of Educational Psychology,* 56, 157-63.

Clark, P.M. and Mirels, H.L. (1970). Fluency as a Pervasive Element in the Measurement of Creativity. *Journal of Educational Measurement*, 7, 2.

Cline, V.B., Richards, J.M. and Needham, W.E. (1963). Creativity Tests and Achievement in High School Science. *Journal of Applied Psychology,* 47 (3), 184-89.

Coleman, L.J. (1992). Reflections on the Cognitive Map of Master Teacher Conducting Discussion with Gifted Students. *Exceptionality,* 3 (l), 49-53.

Cornish, I.M. (1989). The Relationship between Convergence-Divergence and the Free Recall of Discourse. *British Journal of Educational-Psychology,* 59(2), 258-61.

Coomarswamy, K.A. (1924). The dance of Shiva. Sunrise Turn.

Crawford, R.P. (1954). The Techniques of Creative Thinking. New York : Hawthorn Books Inc.

Cropley, A.J. (1966). Creativity and Intelligence. *The British Journal of Educational Psychology,* XXXVI (3), 259-65.

Davidow, J.R. (1995). The Aims of Intervention. *Psychology in the Schools,* 31(4), 305-08.

Davis, C.A. and Belcher, T.L. (1971). How shall Creativity by easured? Torrance Tests, RAT, Alpha Biographical, and IQ. *The Journal of Creative Behavior,* 15(3), 153-61.

Dececco, J.P. and Crawford, W.R. (1988). The Psychology of Learning and Instruction. New Jersy : Prentice-Hall International Inc.

De Haan, R.F. and Havighurst, R.J. (1957). Educating Gifted Children. Chicago : Chicago University Press.

Dewey, J. (1933). How we Think a Restatement of Relationship of Reflective Thinking to the Educative Process. Lexington, M.A : Heath.

Dewing, K. (1970). Some Correlates of Creativity Test Performance in Seventh Grade Children. *American Journal of Psychology,* 22(3), 269-76.

Drevadahl, E.J. (1962). Educational Etiology of Creativity. *The Gifted Child Quarterly*, 6, 91-94.

Duffy, J.A. (1971). Teaching of Creative Writing. In L.C. Deighton (Ed.). Aging in the 1970s; The Encyclopedia of Education, 2, (pp. 548-52). USA : The Mac Millan Company and The Free Press.

Edward, M.P. and Tyler, L.E. (1965). Intelligence, Creativity and Achievement in a Non-selective Public Junior High School. *Journal of Educational Psychology*, 56 (2), 96-99.

Ekvall, G. and Parnes, S.J. (1989). Creative Problem-solving Methods in Product Development—A Second Experiment. *Creativity and Innovation Yearbook*, 2, 122-42.

Feldhusen, J.F. and Clinkenbeard, P.R. (1986). Creativity Instructional Materials : A Review of Research. *The Journal of Creative Behavior*, 20(3), 153-181.

Ferrel, S.D. (1991). Critical Thinking as a Function of Teacher Questions. Unpublished Doctoral Dissertation in Education. University of Georgia.

Flescher, I. (1963). Anxiety and Achievement of Intellectually Gifted and Creatively Gifted Children. *The Journal of Psychology*, 56, 251-68.

Foshay, W.R. and Foshay, A.W. (1981). Curriculum Development and Instructional Development. *Educational Leadership*, 38 (8), 621-25.

Frasier, M.M. (1987). Creativity. In Cecil R. Reynolds (Ed.). Aging in the 1980s : Encyclopedia of Special Education, I, (pp. 422-24). New York : John Wiley and Sons.

Freeman, F.S. (1962). Theory and Practice of Psychological Testing. New Delhi : Oxford and IBH Publishing Co.

Freeman, J., Butcher, H.J. and Christie, T. (1971). Creativity—A Selective Review of Research (Second Ed.). Monograph 5, London : Society for Research into Higher Education Ltd.

Freeman, J. (1995). Gifted School Performance and Creativity. *Psychological Abstracts*, 82, 3, 1417.

Gakhar, S.C. (1985). Intelligence, Creativity and Achievement in Mathematics : A Regression Analysis. *Journal of the Institute of Educational Research*, B(3), 17-20.

Gaekwad, A., Nautiol, S., Pai, S. and Paremu, B. (1994). The Effect of Brainstorming on the Creativity Scores of Institutionalized and Non-institutionalized Girls. *Indian Journal of Psychology*, 69 (1&2), 51-56.

Gallaghar, J.J. (1964). Teaching the Gifted Child. Boston : Allyn and Bacon Inc.

Gallaghar, J.J. (1982). Gifted Persons. In M.C. Alkin (Ed.). Aging in 1980s : Encyclopedia of Educational Research, 2, (pp. 544-48). New York : McMillan.

Garrett, H.E. (Sixth U.S. ed.). (1966). Statistics in Psychology and Education. Bombay : Vakils, Feffer and Simons Pvt. Ltd.

Gay, L.R. (1990). Educational Research : Competencies for Analysis and Application. Singanpore : Maxwell Macmillan Publishing Pvt. Ltd.

Gehlbach, R.D. (1987). Creativity and Instruction—The Problem of Task Design. *The Journal of Creative Behavior*, 21 (1), 34-47.

Gehlbach, R.D. (1991). Play, Piaget, and Creativity: The Promise of Design. *The Journal of Creative Behavior*, 25(2), 137-44.

Gelade, G. (1995). Creative Style and Divergent Production. *The Journal of Creative Behavior*, 26(1), 36-53.

Getzels, J.W. and Jackson, P.W. (1962). Creativity and Intelligence-Exploration with Gifted Students. New York: John Wiley and Sons.

Ghiselin, B. (ed.). (1952). The Creative Process. Berkeley : University of California Press.

Gill, S., Singh, M.B. and Chauhan, N. (1990). Effect of an Intervention Programme on Selected Cognitive Abilities 3f Pre-school Children. *Indian Journal of Social Sciences*, 1(1), 97-106.

Ginsburg, G.P. and Whittemore, R.G. (1968). Creativity and Verbal Ability : A Direct examination of their Relationship. *The British Journal of Educational Psychology*, 18 (2), 133-39.

Goldberg, C. (1986). The Interpersonal Aim of Creative Endeavor. *The Journal of Creative Behavior* 20(1), 15-48.

Golub, S. and Hahn, K.S. (1983). Training Creative Thinking in the Open and Traditional Classroom. *The Journal of Creative Behavior*, 17(3), 217-18.

Gowan, J.C. (1977). Some New thoughts on the Development of Creativity. *The Journal of Creative Behavior*, 11(2), 77-90.

Greer, M. and Levine, E. (1991). Enhancing Creative Performance in College Students. *The Journal of Creative Behavior*, 25(3), 250-55.

Grossman, S. and Wiseman, E.E. (1993). Seven Operating Principles for Enhanced Creative Problem-solving Training. *The Journal of Creative Behavior*, 67(1), 01-17.

Guilford, J.P. (1950). Creativity. *The Americalr Psychologist*. 5, 8.

———, (1950). Creativity. *American Psychologist*, 5, 444-54.

———, (1956). Fundamental Statistics in Psychology and Education. (Third Edition), New York : McGraw Hill.

———, (1959). Three Faces of Intellect. *American Psychologist*, 14, 469-79.

———, (1967). The Nature of Human Intelligence. New York : McGraw Hill.

———, (1971). Testing for Creativity. In Lee C. Deignton (Ed.). Aging in 1970s ; The Encyclopedia of Education, 2, (pp. 557-60). USA : The McMillan Company and The Free Press.

———, (1983). Transformation Abilities or Functions. *The Journal of Creative Behavior*, 17(2), 75-83.

——— and Christensen, P.R. (1974). Creative Potential as Related to Measures of IQ and Verbal Comprehension. *The Journal of Creative Behavior*, (S), 247-52.

Gupta, A.K. (1974). Creativity Research in India—Its Past and Future. *Creativity Newsletter*, (l), 18-24.

———, (1990). Development and Evaluation of Creative Training Programme for Sixth Grade Children. *Indian Educational Review*, 65(1), 95-99.

Gupta, R. (1972). Creativity : Its Relation with Intelligence. *Creativity Newsletter*, 1, 1.

Gurman, E.B. (1988). The Effect of Foreign Travel on Creativity. *The Journal of Creative Behavior*, 22(4), 281.

Gurnani, L., Bala, M. and Golwalkar, S. (1995). Comparison between Creativity of Physically Handicapped Students Studying in Senior Higher Secondary Classes in Rajasthan with Settled Physically Handicapped Persons. *The Educational Review*, C(8), 135-37.

Hany, E.A. (1994). The Development of Basic Cognitive Components of Technical Creativity : A Longitudinal Comparison of Children and Youth with High and Average Intelligence. *Psychological Abstracts*, 61(8), 3507.

Hennessey, B.A. and Amabile, T.M. (1988). Story-telling: A Method for Assessing Children's Creativity. *The Journal of Creative Behavior*, 22(3), 235-46.

Holland, J.L. (1961). Creative and Academic Performance among Talented Adolescents. *Journal of Educational Psychology*, 52 (3), 136-47.

Hooda, R.C. and Jarial, G.S. (1983). Development of Creativity through the Techniques of Role Playing. *The Rajasthan Board Journal of Education*, Oct.-Dec., 16-21.

Hooda, R.C. and Jarial, G.S. (1986). Effect of Teaching through Mastery Learning Strategy on the Creativity of Students. *The Journal of Creative Behaviour*, 20(2), 143.

Hota, A.K. (1993). Creative Potential, Achievement Motivation and Self-concept of Urban, Rural and Tribal Adolescents of Western Orissa. *Indian Educational Review*, 28 (2, 3 and 4), 106-10.

Hullfish, G. and Smith, P.G. (1964). Reflective Thinking : The Method of Education. New Delhi : Do DD, MEAD and Co.

Isaksen, S.G. and Parnes, S.J. (1985). Curriculum Planning for Creative Thinking and Problem-olving. *The Journal of Creative Behavior*, 19(1), 1-29.

Jacobson, M.A. (1966). The Relationship of Creative Thinking Ability, Intelligence and School Performance. *Dissertation Abstracts International*, 26(12), 7157.

Jampole, E.S. (1993). Effects of Imagery Training of the Creative Writings of Academically Gifted Elementary Students, *Psychological Abstracts*, 80(1), 424.

Joseph, P. (1988). The Effect of Creative Divergent Thinking Training on Creative Divergent Thinking and Moral Reasoning. *Dissertation Abstracts International*, 29(1), 39.

Kaha, C.W. (1983). The Creative Mind : Form and Process. *The Journal of Creative Behavior*, 17(2), 84-94.

Kaile, H.S. (1987). Intelligence and Creativity as Predictors of Scholastic Achievement in Mother Tongue and Foreign Language at different Levels of Socio-economic Status. Unpublished Doctoral Dissertation in Education, Punjab University, India.

Kamila, B.B. (1986). Creative Thinking Abilities of Blind School Children. *Indian Educational Review*, 21(2), 111-16.

Kapoor, K. (1996). A Study of Creative Thinking Ability of High School Pupils of Arunachal Pradesh in Relation to their Sex and Academic Achievement. *The Progress of Education*, LXX (8), 172-75.

Katiyar, P.C. and Jarial, G.S. (1985). Programme for Developing Creativity in School Children. *The Journal of Creative Behavior*, 19(3), 219-20.

Kaur, P. and Kharb, D. (1993). Creativity in Children: The Impact of School and Home Environment. *Journal of Indian Education*, 18(6), 46-49.

Kerlinger, F.N. (1989). Foundations of Behavioral Research. New York : Rinehart and Winston Inc.

Khandwalla, P.N. (Second ed.). (1995). Fourth Eye-excellence through Creativity. New Delhi : Wheeler and Co. Ltd.

King, A. (1991). Efforts of Training in Strategic Questioning on Children's Problem-solving Performance. *Journal of Educational Psychology*, 83(3), 307-17.

Klausmeier, H.J. and Wiersma, W. (1964). Relationship of Sex, Grade Level and Locale to Performance of High IQ Students on Divergent Thinking Tests. *Journal of Educational Psychology*, 15 (2), 114-19.

Kumar, M.A.S. (1992). Socio-educational Correlates of Creativity among Secondary School Students in Arunachal. *Indian Educational Review*, 76, 98-106.

Kuppuswamy, B. (1961). The Manual of Socio-economic Status Scale. New Delhi : Manasayan.

Lesner, W.J. and Hillman, D. (1983). A Developmental Schema of Creativity. *The Journal of Creative Behavior*, 17(2) 103-14.

Lindquist, E.F. (1953). Design and Analysis of Experiments in Psychology and Education. New York : Houghton Mifflin Co.

Loomba, S. and Tyerma, S. (1990). Learning Abilities as a Function of Creativity and Attention Span in Children. *Indian Educational Review*, 25(4), 74-83.

Londner, L. (1991). Connection-making Processes during Creative Task Activity. *The Journal of Creative Behavior*, 25(1), 20-26.

Lutzer, V.D. (1991). Gender Differences in Preschooler's Ability to Interpret Common Metaphors. *The Journal of Creative Behavior*, 25 (l), 69-74.

Madaus, G.F. (1967). Divergent Thinking and Intelligence : Another Look at a Controversial Question. *Journal of Educational Measurement*, 4, 4.

Mangal, S.K. (1993). Advanced Educational Psychology. New Delhi: Prentice Hall of India Pvt. Ltd.

Mann, C. (1994). New Technology and Gifted Education. *Psychological Abstracts*, 8(8), 3796.

Marsh, R.W. (1964). Research Note : A Statistical Reanalysis of Getzels and Jackson's Data. *The British Journal of Educational Psychology*, XXXIV (1), 91-93.

Massad, C.E. (1969). A Comparative Study of Creativity, Language Aptitude and Intelligence in Sixth Grade Children from Low Socio-economic and Middle Socio-economic Levels. Dissertation Abstracts International, 29(12), 4331-A.

Matson, J.V. (1991). Failure 101 : Rewarding Failure in the Classroom to Stimulate Creative Behavior. *The Journal of Creative Behavior*, 25 (1), 82-85.

May, R. (1959). The Nature of Creativity. In Anderson, H.H. (ed.). Creativity and its Cultivation. New York : Harper and Bros.

Mayhon W.C. (1966). The Relationship of Creativity to Achievement and Other Student Variables. *Dissertation Abstracts International*, 27 (6), 1713-A.

McCabe M.P. (1991). Influence of Creativity and Intelligence on Academic Performance. *The Journal of Creative Behavior*, 25(2), 116-22.

Mcnemar, Q. (1964). Lost : Our intelligence. Why? *American Psychologist*, 19, 871-82.

Mednick, M.T. and Andrews, F.M. (1967). Creative Thinking and Level of Intelligence. *The Journal of Creative Behavior*, 1(4), 428-31.

Mehdi, B. (1973). Creativity and intelligence : The Evidence of Present Research. The Educational Trends, 8 (1-4), 150-56.

———, (1978). Socio-psychological Factors in Creativity among School Children. Unpublished Project Report, Indian Council of Social Science Research, New Delhi.

———, (1985). Manual of Verbal Test of Creative Thinking. (Rev. ed.). Agra : National Psychological Corporation.

Mille, R.D. and Merrifield, P.R. (1962). Book Reviews—Creativity and Intelligence : Exploration with Gifted Students by Jackob W. Getzels and Phillip W. Jackson. *Educational and Psychological Measurement*, XXII, 4.

Mishra, B.C. (1986). Relationship between Creativity and Problem-solving Ability at different Levels of Intelligence. *Indian Educational Review*, 21 (4), 112-18.

Mishra, D.P. (1993). A Study of the Creativity of Educable Mentally Retarded Children. *The Educational Review*. XCIX (2), 26-30.

Mitchell, B.M. and Wilkens, R.F. (1986). Changes in Hemispheric Functioning through Direct Training in Creative Thinking. *The Journal of Creative Behavior*, 20(2), 144-45.

Mohanty, J. (1989). Creativity : Meaning, Nature and Identification. *Journal of Indian Education*, 14 (6), 8-12.

Motlagh, H. (1968). Selected Non-academic Factors Related to Creativity. *Dissertation Abstracts International*, 22(5), 1453-A.

Moukwa, M. (1995). A Structure to Foster Creativity: An Industrial Experience. *The Journal of Creative Behavior*. 29(1), 54-63.

Mukhopadhyay, K.K., Chakrabarti, P.K. and Kundu, R. (1990). Creative Development of Children: Effects of Parental Sex, Education and Hobbies, *Indian Educational Review*, 25(3), 75-80.

Mumford, M.D., Connelly, M.S., Baughman, W.A. and Marks, M.A. (1995). Creativity and Problem-solving : Cognition, Adaptability and Wisdom. *Psychological Abstracts*, 443.

Murdock, M.C., Isaken, S.G., Lauer, K.J. (1993). Creativity Training and the Stability and Internal Consistency of the Kirton Adaption-Innovation Inventory. *Psychological Reports*, T2, 1123-30.

Nosanchuk, T.A., Ogrodink, J.A., and Henigan, T. (1988). A Preliminary Investigation of Incubation in Story Writing. *The Journal of Creative Behavior*, 22(4), 279-80.

Ochse, A. (1991). Why there were Relatively Few Eminent Women Creators? *The Journal of Creative Behavior*, 25(4), 334-342.

Ogletree, E.J. (1968). A Cross-cultural Exploratory Study of the Creativeness of Steiner and State School Pupils in England, Scotland and Germany. *Dissertation Abstracts*, 29(2), 516-A.

Osborn, A. (1963). Applied Imagination. New York : Charles Scribner's Sons.

Padhi, J.S. (1995). Influence of Creativity on Academic Performance. *Journal of Indian Education*, 20 (6), 46-51.

Panda, K.C. (1988). Elements of Child Development. New Delhi: Kalyani Publishers.

Pandey, A.K. (1992). Divergent Thinking in Relation to Scholastic Achievement, Cognitive Style, Self-concept and Interest Pattern. *Indian Educational Review*, 27(1), 56-60.

Pal, Y. (1991). Interdomain Relationship between Creativity and Intelligence by Canonical Analysis. *Indian Educational Review*, 26 (1), 20-27.

Pandey, R.C. (1990). Study of Creating Thinking Abilities of 8th Class Students in Kumaon Division in Relation to Intelligence and Socio-economic Status. New Delhi : Indian Council of Social Science Research.

Pandey, R.C. and Rai, R.N. (1995). Sex Difference in Creativity of Tribals and Non-tribals in Kumaon Hills. *The Educational Review*, CI (4), 70-73.

Paramjeet, D. and Saxena, S. 1995). Are Values Denote Creativity? *The Progress of Education*, LXIX (7), 124-26.

Passi, B.K. (1972). An Exploratory Study of Creativity and its Relationship with Intelligence and Achievement in School Subjects at Higher Secondary Stage. Unpublished Doctoral Dissertation, Punjab University, India.

Passi, S. (1996). Thinking Skills and Educational Management : New Perspective. *Progressive Education Herald*, 10(2), 9-17.

Pathak, P. (1962). Experimental Study of Creativity and Intelligence and School Achievement. Psychological Studies, 17, 1-9.

Patwardhan, V. (1995). A Comparative Study of Thinking Processes of Rural and Urban Women with Special Emphasis on Creative Thinking. *The Progress of Education*, LXX (4), 95.

Pesut, D.J. (1990). Creative Thinking as a Self-regulatory Metacognitive Process—A Model for Education, Training and further Research. *The Journal of Creative Behavior*, 24(3), 105-110.

Pickard, E. (1990). Towards a Theory of Creative Potential. *The Journal of Creative Behavior*, 2A(l), 01-09.

Pogue, B.C. (1965). An Exploration of the Interrelationship among Creativity, Self-esteem and Race. *Dissertation Abstracts*, 26(6), 3155.

Prasad, V. (1979). Promotion of Creativity and Achievement by Discovery Method. *Indian Educational Review*, 14(4), 86-94.

Puccio, G.J. (1989). Rationale for the Study of Creativity : A Review and Summary. *Creativity and Innovation Yearbook*, 2, 13-26.

Raina, M.K. (1969). A Study of Sex difference in Creativity in India. *The Journal of Creative Behavior*, (2) 111-14.

———, (Ed.). (1980). Creativity Research International Perspective. New Delhi : National Council of Educational Research and Training.

———, (1989). Social Change and Changes in Creative Functioning. New Delhi : National Council of Educational Research and Training.

———, (1991). Talent in Perspective (1st ed.). New Delhi : National Council of Educational Research and Training.

Rajendran, P. and Krishnan, S.S. (1992). Impact of Sex and Standards on Creative Thinking Ability. *Indian Journal of Psychometry and Education*, 23(1), 57-60.

Rajyalakshmi (1972). A Study of the Relationship among Creativity, Intelligence and Non-professional Achievement of Industrial Workers. *Creativity Newsletter*, 1(1), 24.

Rao, V. (1988). Standardization of a Test of Literary Creativity in Telgu for Students of Secondary Schools. *Indian Educational Review*, 23(4), 82-86.

Renzulli, J. and Callahan, C. (1973). New Directions in Creativity; Mark III. NYC : Harper and Row.

Renzulli, J.S. (1993). A General Theory for the Development of Creative Productivity through the Persuit of Ideal act of Learning. *Psychological Abstracts*, 80(6), 2834.

Richardson, A.G. (1986). Sex difference in Creativity among a Sample of Jamaican Adolescents. *The Journal of Creative Behavior*, 20 (2), 147-48.

———, (1989). Approaches to studying and Creativity : Is there a Link? *Psychological Report*, 65, 1089-90.

Ritchie S.M. and Edwards, J. (1996). Creative Thinking Instruction for Aboriginal Children. *Learning and Instruction*, 6(I), 59-75.

Rogers, C.R. (1959). Towards a Theory of Creativity. In Anderson, H.H. (ed.), Aging in 1950s; Creativity and Its Cultivation, New York : Harper and Bros.

Roy, O.K. (1993, April-Oct.). Personality Differentials of Adolescents with Scientific Creativity in Relation to Environment. *Indian Educational Review.* 123-126.

Rubenstein, I.R. (1966). An Experimental Study of the Effect of a Creative Problem-solving Course on the Creativity and Intelligence Test-scores of Fourth Grade Children from three different Socio-economic Levels. *Dissertation Abstracts,* 67(6), 1669-A.

Runco, M.A. and Nemiro, J. (1995). Problem Finding, Creativity and Giftedness. *Psychological Abstracts,* 82 (1), 443.

Russel, S. (1994). Effect of Creativity Training upon Concept Map Complexity : SLD, Gifted and Regular Education 5th, 6th and 7th Grade Students. *Dissertation Abstracts International,* 54(11), 4062.

Sandhu, T.S. (1979). Relationship of Creativity with Academic Achievement in Science Subjects. *Creativity Newsletter,* 7-8 (1&2), 1-10.

Schachtel, E.G. (1959). Metamorphosis on the Development of Affect, Perception, Attention and Memory. New York : Basic Books.

Schrag, F. (1982). Critical Thinking. In Alkesh, M.C. (ed.) Aging in 1980s : Encylopedia of Educational Research (1), USA : MacMillan Company and Free Press.

Scobee, V.J. (1983). Metacognitive Awareness of Brain Hemispheric Functions during the Composing Process : A Comparison between Eminent Scientist-authors and Gifted Students with Similar Career Operations. (Dissertation, Texas A & M University, 1983). University Microfilms, No. 8323715.

Selby, E.G., Treffinger, D.J., Isaksen, S.G. and Powers, S.V. (1993). Use of Kirton Adaption-Innovation Inventory with Middle School Students. *The Journal of Creative Behavior,* 27(4), 223-235.

Setia, R. (1984). Intelligence, Creativity and Achievement in Mathematics : A Regression Analysis. Unpublished M.Ed. Thesis, Panjab University, Chandigarh.

Shan, H.R. (1992). Effectiveness of Certain Curricular Activities in the Development of Creative Thinking of High School Students of Backward Hilly Region of Jammu. *Indian Educational Review,* 27 (2), 68-72.

Sharma, K.A. (1972). Creativity as a Function of Intelligence, Interest and Culture. Unpublished Ph.D. Thesis. Agra University, India.

Sharma, R.A. and Bhartiya, A. (1988). Mathetical Performance of Convergent and Divergent Thinkers. *Indian Educational Review*, 23(i), 116-21.

Shaw, J. and Cliatt, M.J.P. (1986). A Model for Training Teachers to Encourage Divergent Thinking in Young Children. *The Journal of Creative Behavior*, 20(2), 81-88.

Silcock, P. (1994). The Process of Reflective Thinking. *British Journal of Educational Studies*, XXXXII(3), 273-83.

Singer, E. (1992). Teacher Consultation to Develop Students' Higher Level Thinking Skills. *Dissertation Abstracts International*, 52(7), 2476.

Singh, A. (1986). Sex Difference in Verbal Creativity of Science Teachers. *Indian Educational Review*, 21(3), 113-15.

Singh, B. (1988). Mathematical Creativity and Some Socio-psychological Factors of Hindus and Muslims. *Indian Educational Review*, 23 (4), 121-29.

Singh, K. and B. Goutam (1988). A Study of Development of Creative Thinking among High School Students of Himachal Pradesh in Relation to Residential Background and Economic Status. *Prachi Journal of Psycho-Cultural Dimensions*, 4 (2).

Singh, R.P. (1978). Divergent Thinking Abilities and Creative Personality Dimensions of Bright Adolescent Boys and Girls. *Indian Educational Review*, 13 (4), 82-91.

Snyman, R. and Dekock, D.M. (1991). Problem-solving and Creative Thinking in Structured Second Language Teaching. *The Journal of Creative Behavior*, 25 (3), 28-37.

Soliman, A.M. (1968). A Study of Relationships between Creativity/Social Class, Social Mobility and Vocational Goals of High School Seniors. *Dissertation Abstracts*-A, 28(9), 3518.

Soloman, A.O. (1968). A Comparative Analysis of Creative and Intelligent Behavior of Elementary School Children with different Socio-economic Background. *Dissertation Abstracts International*, 29 (51), 1457-A..

Stein, M.I. (1962). Creativity as an Intra and Interpersonal Process. In Parnes, S.J., and Harding, H.F. (eds.), Aging in 1960s; A Source Book of Creating Thinking, New York: Charls Scribners Sons.

Stockley, D. (1993). Being Productive, being Cleaver : The Enchanted Forest of Intellectual Property. *Australian Journal of Education*, 96-111.

Sudhir, M.A. and Khiangte, V. (1991). Testing Creativity in India. *Journal of Creative Behavior*, 25(1), 27-33.

Torrance, E.P. (1959). Exploration in Creative Thinking in Early School Years (VIII) IQ, and Creativity in School Achievement. Minneapollis : Bureau of Educational Research, University of Minnesota.

———, (1961). Factors Affecting Creative Thinking in Children : An Interim Report. *Merrill-Palmer Quarterly*, 171-80.

———, (1962). Guiding Creative Talent. Englewood Cliffs, New Jersey : Prentice Hall.

———, (1963). Essay Review : Creativity and Intelligence. The School Review, 71, 1.

———, (1965). Rewarding Creative Behavior; Experiment in Classroom Creativity. New Jersy: Prentice-Hall.

———, (1968). Examples and Rationales of Test Tasks for Assessing Creative Abilities. *The Journal of Creative Behavior*, 2 (3).

Torrance, E.P. and Myers, R.E. (1970). Creative Learning and Teaching, New York : Dodd, Mead and Co.

Torrance, E.P. and Safter, H.T. (1986). Are Children Becoming more Creative? *The Journal of Creative Behavior*, 20 (1), 01-13.

Torrance, E.P. (1971). The Creative Person. In Deighton, L.C. (ed.), Aging in the 1970s; The Encyclopedia of Education (2) (pp. 552-57). USA : The Macmillan Company and The Free Press.

Toth, S.T. and Baker, S.R. (1990). The Relationship of Creativity and Instructional Style Preferences to Over-achievement and Underachievement in a Sample of Public School Children. *The Journal of Creative Behavior*, 24(3), 190-98.

Treffinger, D.J., Isaksen, S.G. and Firestein R.L. (1983). Theoretical Perspectives on Creative Learning and its Faciliation : An overview. *The Journal of Creative Behavior*, 17 (1), 9-17.

Tuli, M.R. (1988). Mathematical Creativity and Personality. *Indian Educational Review,* 23 (4), 144-49.

Tylor, C.W. (ed). (1972). Climate for Creativity—Report of the Seventh National Research Conference on Creativity. New York : Pergamon Press.

Verma, B.P. (1995). Creativity Styles of Women Students in Relation to their Rural-urban Background. *The Progress of Education,* LXIX (10), 196-204.

Vernon, P.E. (1964). Creativity and Intelligence. *Educational Research.* VI(3), London: Newnes Educational Publishing Co. Ltd.

Walllach, M.A. and Kogan, N. (1965). A New Look at the Creativity-Intelligence Distinction. *Journal of Personality,* 33, 3.

———, (1965). Modes of Thinking in Young Children : A Study of the Creativity-Intelligence Distinction. New York : Rinehart and Winston.

Weisberg, R.W. (1992). Creativity Beyond the Myth of Genius. New York : W.H. Freeman and Company.

Wertheimer, M. (1959). Productive Thinking. New York: Harper and Row Publishers.

Yadav, R.S. (1986). A Study of Correlation among Intelligence, Academic Achievement and Creativity. *Progress of Education,* LXI (3), 50-53.

Yamamoto, K. (1964). Threshold of Intelligence in Academic Achievement of Highly Creative Students. *The Journal of Experimental Education,* 32, 4.

Yamamoto, K. (1964). Creative Thinking: Some Thoughts on Research. *Exceptional Children,* 30(a), 403-10.

Yamamoto, K., Lenbright, M.L. and Corrigan, A.M. (1966). Intelligence, Creative Thinking and Socio-metric Choice among Fifth Grade Children. *The Journal of Experimental Education,* 34; 3.

Young, J.G. (1985). What is Creativity? *The Journal of Creative Behavior,* 19(2), 77-87.

Index